The Catholic Hymn Book

The Catholic Hymn Book

Melody Edition

Compiled and edited at
The London Oratory

First published in 1998

Gracewing
Fowler Wright Books
2 Southern Avenue, Leominster
Herefordshire HR6 0QF

All rights reserved. No part of this publication may be reproduced,
stored in a retrieval system, or transmitted in any form, or by any
means, electronic, mechanical, photocopying, recording, or otherwise,
without the written consent of the publisher.

Compilation and editorial material
© Trustees of the London Oratory 1997

The right of the editors to be identified with
this work has been asserted in accordance with
the Copyright, Designs and Patents Act 1988.

ISBN 0 85244 358 7

Typesetting by Reesprint
Radley, Oxfordshire, OX14 3AJ

Printed by Cromwell Press
Trowbridge, Wiltshire, BA14 0XB

Contents

Foreword . . . . *vii*
Preface . . . . *ix*
Musical Editor's Note . . . . *xi*
Acknowledgements and Copyrights . . . . *xiii*
Advent 1–10
Christmas 11–40
Epiphany 41–49
Lent 50–58
Passiontide and Holy Week 59–72
Easter 73–86
Ascension 87–90
Pentecost 91–95
Trinity 96–99
Transfiguration 100
Offertory at Mass 101–111
Blessed Sacrament 112–132
Sacred Heart 133–137
Precious Blood 138–140
Christ the King 141–143
Blessed Virgin Mary 144–165
Saints 166–177
Angels 178–180
Departed 181–182
Church 183–188
Morning 189–191
Evening 192–197
General 198–275
Benediction 276–280
Antiphons of the Blessed Virgin Mary 281–284
Mass Ordinary 285–290
Latin Hymns 291–316
Index of First Lines and Tunes . . . . *xvii*

This hymn book is dedicated to

THE IMMACULATE HEART OF MARY

The publication of this hymn book was made possible
by a generous legacy from the estate of the late
RALPH DOWNES CBE, KSG
distinguished musician, faithful servant of the Church
and Organist of the London Oratory 1936–1977.

Foreword

ARCHBISHOP'S HOUSE,
WESTMINSTER, LONDON, SW1P 1QJ

The singing of hymns in its different forms has been for centuries an important part of worship.

In the last thirty years, our Catholic repertoire of hymns has been greatly enriched. We have been able to borrow from the great tradition of hymnody, developed by Christians from other denominations. We have been exposed to new styles of music. We have witnessed a considerable growth of new music, tailor-made for the modern liturgy. Inevitably, the great diversity of material can make it hard to find music that everybody knows. There is a need in the Church for a good and wide-ranging collection of hymns that have stood the test of time.

It is my hope that many parishes and schools will find in *The Catholic Hymnbook* a resource that will help our people sing with one voice to the praise and glory of God.

Basil Hume
Archbishop of Westminster

Preface

*Sing psalms and hymns and spiritual songs
with thankfulness in your hearts to God.*
Colossians 3:16

He who sings prays twice.
St Augustine

It is not at all far-fetched to say that music can lift our souls, our minds and our hearts in praise and thanksgiving to God, our Creator. It is he who gives us the power to make music, to listen to music, to respond to music. Music is one of our greatest gifts from God; it is one of the least tangible expressions of our human mind and therefore, in a sense, one that is by its nature closest to the intangible God who made us and who loves us. Music can answer the desires and longings of our hearts, desires placed there by our Creator and which, ultimately, can be perfectly satisfied only by him; but music can help us. So music has a special role to play in our worship.

The Constitution on the Sacred Liturgy promulgated by the Second Vatican Council states that '*the musical tradition of the universal Church is a treasure of inestimable value, greater even than that of any other art. The main reason for the pre-eminence is that, as a combination of sacred music and words, it forms a necessary or integral part of solemn liturgy. . . . Religious singing by the faithful is to be fostered. The texts intended to be sung must always be in conformity with Catholic doctrine.*' One of the principal components of this musical tradition is the singing of hymns, originally in Latin, but for several centuries now, in the vernacular, that is, in the everyday language of a place. The treasury of English hymnody is especially rich and varied, but has been rather neglected in recent years. It is for this reason that we have produced a new hymn book, which contains

Preface

many traditional Catholic hymns, a number which have their origins in other Christian communities, and several written more recently which we believe will stand the test of time. We hope that this new selection will encourage people to sing hymns — whether familiar and much-loved, or thought-provoking in their unfamiliarity — which contain such theological and devotional riches.

This is an aspiration dear to the heart of Saint Philip Neri, the founder of the Congregation of the Oratory, who introduced into the Rome of his time the singing of *laudi*, or spiritual praises sung in Italian to attractive melodies. In this way, the words of these hymns would remain in the mind as a great source of inspiration and of Christian doctrine. In the English Oratories, Cardinal Newman and Father Caswall of the Birmingham Oratory and Father Faber of the London Oratory have given to us a great number of hymns, which are widely represented among those chosen for this book. We have also included a section of Latin hymns (often with a translation suitable for singing to the original melody), and three complete settings in Gregorian chant of the Mass in Latin. It is our hope that the provision of these settings in modern notation with accompaniments for organ will mean that many parishes make use of them in their liturgy.

In a small number of hymns, we have provided words which include slight variations from the author's original text; these are marked with an asterisk beside the attribution at the end of the hymn. However, wherever possible, we have provided the full original texts of the hymns. These have often been modified or adapted by editors and publishers of hymnbooks over the years. We hope that the restoration of original texts will encourage those who sing them to consider anew the intentions of the authors. As we sing these and indeed all the hymns included in this book, let us make use of these wonderful words and melodies to raise our voices in praise of our heavenly Father, for 'it is right to give him thanks and praise' through the great gift of music, which raises our hearts to God in a way unmatched in all creation.

The London Oratory
August 1997

Musical Editor's Note

The varied evolution of many hymn melodies has prompted the following shorthand for attributions in *The Catholic Hymn Book:*
- the name of the composer or source alone indicates the melody is in its original form;
- 'adapted' indicates the original melody has been thoroughly re-sculpted and/or transferred by the adapter from one musical genre to the present one;
- 'arranged' indicates melodic and/or rhythmic details of the original tune have been retouched by the arranger within the context of a complete musical setting, given in its entirety in the Harmony Edition of *The Catholic Hymn Book.*

Commas have been added to the tunes to help indicate, together with double bar-lines, the ends of musical phrases. These are generally effective breathing points too. However, where the verbal sense runs on at the end of a line, no break should be made in the music.

Gregorian chant

The chant melodies and texts are given in the form of the Vatican Edition, familiar to previous generations from the *Liber Usualis* and *Plainsong for Schools.* The melodies have been transcribed into modern notation in a simple manner, though the following signs retain their meaning as in traditional Gregorian notation:
- bar-lines: a small dash through the top line of the stave (quarter bar-line) indicates an opportunity for a quick breath, like a comma in speech; a small dash in the middle of the stave (half bar-line) indicates a longer breath, like a colon or semi-colon; a full bar-line indicates the end of a musical sentence, like a full-stop in speech; double bar-lines normally indicate the end of a musical paragraph, except in long pieces like the *Gloria, Credo* or *Te Deum* where their

Musical Editor's Note

frequent appearances indicate possible points of alternation between two groups of singers;
- a horizontal line (*episema*) above a note or notes: this indicates not emphasis but a slight lengthening or lingering;
- an asterisk in the text: this indicates the end of an intonation (by cantors or celebrant), after which all join in;
- vowels printed in italics in hymn verses: these should be either left unpronounced when sung, or compressed with the following vowel in order to effect an elision, preserving the poetic scansion.

The chant is best sung with an animated smoothness, while observing both the sense and natural accentuation of the text. It should never drag or seem heavy. Even in sombre mood quavers flow forward in shapely groups, and joyful texts should be delivered with supple rhythmic vitality. The ends of important phrases, sections or verses should be marked by plenty of time to breathe, before the progress of the melody is alertly resumed.

The 'translations suitable for singing' can all be fitted to their proper chant melody.

Patrick Russill

Acknowledgments and Copyrights

Editorial material and compilation of this work are the copyright of the London Oratory. All material designated PR, all Gregorian chant accompaniments except for No. 298, and all transcriptions of Gregorian chant into modern notation except for Gloria XV and Sanctus XVIII of No. 288 are by Patrick Russill and are the copyright of the London Oratory.

For permission to reproduce copyright material, whether in permanent or temporary form, application must be made to the respective copyright holders. The material listed below is copyright, and used by permission.

Every effort has been made to trace copyright holders for material included in this book. If, through obscurity of ownership or through inadvertence, any rights still surviving have not been acknowledged, pardon is sought and apology made. A correction will be made in any reprint of this book.

Agnes, Sr: *Hail, Glorious Saint Patrick* (words) Burns & Oates
Alington, C.A.: *Good Christian men rejoice and sing* (words) Hymns Ancient & Modern Ltd
Bévenot, Laurence: *Christus Vincit* (arrangement) Ampleforth Abbey Trustees
Brennan, Patrick: *Hail Redeemer, King Divine* (words) Burns & Oates
Bridges, Robert: *Ah, Holy Jesus! How Hast Thou Offended* (translation) Oxford University Press
   All My Hope on God is Founded (words) Oxford University Press
   Come, O Creator Spirit, come (translation) Oxford University Press
   Love of the Father, Love of God the Son (translation) Oxford University Press
   O Sacred Head, Sore Wounded (translation) Oxford University Press
Buck, P.C.: *Gonfalon Royal* (music) Oxford University Press
Burkitt, F.C.: *Wake, O wake! with tidings thrilling!* (translation) Oxford University Press
Chesterton, G.K.: *O God of Earth and Altar* (words) Oxford University Press
Coles, V.S.S.: *Ye Who Own the faith of Jesus* (words) Oxford University Press
Crum, J.M.C.: *Now the Green Blade Riseth* (words) © Oxford University Press 1928
Davis, R.F.: *Of the Father's Heart Begotten* (translation) J.M. Dent & Sons
Décha, Paul: *Vierge Sainte* (music) (arrangement, S. Dean) Kevin Mayhew Ltd

Acknowledgements and Copyrights

Dearmer, Percy: *Father, we praise thee, now the night is over* (words) Oxford University Press
Jesus, good above all other (words) Oxford University Press
O little One Sweet (translation) © Oxford University Press 1928
Sing, my Tongue, the Glorious Battle (words) Oxford University Press

Draper, W.: *All Creatures of our God and King* (words, translation) Roberton Publications (for J. Curwen)

Dudley-Smith, Timothy: *Tell out, my Soul* (words) author

Elgar, Edward: *Drakes Boughton* (music) Burns & Oates

Evers, J.C.: *Accept, Almighty Father* (words) World Library Publications Inc., Cincinnati, USA
Lord, we gather at thy altar (words) World Library Publications Inc., Cincinnati, USA

Farjeon, Eleanor: *Morning has Broken* (words) David Higham Associates

Farrell, M.: *Merciful Saviour, hear our humble prayer* (words) World Library Publications Inc., Cincinnati, USA

Ferguson, W.H.: *Wolvercote* (music) Oxford University Press

Foley, Brian: *Holy Spirit, Come Confirm Us* (words) Faber Music Ltd

Greatorex, Walter: *Woodlands* (music) Oxford University Press

Griffiths, Vernon: *Dunedin* (music) Faber Music Ltd

Gurney, Dorothy F.: *O Perfect Love, all Human Thought Transcending* (words) Oxford University Press

Harris, W.H.: *Alberta* (music) Oxford University Press

Harwood, Basil: *Luckington* (music) The Public Trust Office
Thornbury (music) The Public Trust Office

Holst, Gustav: *Cranham* (music) Oxford University Press
Personent hodie (arrangement) J Curwen & Sons
Thaxted (music) Novello & Co Ltd

Housman, Laurence: *O Christ, Our Joy, to Whom is Given* (translation) Oxford University Press

Howell, Clifford: *O God, we give ourselves today* (words) Trustees of Revd Clifford Howell SJ
See us Lord about thine altar (words) Trustees of Revd Clifford Howell SJ

Howells, Herbert: *Michael* (music) Novello & Company Ltd

Hughes, John: *Cwm Rhondda* (music) Mrs D Webb

Ireland, John: *Love Unknown* (music) The John Ireland Trust

Jacob, Dominic & Amanda Hill *When many sought a guide* (words) The Oxford Oratory

Knox, Ronald: *The Battle is O'er* (translation) Burns & Oates
Maiden yet a Mother (translation) Burns & Oates

Acknowledgements and Copyrights

O English Hearts (words) Burns & Oates
Wouldst thou a Patron See (translation) Burns & Oates
Lacey, T.A.: *Now is the Healing Time Decreed* (words) Oxford University Press
Lécot, Jean-Paul: *Holy Virgin, by God's Decree* (words, translated by W.R. Lawrence) © 1988 Kevin Mayhew Ltd
Mass XVIII (English texts) Excerpts from the English translation of *The Roman Missal* © 1973, International Committee on English in the Liturgy, Inc. All rights reserved.
Mass XVIII (music) *Gloria* from *English Kyriale*
Sanctus from *English Roman Missal* Collins
Mostyn, F.E.: *O Great St David* (words) Burns & Oates
Murray, Gregory Dom: *Surrexit* (music) Downside Abbey Trustees
O King of Might and Splendour (words) Downside Abbey Trustees
St David (music) Burns & Oates
Nicholson, Sydney: *Bow Brickhill* (music) The Canterbury Press
Pettman, Edgar: *Gabriel's Message* (arrangement) EMI Music Publishers Ltd
Phillips, C.S.: *Thou whom shepherds worshipped* (translation) The Canterbury Press
Quinn, James: *Father of mercy, God of consolation* (words) Geoffrey Chapman (Cassell plc)
Loving Father, from thy bounty (words) Geoffrey Chapman (Cassell plc)
Rigby, Charles: *King Divine* (music) Burns & Oates
Riley, Athelstan: *Christ, the Fair Glory* (translation) Oxford University Press
O Food of Men Wayfaring (translation) Oxford University Press
Ye Watchers and Ye Holy Ones (words) Oxford University Press
Robinson, J.A.: *'Tis good, Lord, to be here* (words) Oxford University Press
Rowlands, William: *Blaenwern* (music) G.A. Gabe, Swansea
Shaw, Martin: *Marching* (music) Oxford University Press
Shewring, Walter: *To Christ, the Lord of Worlds* (translation) Burns & Oates
Sparrow-Simpson, William: *Cross of Jesus, cross of sorrow* (words) Novello & Co. Ltd
Slater, Gordon: *St Botolph* (music) Oxford University Press
Struther, Jan: *Lord of all Hopefulness, Lord of all Joy* (words) Oxford University Press
Somervell, Arthur: *Chorus Angelorum* (music) Boosey & Hawkes
Taylor, Cyril: *Abbot's Leigh* (music) Oxford University Press
Teresine, Sister M.: *Lord, accept the gifts we offer* (words) the author
Terry, R.R.: *Aquinas* (music) Burns & Oates
Arfon (arrangement) Burns & Oates
Billing (music) Oxford University Press
Everlasting Love (music) Burns & Oates

Acknowledgements and Copyrights

    Laurence (music) Burns & Oates
    Highwood (music) Oxford University Press
    Providence (music) Burns & Oates
Tucker, Bland F.: *Father we Thank Thee* (words) The Church Hymnal Corporation
Turton, W.: *O thou, who at thy Eucharist did pray* (words) Canterbury Press
Vaughan Williams, Ralph: *Down Ampney* (music) Oxford University Press
    Forest Green (arrangement) Oxford University Press
    Kings Lynn (arrangement) Oxford University Press
    Lasst uns Erfreuen (arrangement) Oxford University Press
    Monks Gate (arrangement) Oxford University Press
    Shipston (arrangement) Oxford University Press
    Sine Nomine (music) Oxford University Press
    Sussex (arrangement) Oxford University Press
    Sussex Carol (arrangement) Stainer & Bell Ltd
Wetherell, F.W.: *Mary Immaculate, star of the morning* unable to trace
Williams, Derek: *San Rocco* (music) composer
Woodward, George R.: *Dearest Jesu, we are here* (words) Mowbray (Cassell plc)
    Ding Dong Merrily on High (words) SPCK
    This joyful Eastertide (words) Cassell plc
Wright, Ralph: *Star of sea and ocean* (translation) author

Advent

1 CROSS OF JESUS   87 87   JOHN STAINER 1840–1901

1. Come, thou long-expected Jesus,
   Born to set thy people free,
   From our fears and sins release us,
   Let us find our rest in thee.

2. Israel's strength and consolation,
   Hope of all the earth thou art,
   Dear Desire of every nation,
   Joy of every longing heart.

3. Born thy people to deliver,
   Born a Child and yet a King,
   Born to reign in us for ever,
   Now thy gracious kingdom bring.

4. By thine own eternal Spirit,
   Rule in all our hearts alone;
   By thine all-sufficient merit
   Raise us to thy glorious throne.

CHARLES WESLEY 1707–88

Advent

2 CREATOR ALME

Mode IV

1. Dear Maker of the starry skies,
   Light of believers evermore,
   Jesu, Redeemer of mankind,
   Be near us who thine aid implore.

2. When man was sunk in sin and death,
   Lost in the depths of Satan's snare,
   Love brought thee down to cure our ills,
   By taking of those ills a share.

3. Thou, for the sake of guilty men,
   Permitting thy pure Blood to flow,
   Didst issue from thy virgin shrine,
   And to the Cross a victim go.

4. So great the glory of thy might,
   If we but chance thy name to sound,
   At once all heaven and hell unite
   In bending low with awe profound.

5. Great Judge of all! in that last day,
   When friends shall fail, and foes combine,
   Be present then with us, we pray,
   To guard us with thine arm divine.

6. To God the Father, with the Son,
   And Holy Spirit, One and Three,
   Be honour, glory, blessing, praise,
   All through the long eternity.

Creator alme siderum 7th century
tr. EDWARD CASWALL Cong. Orat. 1814–78

Advent

3 CRÜGER 76 76 D

JOHANN CRÜGER 1598–1662
adapted WILLIAM HENRY MONK 1823–89

1. Hail to the Lord's Anointed!
   Great David's greater Son;
   Hail, in the time appointed,
   His reign on earth begun!
   He comes to break oppression,
   To set the captive free;
   To take away transgression,
   And rule in equity.

2. He comes with succour speedy
   To those who suffer wrong;
   To help the poor and needy,
   And bid the weak be strong;
   To give them songs for sighing,
   Their darkness turn to light,
   Whose souls, condemned and dying,
   Were precious in his sight.

3. He shall come down like showers
   Upon the fruitful earth,
   And love, joy, hope, like flowers,
   Spring in his path to birth:
   Before him on the mountains,
   Shall peace the herald go:
   And righteousness in fountains
   From hill to valley flow.

4. Kings shall fall down before him,
   And gold and incense bring;
   All nations shall adore him,
   His praise all people sing;
   To him shall prayer unceasing
   And daily vows ascend;
   His kingdom still increasing,
   A kingdom without end.

5. O'er every foe victorious,
   He on his throne shall rest;
   From age to age more glorious,
   All-blessing and all-blest:
   The tide of time shall never
   His covenant remove;
   His name shall stand for ever,
   That name to us is Love.

based on *Psalm 72*
JAMES MONTGOMERY 1771–1854

Advent

4 MERTON   87 87   William Henry Monk 1823–89

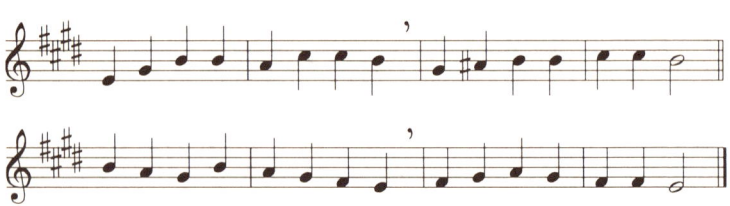

1. Hark! a herald voice is sounding;
    'Christ is nigh!' it seems to say;
   'Cast away the dreams of darkness,
    O ye children of the day!'

2. Startled at the solemn warning,
    Let the earth-bound soul arise;
   Christ her Sun, all sloth dispelling,
    Shines upon the morning skies.

3. Lo! the Lamb so long expected,
    Comes with pardon down from heaven;
   Let us haste, with tears of sorrow,
    One and all to be forgiven.

4. So when next he comes with glory,
    Shrouding all the earth in fear,
   May he then as our defender
    On the clouds of heaven appear.

5. Honour, glory, virtue, merit,
    To the Father and the Son,
   With the co-eternal Spirit
    While eternal ages run.

Vox clara ecce intonat 5th or 6th century
tr. Edward Caswall Cong. Orat. 1814–78 *

Advent

5 BRISTOL   CM   Thomas Ravenscroft's *Psalmes* 1621

1   Hark the glad sound! the Saviour comes,
       The Saviour promised long;
   Let every heart prepare a throne,
       And every voice a song.

2   He comes the prisoners to release
       In Satan's bondage held;
   The gates of brass before him burst,
       The iron fetters yield.

3   He comes the broken heart to bind,
       The wounded soul to cure,
   And with the treasures of his grace
       To enrich the humble poor.

4   The silver trumpets publish loud
       The Jub'lee of the Lord;
   Our debts are all remitted now,
       Our heritage restored.

5   Our glad hosannas, Prince of Peace,
       Thy welcome shall proclaim;
   And heaven's eternal arches ring
       With thy belovèd name.

based on *Luke 4: 18–19*
PHILIP DODDRIDGE 1702–51

Advent

6 OUR LADY'S EXPECTATION 87 87 D

William Pitts's
Oratory Hymn Tunes c. 1870

1 Like the dawning of the morning
   On the mountain's golden heights,
Like the breaking of the moonbeams
   On the gloom of cloudy nights;
Like a secret told by angels,
   Getting known upon the earth,
Is the Mother's expectation
   Of Messiah's speedy birth!

2 Thou wert happy, blessèd Mother!
   With the very bliss of heaven,
Since the angel's salutation
   In thy raptured ear was given;
Since the Ave of that midnight,
   When thou wert anointed Queen,
Like a river overflowing
   Hath the grace within thee been.

Advent

3 On the mountains of Judea,
    Like the chariot of the Lord,
Thou wert lifted in thy spirit
    By the uncreated Word;
Gifts and graces flowed upon thee
    In a sweet celestial strife,
And the growing of thy Burden
    Was the lightening of thy life.

4 And what wonders have been in thee,
    All the day and all the night,
While the angels fell before thee,
    To adore the Light of Light.
While the glory of the Father
    Hath been in thee as a home,
And the sceptre of creation
    Hath been wielded in thy womb!

5 Thou hast waited, Child of David!
    And thy waiting now is o'er!
Thou hast seen him, blessèd Mother!
    And wilt see him evermore;
Oh, his human face and features,
    They were passing sweet to see;
Thou beholdest them this moment;
    Mother, show them now to me!

              FREDERICK WILLIAM FABER Cong. Orat. 1814–63

Advent

7 HELMSLEY 87 87 47

THOMAS OLIVERS 1725–99
adapted MARTIN MADAN 1726–90

1 Lo! he comes with clouds descending,
   Once for favoured sinners slain;
   Thousand thousand saints attending
   Swell the triumph of his train:
   Alleluia!
   God appears, on earth to reign.

2 Every eye shall now behold him
   Robed in dreadful majesty;
   Those who set at nought and sold him,
   Pierced and nailed him to the tree,
   Deeply wailing
   Shall the true Messiah see.

Advent

3 Those dear tokens of his Passion
    Still his dazzling body bears,
Cause of endless exultation
    To his ransomed worshippers:
        With what rapture
    Gaze we on those glorious scars!

4 Yea, Amen! let all adore thee,
    High on thine eternal throne;
Saviour, take the power and glory:
    Claim the kingdom for thine own:
        O come quickly!
    Alleluia! Come, Lord, come!

JOHN CENNICK 1718–55
and CHARLES WESLEY 1707–88

Advent

8 VENI EMMANUEL 15th century French Franciscan *Processionale*
adapted Thomas Helmore 1811–90

1. O come, O come, Emmanuel,
   And ransom captive Israel,
   That mourns in lonely exile here,
   Until the Son of God appear.
   Rejoice! Rejoice! Emmanuel
   Shall come to thee, O Israel.

2. O come, thou Wisdom, from on high,
   And order all things far and nigh:
   To us the path of knowledge show,
   And teach us in her ways to go.

3. O come, O come, thou Lord of might,
   Who to thy tribes, on Sinai's height,
   In ancient times didst give the law
   In cloud, and majesty, and awe.

4. O come, thou Rod of Jesse, free
   Thine own from Satan's tyranny;
   From depths of hell thy people save
   And give them victory o'er the grave.

Advent

5 O come, thou Key of David, come,
   And open wide our heav'nly home;
   Make safe the way that leads on high,
   And close the path to misery.

6 O come, thou Day-spring, come and cheer
   Our spirits by thine advent here;
   Disperse the gloomy clouds of night,
   And death's dark shadows put to flight.

7 O come, Desire of nations, bind
   In one the hearts of all mankind;
   Bid every strife and sorrow cease
   And fill the world with heaven's peace.

Veni, veni, Emmanuel 13th century
based on the Advent 'O' Antiphons
tr. JOHN MASON NEALE 1818–66 and others

Advent

9 WINCHESTER NEW   LM   *Musikalisches Hand-Buch* Hamburg 1690
adapted William Henry Havergal 1793–1870

1. On Jordan's bank the Baptist's cry
   Announces that the Lord is nigh;
   Come then and hearken, for he brings
   High tidings from the King of kings.

2. Then cleansed be every breast from sin;
   Make straight the way for God within;
   Prepare we in our hearts a home,
   Where such a mighty guest may come.

3. For thou art our salvation, Lord,
   Our refuge, and our great reward;
   Without thy grace we waste away,
   Like flowers that wither and decay.

Advent

4 Stretch forth thine hand, to heal our sore,
   And make us rise, and fall no more;
   Once more upon thy people shine,
   And fill the world with love divine.

5 To him who left the throne of heaven
   To save mankind, all praise be given;
   Like praise be to the Father done,
   And Holy Spirit, Three in One.

Jordanis oras praevia
CHARLES COFFIN 1676–1749
tr. JOHN CHANDLER 1806–76

Advent

10 WACHET AUF   898 898 664 88   PHILIPP NICOLAI 1556–1608
arranged JOHANN SEBASTIAN BACH 1685–1750

1 Wake, O wake! with tidings thrilling
  The watchmen all the air are filling,
    Arise, Jerusalem, arise!
  Midnight strikes! no more delaying,
  'The hour has come!' we hear them saying,
    Where are ye all, ye virgins wise?
      The Bridegroom comes in sight,
      Raise high your torches bright!
        Alleluia!
      The wedding song
      Swells loud and strong:
    Go forth and join the festal throng.

Advent

2 Zion hears the watchmen shouting,
   Her heart leaps up with joy undoubting,
     She stands and waits with eager eyes:
  See her Friend from heaven descending,
  Adorned with truth and grace unending!
     Her light burns clear, her star doth rise,
        Now come, thou precious Crown,
        Lord Jesu, God's own Son!
          Alleluia!
        Let us prepare
        To follow there,
    Where in thy supper we may share.

3 Every soul in thee rejoices;
   From men and from angelic voices
     Be glory giv'n to thee alone!
  Now the gates of pearl receive us,
  Thy presence never more shall leave us,
     We stand with angels round thy throne.
        Earth cannot give below
        The bliss thou dost bestow.
          Alleluia!
        Grant us to raise,
        To length of days,
    The triumph-chorus of thy praise.

Wachet auf
PHILIPP NICOLAI 1556–1608
tr. FRANCIS CRAWFORD BURKITT 1864–1935

Christmas

11 ES IST EIN' ROS' ENTSPRUNGEN 15th century German
76 76 + refrain

1. A great and mighty wonder,
   A full and holy cure!
   The Virgin bears the Infant
   With virgin-honour pure.
   Repeat the hymn again!
   'To God on high be glory,
   And peace on earth to men!'

2. The Word becomes incarnate
   And yet remains on high!
   And cherubim sing anthems
   To shepherds from the sky.

3. While thus they sing your Monarch,
   Those bright angelic bands,
   Rejoice, ye vales and mountains,
   Ye oceans clap your hands.

4. Since all he comes to ransom,
   By all be he adored,
   The Infant born in Bethl'em,
   The Saviour and the Lord.

5. And idol forms shall perish,
   And error shall decay,
   And Christ shall wield his sceptre,
   Our Lord and God for ay.

Greek St Germanus 634–734
tr. John Mason Neale 1818–66 and others

Christmas

12 ADESTE FIDELES   Irregular   John Francis Wade's MS book c. 1740

1. Adeste fideles,
   Laeti triumphantes;
   Venite, venite in Bethlehem;
   Natum videte
   Regem angelorum:
     Venite adoremus,
     Venite adoremus,
     Venite adoremus Dominum!

2. Deum de Deo,
   Lumen de lumine,
   Gestant puellae viscera;
   Deum verum,
   Genitum, non factum:

3. Cantet nunc Io!
   Chorus angelorum:
   Cantet nunc aula
       coelestium,
   Gloria
   In excelsis Deo!

4. Ergo qui natus
   Die hodierna,
   Jesu, tibi sit gloria:
   Patris aeterni
   Verbum caro factum!

John Francis Wade's MS book c. 1740

Christmas

13 ADESTE FIDELES   Irregular   John Francis Wade's MS book c. 1740

1   O come, all ye faithful,
    Joyful and triumphant,
    O come ye, O come ye to
        Bethlehem;
    Come and behold him
    Born the King of angels:
      O come, let us adore him,
      O come, let us adore him,
      O come, let us adore him,
        Christ the Lord!

2   God of God,
    Light of Light,
    Lo! he abhors not the Virgin's
        womb;
    Very God,
    Begotten, not created.

3   Sing, choirs of angels,
    Sing in exultation,
    Sing, all ye citizens of
        heaven above;
    'Glory to God
    In the highest.'

4   Yea, Lord we greet thee,
    Born this happy morning,
    Jesu, to thee be glory given;
    Word of the Father,
    Now in flesh appearing.

Adeste Fideles
John Francis Wade's MS book c. 1740
tr. FREDERICK OAKELEY 1802–80

Christmas

14 WARUM SOLLT' ICH   8336 D   JOHANN GEORG EBELING 1637–76

1. All my heart this night
 rejoices,
   As I hear,
   Far and near,
 Sweetest angel voices:
 'Christ is born!' their choirs
   are singing;
   Till the air
   Everywhere
 Now with joy is ringing.

2. Hark! a voice from yonder
   manger,
   Soft and sweet,
   Doth entreat,
 'Flee from woe and danger!
 Brethren, come! from all
   doth grieve you,
   You are freed;
   All you need
 I will surely give you.'

3. Come then, let us hasten
   yonder;
   Here let all,
   Great and small,
 Kneel in awe and wonder;
 Love him who with love
   is yearning;
   Hail the star
   That from far
 Bright with hope is burning.

4. Thee, dear Lord, with heed
   I'll cherish,
   Live to thee,
   And with thee,
 Dying, shall not perish;
 But shall dwell with thee
   for ever,
   Far on high,
   In the joy
 That can alter never.

Fröhlich soll mein Herze springen
PAUL GERHARDT 1607–76
tr. CATHERINE WINKWORTH 1827–78

Christmas

15 LES ANGES DANS NOS CAMPAGNES 18th century French
77 77 + refrain

Refrain
Glo - - - - - - ri - a in ex-cel-sis De - o, Glo - - - - ri - a in ex-cel-sis De - o.

1 Angels we have heard on high,
    Singing sweetly o'er the plains,
And the mountains in reply,
    Echoing their joyous strains.
      Gloria in excelsis Deo.

2 Shepherds why this jubilee?
    Why your rapturous strain prolong?
What the gladsome tidings be,
    Which inspire your heavenly song?

Christmas

3 Come to Bethlehem and see
    Him whose birth the angels sing:
Come, adore on bended knee
    Christ the Lord, the new-born King.

4 See him in a manger laid,
    Whom the choirs of angels praise;
Mary, Joseph, lend your aid,
    While our hearts in love we raise.

HENRI FRIEDRICH HÉMY 1818–88
after JAMES CHADWICK 1813–82

Christmas

16
FIRST TUNE

CRADLE SONG   11 11 11 11   WILLIAM JAMES KIRKPATRICK 1838–1921

1. Away in a manger, no crib for a bed,
   The little Lord Jesus laid down his sweet head.
   The stars in the bright sky looked down where he lay,
   The little Lord Jesus asleep on the hay.

2. The cattle are lowing, the Baby awakes,
   But little Lord Jesus no crying he makes.
   I love thee, Lord Jesus! Look down from the sky,
   And stay by my bedside till morning is nigh.

3. Be near me, Lord Jesus; I ask thee to stay
   Close by me for ever, and love me, I pray.
   Bless all the dear children in thy tender care,
   And fit us for heaven, to live with thee there.

vv. 1, 2 *Little Children's Book* Philadelphia 1885
v. 3 Charles Gabriel's *Vineyard Songs* Louisville 1892

Christmas

16 SECOND TUNE

NORMANDY CAROL   11 11 11 11   traditional Normandy

1. Away in a manger, no crib for a bed,
   The little Lord Jesus laid down his sweet head.
   The stars in the bright sky looked down where he lay,
   The little Lord Jesus asleep on the hay.

2. The cattle are lowing, the Baby awakes,
   But little Lord Jesus no crying he makes.
   I love thee, Lord Jesus! Look down from the sky,
   And stay by my bedside till morning is nigh.

3. Be near me, Lord Jesus; I ask thee to stay
   Close by me for ever, and love me, I pray.
   Bless all the dear children in thy tender care,
   And fit us for heaven, to live with thee there.

vv. 1, 2 *Little Children's Book* Philadelphia 1885
v. 3 Charles Gabriel's *Vineyard Songs* Louisville 1892

Christmas

17 STOCKPORT   10 10 10 10 10 10   JOHN WAINWRIGHT 1723–68

1. Christians awake! salute the happy morn
   Whereon the Saviour of the world was born;
   Rise to adore the mystery of love
   Which hosts of angels chanted from above;
   With them the joyful tidings first begun
   Of God incarnate and the Virgin's Son.

2. Then to the watchful shepherds it was told,
   Who heard the angelic herald's voice, 'Behold,
   I bring good tidings of a Saviour's birth
   To you and all the nations of the earth:
   This day hath God fulfilled his promised word,
   This day is born a Saviour, Christ the Lord.'

Christmas

3   He spake; and straightway that celestial choir
     In hymns of joy, unknown before, conspire;
     The praises of redeeming love they sang,
     And heaven's whole orb with alleluias rang:
     God's highest glory was their anthem still,
     Peace on the earth, and unto men goodwill.

4   To Bethl'em straight the enlightened shepherds ran
     To see the wonder God had wrought for man,
     And found, with Joseph and the blessèd Maid,
     Her Son, the Saviour, in a manger laid:
     They to their flocks, still praising God, return,
     And their glad hearts within their bosoms burn.

5   Like Mary let us ponder in our mind
     God's wondrous love in saving lost mankind;
     Trace we the Babe, who hath retrieved our loss,
     From his poor manger to his bitter Cross;
     Treading his steps, assisted by his grace,
     Till man's first heavenly state again takes place.

6   Then may we hope, the angelic hosts among,
     To sing, redeemed, a glad triumphal song;
     He that was born upon this joyful day
     Around us all his glory shall display;
     Saved by his love, incessant we shall sing
     Eternal praise to heaven's almighty King.

JOHN BYROM 1691–1763

Christmas

18 PUER NOBIS NASCITUR LM medieval German
adapted MICHAEL PRAETORIUS 1571–1621

1 Come, thou Redeemer of the earth,
And manifest thy virgin-birth:
Let every age adoring fall,
Such birth befits the God of all.

2 Begotten of no human will,
But of the Spirit, thou art still
The Word of God in flesh arrayed,
The promised fruit to man displayed.

3 The virgin womb that burden gained
With virgin honour all unstained;
The banners there of virtue glow,
God in his temple dwells below.

4 O equal to thy Father, thou!
Gird on thy fleshly mantle now,
The weakness of our mortal state
With deathless might invigorate.

5 Thy cradle here shall glitter bright,
And darkness breathe a newer light,
Where endless faith shall shine serene,
And twilight never intervene.

6 All laud to God the Father be,
All praise, eternal Son, to thee:
All glory, as is ever meet,
To God the Holy Paraclete.

Veni, Redemptor gentium
ST AMBROSE 340–97
tr. JOHN MASON NEALE 1818–66 and others

Christmas

19 BRANLE DE L'OFFICIAL 77 77 + refrain 16th century dance
in Thoinot Arbeau's *Orchésographie* 1589

Refrain

Glo - - - - - ri - a, Ho - san - na in ex - cel - sis!

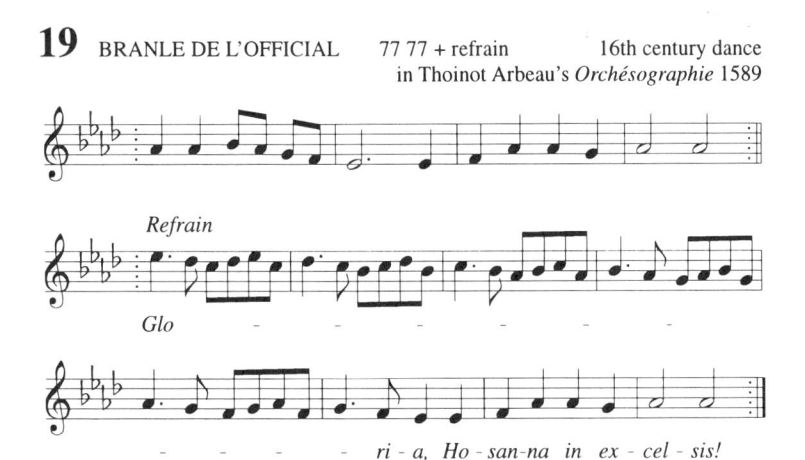

1. Ding dong! merrily on high in heav'n the bells are ringing:
Ding dong! verily the sky is riv'n with angels singing.
   Gloria,
   Hosanna in excelsis.

2. E'en so here below, below, let steeple bells be swungen,
And *io,** io, io,* by priest and people sungen.

3. Pray you, dutifully prime your matin chime, ye ringers;
May you beautifully rime your evetime song, ye singers.

GEORGE RATCLIFFE WOODWARD 1848–1934

* *io* pronounced as *ee-o*

Christmas

20 GOD REST YOU MERRY
86 86 86 + refrain

traditional English

1. God rest you merry, gentlemen,
   Let nothing you dismay,
   Remember Christ our Saviour
   Was born on Christmas Day,
   To save us all from Satan's power
   When we were gone astray.
   O tidings of comfort and joy,
   comfort and joy!
   O tidings of comfort and joy!

2. From God our heavenly Father
   A blessèd angel came,
   And unto certain shepherds
   Brought tidings of the same,
   How that in Bethlehem was born
   The Son of God by name.

Christmas

3 And when they came to Bethlehem
    Where our dear Saviour lay,
They found him in a manger,
    Where oxen feed on hay;
His mother Mary kneeling down,
    Unto the Lord did pray.

4 The shepherds at those tidings
    Rejoicèd much in mind,
And left their flocks a-feeding
    In tempest, storm and wind,
And went to Bethlehem straightway
    This blessèd Babe to find.

5 Now to the Lord sing praises,
    All you within this place,
And with true love and brotherhood
    Each other now embrace;
The holy tide of Christmas
    All others doth efface.

                            West Country traditional
              in William Sandys's *Christmas Carols* 1833

Christmas

21 MENDELSSOHN 7777 7777 77 FELIX MENDELSSOHN 1809–47
adapted WILLIAM HAYMAN CUMMINGS 1831–1915

1. Hark! the herald angels sing
   Glory to the new-born King;
   Peace on earth and mercy mild,
   God and sinners reconciled:
   Joyful all ye nations rise,
   Join the triumph of the skies,
   With the angelic host proclaim,
   Christ is born in Bethlehem.
   Hark! the herald angels sing
   Glory to the new-born King.

Christmas

2 Christ, by highest heaven adored,
　Christ, the everlasting Lord,
　Late in time behold him come
　Offspring of a Virgin's womb!
　Veiled in flesh the Godhead see,
　Hail the incarnate Deity!
　Pleased as man with man to dwell,
　Jesus, our Emmanuel.

3 Hail the heaven-born Prince of Peace!
　Hail the Sun of Righteousness!
　Light and life to all he brings,
　Ris'n with healing in his wings;
　Mild he lays his glory by,
　Born that man no more may die,
　Born to raise the sons of earth,
　Born to give them second birth.

        Charles Wesley 1707–88
            and others

Christmas

22 IN DULCI JUBILO   66 76 76 55   13th century German

1. *In dulci jubilo*
   Now sing with hearts aglow!
      Our hearts' joy and pleasure
   Lies *in praesepio;*
      Like sunshine is our treasure
   Matris in gremio.
   Alpha es et O!

2. *O Jesu, parvule,*
   I yearn for thee alway;
      Hear me, I beseech thee,
   O puer optime.
      Lord, grant my prayer may reach thee,
   O princeps gloriae.
   Trahe me post te!

Christmas

3 *O Patris caritas!*
  O Nati lenitas!
    Deeply were we stainèd
  Per nostra crimina;
    But thou for us hast gainèd
  Coelorum gaudia.
  O that we were there!

4 *Ubi sunt gaudia*
  What other place but there?
    Angels ever singing
  Their *nova cantica*;
    In heaven the bells are ringing
  In Regis curia.
  O that we were there!

Latin and German 13th century
tr. cento arranged P.R.

Christmas

23 CRANHAM Irregular   Gustav Holst 1874–1934

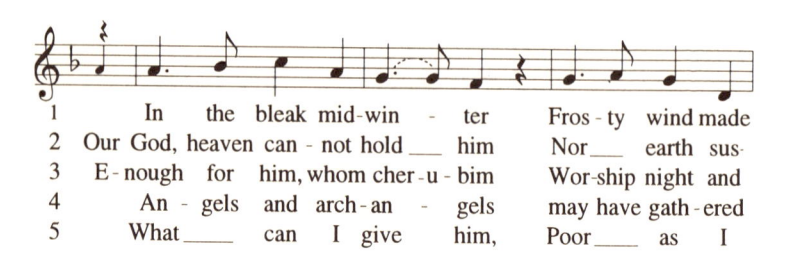

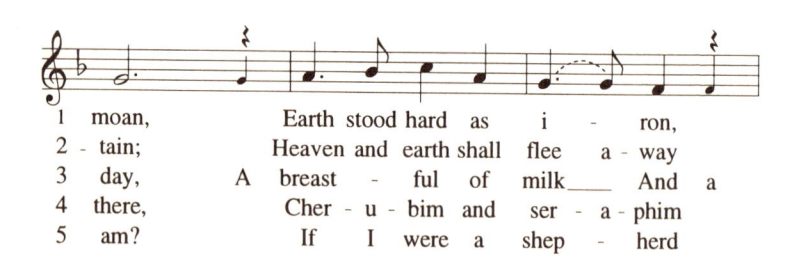

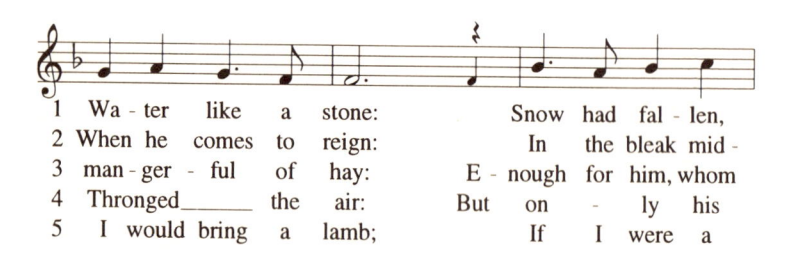

1. In the bleak mid-winter
Frosty wind made moan,
Earth stood hard as iron,
Water like a stone:
Snow had fallen,
Snow on snow,
Snow on snow,
In the bleak mid-winter
Long ago.

2. Our God, heaven cannot hold him
Nor earth sustain;
Heaven and earth shall flee away
When he comes to reign:
In the bleak mid-winter
A stable-place sufficed
The Lord God Almighty,
Jesus Christ.

3. Enough for him, whom cherubim
Worship night and day,
A breast-ful of milk
And a manger-ful of hay:
Enough for him, whom angels
Fall down before,
The ox and ass and camel
Which adore.

4. Angels and archangels
May have gathered there,
Cherubim and seraphim
Thronged the air:
But only his mother
In her maiden bliss
Worshipped the Beloved
With a kiss.

5. What can I give him,
Poor as I am?
If I were a shepherd
I would bring a lamb;
If I were a wise man
I would do my part;
Yet what I can I give him —
Give my heart.

Christmas

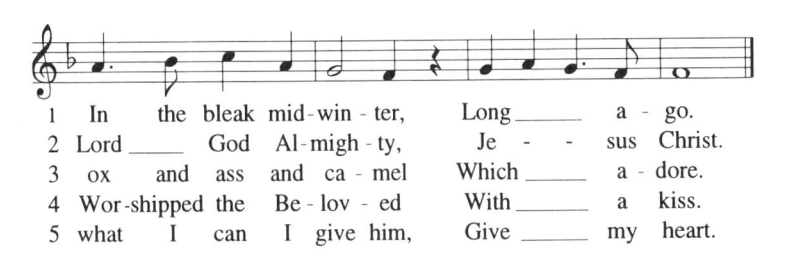

1. snow on snow, Snow on snow, In the bleak mid-winter, Long ago.
2. -winter A stable-place sufficed The Lord God Almighty, Jesus Christ.
3. angels Fall down before, The ox and ass and camel Which adore.
4. Mother In her maiden bliss Worshipped the Beloved With a kiss.
5. wise man I would do my part; Yet what I can I give him, Give my heart.

CHRISTINA ROSSETTI 1830–94

Christmas

24 W ŻŁOBIE LEŻY 87 87 88 7 traditional Polish

1. Infant holy,
   Infant lowly,
   For his bed a cattle stall;
   Oxen lowing,
   Little knowing
   Christ the Babe is Lord of all.
   Swift are winging
   Angels singing,
   Nowells ringing,
   Tidings bringing,
   Christ the Babe is Lord of all.

2. Flocks were sleeping,
   Shepherds keeping
   Vigil till the morning new;
   Saw the glory,
   Heard the story,
   Tidings of a gospel true.
   Thus rejoicing,
   Free from sorrow,
   Praises voicing,
   Greet the morrow,
   Christ the Babe was born for you!

W żłobie leży traditional Polish
tr. EDITH REED 1885–1933

Christmas

25 NOEL   DCM   ARTHUR SULLIVAN 1842–1900
after a traditional English melody

1. It came upon the midnight clear,
   That glorious song of old,
   From angels bending near the earth
   To touch their harps of gold:
   'Peace on the earth, good-will to men,
   From heaven's all-gracious King!'
   The world in solemn stillness lay
   To hear the angels sing.

2. Still through the cloven skies they come,
   With peaceful wings unfurled;
   And still their heavenly music floats
   O'er all the weary world;
   Above its sad and lowly plains
   They bend on hovering wing;
   And ever o'er its Babel sounds
   The blessèd angels sing.

3. Yet with the woes of sin and strife
   The world has suffered long;
   Beneath the angel-strain have rolled
   Two thousand years of wrong;
   And man, at war with man, hears not
   The love-song which they bring:
   O hush the noise, ye men of strife,
   And hear the angels sing!

4. For lo! the days are hastening on,
   By prophet-bards foretold,
   When, with the ever-circling years,
   Comes round the age of gold;
   When peace shall over all the earth
   Its ancient splendours fling,
   And the whole world send back the song
   Which now the angels sing.

EDMUND HAMILTON SEARS 1810–76

Christmas

26 O JESULEIN SÜSS 10 9 88 10   Samuel Scheidt's *Tabulatur-Buch* 1650

1. O Little One sweet, O Little One mild,
   Thy Father's will thou hast fulfilled;
     Thou cam'st from heaven to mortal ken,
     Equal to be with us poor men,
   O Little One sweet, O Little One mild.

2. O Little One sweet, O Little One mild,
   With joy thou hast the whole world filled;
     Thou camest here from heaven's domain,
     To bring men comfort in their pain,
   O Little One sweet, O Little One mild.

3. O Little One sweet, O Little One mild,
   Help us to do as thou hast willed.
     Lo! all we have belongs to thee!
     Ah, keep us in our fealty!
   O Little One sweet, O Little One mild.

O Jesulein süss
Samuel Scheidt's Tabulatur-Buch 1650
tr. PERCY DEARMER 1867–1936

Christmas

27 FOREST GREEN DCM

English folk tune
adapted RALPH VAUGHAN WILLIAMS 1872–1958

1 O little town of Bethlehem,
  How still we see thee lie!
 Above thy deep and dreamless sleep
  The silent stars go by.
 Yet in thy dark streets shineth
  The everlasting light;
 The hopes and fears of all the years
  Are met in thee tonight.

2 O morning stars, together
  Proclaim the holy birth,
 And praises sing to God the King,
  And peace to men on earth;
 For Christ is born of Mary;
  And, gathered all above,
 While mortals sleep, the angels keep
  Their watch of wondering love.

3 How silently, how silently
  The wondrous gift is given!
 So God imparts to human hearts
  The blessings of his heaven.
 No ear may hear his coming;
  But in this world of sin,
 Where meek souls will receive him, still
  The dear Christ enters in.

4 Where children pure and happy
  Pray to the blessèd Child,
 Where misery cries out to thee,
  Son of the Mother mild;
 Where charity stands watching
  And faith holds wide the door,
 The dark night wakes, the glory breaks,
  And Christmas comes once more.

5 O holy Child of Bethlehem
  Descend to us, we pray;
 Cast out our sin, and enter in,
  Be born in us today.
 We hear the Christmas angels
  The great glad tidings tell:
 O come to us, abide with us,
  Our Lord Emmanuel.

PHILLIPS BROOKS 1835–93

Christmas

28 DIVINUM MYSTERIUM   87 87 87 7   13th century *Sanctus* trope
adapted *Piae Cantiones* Griefswald 1582

1. Of the Father's heart begotten,
    Ere the world from chaos rose,
   He is Alpha: from that Fountain
    All that is and hath been flows;
   He is Omega, of all things
    Yet to come the mystic Close,
      Evermore and evermore.

2. By his word was all created;
    He commanded and 'twas done;
   Earth and sky and boundless ocean,
    Universe of three in one,
   All that sees the moon's soft radiance,
    All that breathes beneath the sun,

Christmas

3 He assumed this mortal body,
  Frail and feeble, doomed to die,
That the race from dust created
  Might not perish utterly,
Which the dreadful Law had sentenced
  In the depths of hell to lie,

4 O how blest that wondrous birthday,
  When the Maid the curse retrieved,
Brought to birth mankind's salvation,
  By the Holy Ghost conceived;
And the Babe, the world's Redeemer,
  In her loving arms received,

5 This is he, whom seer and sybil
  Sang in ages long gone by;
This is he of old revealèd
  In the page of prophecy;
Lo! he comes, the promised Saviour;
  Let the world his praises cry,

6 Sing, ye heights of heaven, his praises;
  Angels and archangels, sing!
Wheresoe'er ye be, ye faithful,
  Let your joyous anthems ring,
Every tongue his name confessing,
  Countless voices answering,
    Evermore and evermore.

Corde natus ex parentis
AURELIUS PRUDENTIUS 348–413
tr. ROBY FURLEY DAVIS 1866–1937

Christmas

29 SUSSEX CAROL   88 88 88   traditional English

1. On Christmas night all Christians sing
To hear the news the angels bring:
    On Christmas night all Christians sing
    To hear the news the angels bring:
News of great joy, news of great mirth,
News of our merciful King's birth.

2. Then why should men on earth be sad,
Since our Redeemer made us glad,
    Then why should men on earth be sad,
    Since our Redeemer made us glad,
When from our sin he set us free,
All for to gain our liberty?

Christmas

3 When sin departs before his grace,
　Then life and health come in its place;
　　When sin departs before his grace,
　　Then life and health come in its place;
　Angels and men with joy may sing,
　All for to see the new-born King.

4 All out of darkness we have light,
　Which made the angels sing this night:
　　All out of darkness we have light,
　　Which made the angels sing this night:
　'Glory to God and peace to men,
　Now and for evermore—Amen.'

Sussex traditional
after LUKE WADDING died 1686

Christmas

30 IRBY   87 87 77   Henry John Gauntlett 1805–76

1. Once in royal David's city
   Stood a lowly cattle shed,
   Where a Mother laid her Baby
   In a manger for his bed:
   Mary was that Mother mild,
   Jesus Christ her little Child.

2. He came down to earth from heaven,
   Who is God and Lord of all,
   And his shelter was a stable,
   And his cradle was a stall;
   With the poor, and mean, and lowly,
   Lived on earth our Saviour holy.

3. And through all his wondrous childhood
   He would honour and obey,
   Love and watch the lowly Maiden,
   In whose gentle arms he lay;
   Christian children all must be
   Mild, obedient, good as he.

Christmas

4 For he is our childhood's pattern,
　Day by day like us he grew,
　He was little, weak, and helpless,
　Tears and smiles like us he knew;
　And he feeleth for our sadness,
　And he shareth in our gladness.

5 And our eyes at last shall see him,
　Through his own redeeming love,
　For that Child so dear and gentle
　Is our Lord in heaven above;
　And he leads his children on
　To the place where he is gone.

6 Not in that poor lowly stable,
　With the oxen standing by,
　We shall see him; but in heaven,
　Set at God's right hand on high;
　When like stars his children crowned,
　All in white shall wait around.

CECIL FRANCES ALEXANDER 1818–95

Christmas

31 PERSONENT HODIE 666 66 55 66 *Piae Cantiones* Griefswald 1582
arranged Gustav Holst 1874–1934

1 Personent hodie
  Voces puerulae,
  Laudantes jucunde
    Qui nobis est natus,
    Summo Deo datus,
  Et de vir- vir- vir-,
  Et de vir- vir- vir-,
  Et de virgineo
    Ventre procreatus.

2 In mundo nascitur;
  Pannis involvitur,
  Praesepi ponitur
    Stabulo brutorum,
    Rector supernorum.
  Perdidit, -dit, -dit,
  Perdidit, -dit, -dit,
  Perdidit spolia
    Princeps infernorum.

3 Magi tres venerunt;
  Parvulum inquirunt;
  Bethlehem adeunt;
    Stellulam sequendo,
    Ipsum adorando,
  Aurum, thus, thus, thus,
  Aurum, thus, thus, thus,
  Aurum, thus et myrrham
    Ei offerendo.

4 Omnes clericuli,
  Pariter pueri,
  Cantent ut angeli:
    Advenisti mundo,
    Laudes tibi fundo.
  Ideo, -o, -o,
  Ideo, -o, -o,
  Ideo gloria
    In excelsis Deo!

Piae Cantiones Griefswald 1582

Christmas

32 QUEM PASTORES   88 87   14th century German

1. Quem pastores laudavere,
   Quibus angeli dixere:
   'Absit vobis jam timere:
   Natus est Rex Gloriae!'

2. Ad quem magi ambulabant,
   Aurum thus, myrrham portabant;
   Immolabant haec sincere;
   Leoni victoriae;

3. Exsultemus cum Maria
   In caelesti hierarchia:
   Natum promant voce pia
   Dulci cum melodia;

4. Christo Regi, Deo nato,
   Per Mariam nobis dato,
   Merito resonet vere:
   'Laus, honor, et gloria!'

14th century German

Christmas

33 QUEM PASTORES   88 87   14th century German

1 Thou whom shepherds worshipped, hearing
    Angels tell their tidings cheering,
    'Sirs, away with doubt and fearing!
    Christ the King is born for all.'

2 Thou to whom came wise men faring,
    Gold and myrrh and incense bearing,
    Heartfelt homage thus declaring
    To the King that's born for all.

3 Bending low in adoration,
    Thee we greet, for our salvation
    Giv'n by wondrous incarnation,
    King of Glóry, born for all.

> based on *Quem pastores*
> 14th century German
> *tr.* CHARLES STANLEY PHILLIPS 1883–1949

Christmas

34 OXFORD 77 77 D

JOHN GOSS 1800–80

1. See, amid the winter's snow,
   Born for us on earth below,
   See, the tender Lamb appears,
   Promised from eternal years.
   Hail, thou ever-blessèd morn,
   Hail redemption's happy dawn!
   Sing through all Jerusalem,
   Christ is born in Bethlehem.

2. Lo, within a manger lies
   He who built the starry skies;
   He who, throned in height sublime,
   Sits amid the cherubim.

3. Say, ye holy shepherds, say,
   What your joyful news today?
   Wherefore have ye left your sheep
   On the lonely mountain steep?

4. 'As we watched at dead of night,
   Lo, we saw a wondrous light;
   Angels, singing peace on earth,
   Told us of the Saviour's birth.'

5. Sacred Infant, all divine,
   What a tender love was thine,
   Thus to come from highest bliss,
   Down to such a world as this!

6. Teach, oh teach us, holy Child,
   By thy face so meek and mild;
   Teach us to resemble thee,
   In thy sweet humility.

7. Virgin Mother, Mary blest,
   By the joys that fill thy breast,
   Pray for us, that we may prove
   Worthy of the Saviour's love.

EDWARD CASWALL Cong. Orat. 1814–78

Christmas

35 STILLE NACHT Irregular Franz Xaver Gruber 1787–1863
later form A.R. Friese Dresden 1833

1. Silent night, holy night,
   All is calm, all is bright:
   'Round yon Virgin Mother and Child,
   Holy Infant, so tender and mild,
   Sleep in heavenly peace,
   Sleep in heavenly peace.

2. Silent night, holy night,
   Shepherds quake at the sight,
   Glories stream from heaven afar,
   Heav'nly hosts sing Alleluia;
   Christ, the Saviour is born,
   Christ, the Saviour is born.

3. Silent night, holy night,
   Son of God, love's pure light
   Radiant beams from thy holy face,
   With the dawn of redeeming grace,
   Jesus, Lord at thy birth,
   Jesus, Lord at thy birth.

Stille Nacht
Joseph Mohr 1792–1849
tr. John Freeman Young 1820–85

Christmas

36 GABRIEL'S MESSAGE   10 10 12 10

traditional Basque
arranged EDGAR PETTMAN 1865–1943

1. The angel Gabriel from heaven came,
   His wings as drifted snow, his eyes as flame;
   'All hail,' said he, 'thou lowly maiden Mary,
   Most highly favoured lady!' Gloria!

2. 'For know a blessèd Mother thou shalt be,
   All generations laud and honour thee,
   Thy Son shall be Emmanuel, by seers foretold,
   Most highly favoured lady!' Gloria!

3. Then gentle Mary meekly bowed her head,
   'To me be as it pleaseth God,' she said.
   'My soul shall laud and magnify his holy name.'
   Most highly favoured lady! Gloria!

4. Of her, Emmanuel the Christ was born
   In Bethlehem, all on a Christmas morn,
   And Christian folk throughout the world will ever say
   'Most highly favoured lady!' Gloria!

SABINE BARING-GOULD 1834–1924
after the Basque *Birjina gaztettobat zegoen*

Christmas

37 THE FIRST NOWELL   Irregular   traditional English

1. The first Nowell the angel did say
   Was to certain poor shepherds in fields as they lay;
   In fields where they lay keeping their sheep,
   On a cold winter's night that was so deep.
   Nowell, Nowell, Nowell, Nowell,
   Born is the King of Israel.

2. They lookèd up and saw a star,
   Shining in the east, beyond them far:
   And to the earth it gave great light,
   And so it continued both day and night.

Christmas

3 And by the light of that same star,
   Three wise men came from country far;
   To seek for a king was their intent,
   And to follow the star wheresoever it went.

4 This star drew nigh to the north-west,
   O'er Bethlehem it took its rest,
   And there it did both stop and stay
   Right over the place where Jesus lay.

5 Then entered in those wise men three,
   Full reverently upon their knee,
   And offered there in his presence
   Their gold and myrrh and frankincense.

6 Then let us all with one accord
   Sing praises to our heavenly Lord,
   That hath made heaven and earth of nought,
   And with his Blood mankind hath bought.

traditional English
in William Sandys's *Christmas Carols* 1833

Christmas

38 A VIRGIN UNSPOTTED   11 11 11 11 + refrain   traditional English

1. The great God of heaven is come down to earth,
   His mother a Virgin, and sinless his birth;
   The Father eternal his Father alone:
   He sleeps in the manger; he reigns on the throne:
   Then let us adore him, and praise his great love:
   To save us poor sinners he came from above.

2. A Babe on the breast of a Maiden he lies,
   Yet sits with the Father on high in the skies;
   Before him their faces the seraphim hide,
   While Joseph stands waiting, unscared, by his side:

3. Lo! here is Emmanuel, here is the Child,
   The Son that was promised to Mary so mild;
   Whose power and dominion shall ever increase,
   The Prince that shall rule o'er a kingdom of peace:

Christmas

4 The Wonderful Counsellor, boundless in might,
  The Father's own image, the beam of his light;
  Behold him now wearing the likeness of man,
  Weak, helpless, and speechless, in measure a span:

5 O wonder of wonders, which none can unfold:
  The Ancient of Days is an hour or two old;
  The maker of all things is made of the earth,
  Man is worshipped by angels, and God comes to birth:

6 The Word in the bliss of the Godhead remains,
  Yet in flesh comes to suffer the keenest of pains;
  He is that he was, and for ever shall be,
  But becomes what he was not, for you and for me.

HENRY RAMSDEN BRAMLEY 1833–1917

Christmas

39 PUER NOBIS 76 77

medieval *Benedicamus* trope
adapted *Piae Cantiones* Griefswald 1582

1. Unto us is born a Son,
    King of quires supernal;
   See on earth his life begun,
    Of lords the Lord eternal.

2. Christ, from heav'n descending low,
    Comes on earth a stranger:
   Ox and ass their Owner know
    Becradled in a manger.

3. This did Herod sore affray,
    And grievously bewilder;
   So he gave the word to slay,
    And slew the little childer.

4. Of his love and mercy mild
    This the Christmas story:
   And oh, that Mary's gentle Child
    Might lead us up to glory!

5. O and A and A and O,
    Cum cantibus in choro,
   Let our merry organ go,
    Benedicamus Domino.

Puer nobis nascitur 14th century or earlier
tr. GEORGE RATCLIFFE WOODWARD 1848–1934

Christmas

40 WINCHESTER OLD   CM   Thomas East's *Psalms* 1592

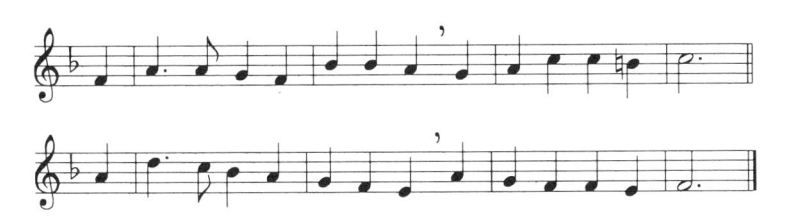

1. While shepherds watched their flocks by night,
    All seated on the ground,
   The angel of the Lord came down,
    And glory shone around.

2. 'Fear not,' said he (for mighty dread
    Had seized their troubled mind);
   'Glad tidings of great joy I bring
    To you and all mankind.

3. 'To you in David's town this day
    Is born of David's line
   A Saviour, who is Christ the Lord;
    And this shall be the sign:

4. 'The heavenly Babe you there shall find
    To human view displayed,
   All meanly wrapped in swathing bands,
    And in a manger laid.'

5. Thus spake the seraph; and forthwith
    Appeared a shining throng
   Of angels praising God, who thus
    Addressed their joyful song:

6. 'All glory be to God on high,
    And to the earth be peace;
   Good-will henceforth from heaven to men
    Begin and never cease.'

NAHUM TATE 1652–1715

Epiphany

41 DIX (Treuer Heiland) 77 77 77 CONRAD KOCHER 1786–1872
adapted WILLIAM HENRY MONK 1823–89

1 As with gladness men of old
   Did the guiding star behold,
   As with joy they hailed its light,
   Leading onward, beaming bright,
   So, most gracious God, may we
   Evermore be led to thee.

2 As with joyful steps they sped
   To that lowly manger-bed,
   There to bend the knee before
   Him whom heaven and earth adore,
   So may we with willing feet
   Ever seek thy mercy-seat.

3 As they offered gifts most rare
   At that manger rude and bare,
   So may we with holy joy,
   Pure, and free from sin's alloy,
   All our costliest treasures bring,
   Christ, to thee our heavenly King.

Epiphany

4 Holy Jesu, every day
　Keep us in the narrow way;
　And, when earthly things are past,
　Bring our ransomed souls at last
　Where they need no star to guide,
　Where no clouds thy glory hide.

5 In the heavenly country bright
　Need they no created light;
　Thou its Light, its Joy, its Crown,
　Thou its Sun which goes not down:
　There for ever may we sing
　Alleluias to our King.

　　　　　　　　　WILLIAM CHATTERTON DIX 1837–98

Epiphany

42 STUTTGART 87 87 Christian Friedrich Witt's *Psalmodia Sacra* 1715
adapted Henry John Gauntlett 1805–76

1. Bethlehem, of noblest cities
   None can once with thee compare;
   Thou alone the Lord from heaven
   Didst for us incarnate bear.

2. Fairer than the sun at morning
   Was the star that told his birth;
   To the lands their God announcing,
   Hid in human form on earth.

3. By its lambent beauty guided,
   See, the eastern kings appear;
   See them bend, their gifts to offer,
   Gifts of incense, gold and myrrh.

4. Solemn things of mystic meaning!
   Incense doth the God disclose;
   Gold a royal child proclaimeth;
   Myrrh a future tomb foreshows.

5. Holy Jesu, in thy brightness
   To the Gentile world displayed,
   With the Father and the Spirit,
   Endless praise to thee be paid.

O sola magnarum urbium
Aurelius Prudentius 348–413
tr. Edward Caswall Cong. Orat. 1814–78 *

Epiphany

43 EPIPHANY   11 10 11 10   JOSEPH FRANCIS THRUPP 1827–67

An alternative tune will be found at Hymn 156.

1. Brightest and best of the sons of the morning,
    Dawn on our darkness and lend us thine aid;
   Star of the East, the horizon adorning,
    Guide where our infant Redeemer is laid.

2. Cold on his cradle the dew-drops are shining,
    Low lies his head with the beasts of the stall:
   Angels adore him in slumber reclining,
    Maker and Monarch and Saviour of all.

3. Say, shall we yield him, in costly devotion,
    Odours of Edom and offerings divine?
   Gems of the mountain and pearls of the ocean,
    Myrrh from the forest or gold from the mine?

4. Vainly we offer each ample oblation,
    Vainly with gifts would his favour secure;
   Richer by far is the heart's adoration,
    Dearer to God are the prayers of the poor.

5. Brightest and best of the sons of the morning,
    Dawn on our darkness and lend us thine aid;
   Star of the East, the horizon adorning,
    Guide where our infant Redeemer is laid.

REGINALD HEBER 1783–1826

Epiphany

44 ST CECILIA   66 66   LEIGHTON GEORGE HAYNE 1836–83

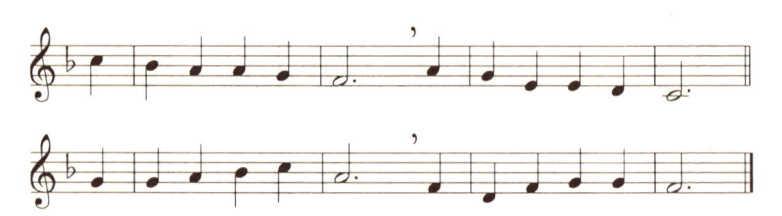

An alternative tune will be found at Hymn 171.

This hymn is most suitable for the Presentation of the Lord.

1. Hail to the Lord who comes,
   Comes to his temple gate,
   Not with his angel hosts,
   Nor in his kingly state;

2. But borne upon the throne
   Of Mary's gentle breast;
   Thus to his Father's house
   He comes, a humble guest.

3. There filled with holy joy,
   Old Simeon in his hands
   Takes up the promised Child,
   The glory of all lands.

Epiphany

4 Our bodies and our souls
  Are temples now for him,
  For we are born of grace—
  God lights our souls within.

5 O Light of all the earth!
  We light our lives with thee;
  The chains of darkness gone
  All sons of God are free.

JOHN ELLERTON 1826–93 and others

Epiphany

45 WIE SCHÖN LEUCHTET   887 887 888   Philipp Nicolai 1556–1608
arranged Felix Mendelssohn 1809–47

1. How brightly beams the morning star
   With sudden radiance from afar
      To cheer us with its shining!
   Brightness of God, that breaks our night
   And fills the darkened souls with light
      Who long for truth were pining!
   Thy word, Jesus, inly feeds us,
   Rightly leads us, life bestowing.
   Praise, oh praise such love o'erflowing!

2. Through thee alone can we be blest;
   Then deep be on our hearts impressed
      The love that thou hast borne us;
   So make us ready to fulfil
   With burning zeal thy holy will,
      Though men may mock or scorn us;
   Saviour, let us never lose thee,
   For we choose thee, thirst to know thee;
   All we are and have we owe thee!

Epiphany

3 To him who came on earth to save,
  Who conquered death and burst the grave,
    Each day new praise be given.
  Adore the Lamb who once was slain,
  The Friend whom none shall trust in vain,
    Whose grace from none is hidden.
  Highest heaven, tell the story
  Of his glory, till his praises
  Flood with light earth's darkest places.

> *Wie schön leuchtet der Morgenstern*
> PHILIPP NICOLAI 1556–1608
> and JOHANN ADOLF SCHLEGEL 1721–93
> *tr.* CATHERINE WINKWORTH 1827–78 and others

Epiphany

46 WAS LEBET
13 10 13 10

Johann Reinhardt's *Choral-Buch* Üttingen 1754

1. O worship the Lord in the beauty of holiness!
   Bow down before him, his glory proclaim;
   With gold of obedience, and incense of lowliness,
   Kneel and adore him, the Lord is his name!

2. Low at his feet lay thy burden of carefulness,
   High on his heart he will bear it for thee,
   Comfort thy sorrows, and answer thy prayerfulness,
   Guiding thy steps as may best for thee be.

3. Fear not to enter his courts in the slenderness
   Of the poor wealth thou wouldst reckon as thine:
   Truth in its beauty, and love in its tenderness,
   These are the offerings to lay on his shrine.

4. These, though we bring them in trembling and fearfulness,
   He will accept for the name that is dear;
   Mornings of joy give for evenings of tearfulness,
   Trust for our trembling and hope for our fear.

5. O worship the Lord in the beauty of holiness!
   Bow down before him, his glory proclaim;
   With gold of obedience, and incense of lowliness,
   Kneel and adore him, the Lord is his name!

JOHN SAMUEL BEWLEY MONSELL 1811–75

Epiphany

47 SALZBURG 77 77 D

JAKOB HINTZE 1622–1702
arranged JOHANN SEBASTIAN BACH 1685–1750

1. Songs of thankfulness and praise,
   Jesu, Lord, to thee we raise,
   Manifested by the star
   To the sages from afar;
   Branch of royal David's stem
   In thy birth at Bethlehem;
   Anthems be to thee addressed,
   God in Man made manifest.

2. Manifest at Jordan's stream,
   Prophet, Priest, and King supreme;
   And at Cana wedding-guest
   In thy Godhead manifest;
   Manifest in power divine,
   Changing water into wine;
   Anthems be to thee addressed,
   God in Man made manifest.

3. Manifest in making whole
   Palsied limbs and fainting soul;
   Manifest in valiant fight,
   Quelling all the devil's might;
   Manifest in gracious will,
   Ever bringing good from ill;
   Anthems be to thee addressed,
   God in Man made manifest.

4. Grant us grace to see thee, Lord,
   Mirrored in thy holy word:
   May we imitate thee now,
   And be pure, as pure art thou;
   That we like to thee may be
   At thy great Epiphany,
   And may praise thee, ever blest,
   God in Man made manifest.

CHRISTOPHER WORDSWORTH 1807–85

Epiphany

48 DUNDEE   CM   Scottish *Psalter* 1615

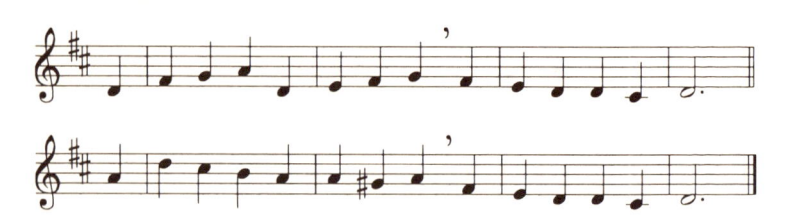

1. The race that long in darkness pined
    Have seen a glorious light;
   The people dwell in day, who dwelt
    In death's surrounding night.

2. To hail thy rise, thou better Sun,
    The gathering nations come,
   Joyous as when the reapers bear
    The harvest-treasures home.

3. To us a Child of hope is born,
    To us a Son is given;
   Him shall the tribes of earth obey,
    Him all the hosts of heaven.

4. His name shall be the Prince of Peace,
    For evermore adored;
   The Wonderful, the Counsellor,
    The great and mighty Lord.

5. His power increasing still shall spread;
    His reign no end shall know:
   Justice shall guard his throne above,
    And peace abound below.

based on *Isaiah 9:2–7*
JOHN MORISON 1750–98

Epiphany

49 ST VENANTIUS   LM   Paris *Antiphonale* 1681

1. What star is this with beams so bright,
   Which shames the sun's less radiant light?
   'Tis sent t'announce a new-born King,
   Glad tidings of our God to bring.

2. 'Tis now fulfilled as God decreed,
   'From Jacob shall a star proceed':
   And lo! the eastern sages stand
   To read in heaven the Lord's command.

3. While outward signs the star displays,
   An inward light the Lord conveys,
   And urges them with force benign
   To seek the Giver of the sign.

4. Impatient love knows no delay,
   Through toil and danger lies their way;
   And yet their home, their friends, their all,
   They leave at once at God's high call.

5. O while the star of heavenly grace
   Invites us, Lord, to seek thy face,
   Let not our stubborn hearts defy
   The light that beckons from on high.

Quae stella sole pulchrior
CHARLES COFFIN 1676–1740
tr. JOHN CHANDLER 1806–76

Lent

50 AUS DER TIEFE 77 77

'M.H.' in Nuremberg *Gesangbuch* 1676
attributed Martin Herbst 1654–1681

1. Forty days and forty nights
   Thou wast fasting in the wild;
   Forty days and forty nights
   Tempted, and yet undefiled:

2. Sunbeams scorching all the day;
   Chilly dew-drops nightly shed;
   Prowling beasts about thy way;
   Stones thy pillow, earth thy bed.

3. Shall not we thy watchings share,
   And from earthly joys abstain,
   Fasting with unceasing prayer,
   Glad with thee to suffer pain?

4. And if Satan, vexing sore,
   Flesh or spirit should assail,
   Thou, his vanquisher before,
   Grant we may not faint nor fail.

5. So shall we have peace divine;
   Holier gladness ours shall be;
   Round us too shall angels shine,
   Such as ministered to thee.

6. Keep, O keep us, Saviour dear,
   Ever constant by thy side;
   That with thee we may appear
   At the eternal Eastertide.

George Hunt Smyttan 1822–70
and Francis Pott 1832–1909

Lent

51 AU SANG QU'UN DIEU   DCM   traditional French
arranged Giovanni Pergolesi 1710–36

1. God of mercy and compassion,
   Look with pity upon me;
   Father, let me call thee Father,
   'Tis thy child returns to thee.
   Jesus, Lord, I ask for mercy;
   Let me not implore in vain;
   All my sins I now detest them,
   Never will I sin again.

2. By my sins I have deservèd
   Death and endless misery,
   Hell with all its pain and torments,
   And for all eternity.

3. By my sins I have abandoned
   Right and claim to heaven above,
   Where the saints rejoice for ever
   In a boundless sea of love.

4. See our Saviour, bleeding, dying,
   On the Cross of Calvary;
   To that Cross my sins have nailed him,
   Yet he bleeds and dies for me.

Edmund Vaughan C.Ss.R. 1827–1908

Lent

52 COMMANDMENTS *Les Commandemens* in the Genevan *Psalter* 1543
LM English form from 1556

An alternative tune will be found at Hymn 201.

1 Hear, O thou bounteous Maker, hear
  Our humble vows with gracious ear:
  Turn not thy saving face away
  Whilst on this solemn fast we pray.

2 Great searcher of our hearts, to thee
  We here deplore our misery;
  Behold, we to thy mercies fly,
  Do thou thy healing grace apply.

3 Great are our sins, O Lord, but thou
  Canst pardon more than we can do;
  May our defects, like shadows, raise
  The beauty and the life of grace.

4 May fasts extinguish in our will
  The fuel and desire of ill,
  And thus our souls, from fetters free,
  May only thirst and follow thee.

5 Grant, O most sacred Trinity,
  One undivided Unity,
  That abstinence may here improve
  Our claim to reign with thee above.

Audi, benigne Conditor
ascribed St Gregory the Great 540–604
tr. Anonymous 18th century

Lent

53 SOUTHWELL SM

William Daman's *Psalmes* 1579
later form of third line

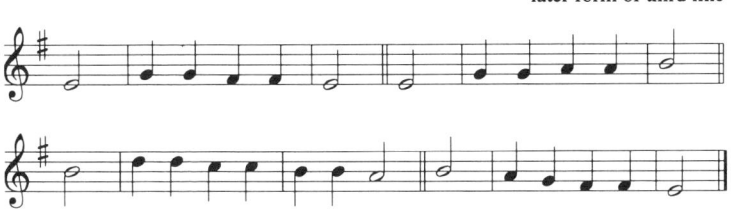

1. Lord Jesus, think on me,
   And purge away my sin;
   From earthborn passions set me free,
   And make me pure within.

2. Lord Jesus, think on me,
   With care and woe oppressed;
   Let me thy loving servant be,
   And taste thy promised rest.

3. Lord Jesus, think on me,
   Amid the battle's strife;
   In all my pain and misery
   Be thou my health and life.

4. Lord Jesus, think on me,
   Nor let me go astray;
   In darkness and perplexity
   Point thou the heavenly way.

5. Lord Jesus, think on me,
   When flows the tempest high:
   When on doth rush the enemy,
   O Saviour, be thou nigh.

6. Lord Jesus, think on me,
   That, when the flood is past,
   I may the eternal brightness see,
   And share thy joy at last.

Greek SYNESIUS OF CYRENE 375–430
tr. ALLEN WILLIAM CHATFIELD 1808–96

Lent

54 ST FLAVIAN   CM

John Day's *Psalmes* 1562
adapted RICHARD REDHEAD 1820–1901

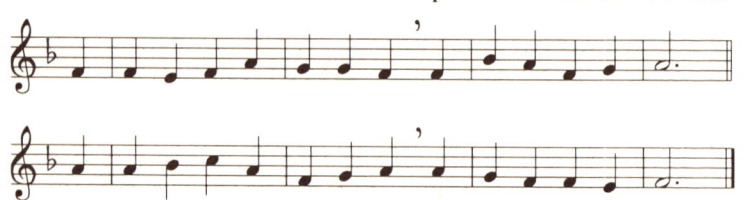

1. Lord, who throughout these forty days
    For us didst fast and pray,
   Teach us with thee to mourn our sins,
    And at thy side to stay.

2. As thou with Satan didst contend,
    And didst the victory win,
   O give us strength in thee to fight,
    In thee to conquer sin.

3. As thirst and hunger thou didst bear,
    So teach us, gracious Lord,
   To die to self, and daily live
    By thy most holy word.

4. And through these days of penitence,
    And through thy Passiontide,
   Yea, evermore, in life and death,
    Jesus, with us abide.

5. Abide with us, that so this life
    Of suffering overpast,
   An Easter of unending joy
    We may attain at last.

CLAUDIA FRANCES HERNAMAN 1838–98

Lent

55 EVERLASTING LOVE   CM   Richard Runciman Terry 1865–1938

An alternative tune will be found at Hymn 245.

1. My God I love thee, not because
    I hope for heaven thereby;
    Nor yet that those who love thee not
    Are lost eternally.

2. Thou, O my Jesus, thou didst me
    Upon the Cross embrace;
    For me didst bear the nails and spear,
    And manifold disgrace.

3. And griefs and torments numberless,
    And sweat of agony;
    E'en death itself—and all for one
    Who was thine enemy.

4. Then why, O blessèd Jesu Christ!
    Should I not love thee well;
    Not for the sake of winning heaven,
    Or of escaping hell;

5. Not with the hope of gaining aught;
    Not seeking a reward;
    But, as thyself hast lovèd me,
    O ever-loving Lord?

6. E'en so I love thee, and will love,
    And in thy praise will sing;
    Solely because thou art my God,
    And my eternal King.

O Deus, ego amo te, nec amo te 17th century
tr. Edward Caswall Cong. Orat. 1814–78

Lent

56 JENA LM Melchior Vulpius's *Kirchen-Gesäng* 1609
(Das neugeborne Kindelein)

1. Now is the healing time decreed
   For sins of heart, of word or deed,
   When we in humble fear record
   The wrong that we have done the Lord.

2. Who, always merciful and good,
   Has borne so long our wayward mood;
   Nor cut us off unsparingly
   In our so great iniquity.

3. Therefore with fasting and with prayer,
   Our secret sorrow we declare;
   With all good striving seek his face,
   And lowly-hearted plead for grace.

4. Cleanse us, O Lord, from every stain,
   Help us the gifts of grace to gain,
   Till with the angels, linked in love,
   Joyful we tread thy courts above.

5. We pray thee, Holy Trinity,
   One God, unchanging Unity,
   That we from this our abstinence
   May reap the fruits of penitence.

Ecce tempus idoneum 12th century or earlier
tr. THOMAS ALEXANDER LACEY 1853–1931 *

Lent

57 WHITEHALL LM HENRY LAWES 1596–1662
(Lawes' Psalm 8)

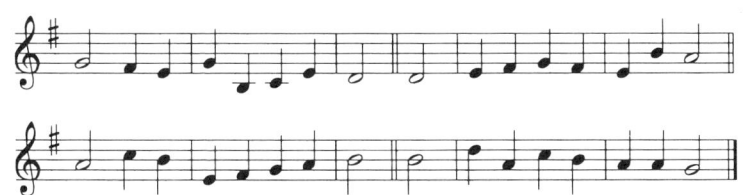

1. O Christ, our true and only light,
   Illumine those who sit in night;
   Let those afar now hear thy voice,
   And in thy fold with us rejoice.

2. And all those who have strayed from thee
   O gently seek; thy healing be
   To every wounded conscience given,
   And let them also share thy heaven.

3. O make the deaf to hear thy word,
   And teach the dumb to speak, dear Lord,
   Who dare not yet the faith avow,
   Though secretly they hold it now.

4. Shine on the darkened and the cold,
   Recall the wanderers from thy fold,
   Those now unite who walk apart,
   Confirm the weak and doubting heart.

5. So they with us may evermore
   Such grace with wondering thanks adore,
   And endless praise to thee be given
   By all thy Church in earth and heaven.

O Jesu Christe, wahres Licht JOHANN HEERMAN 1585–1647
tr. CATHERINE WINKWORTH 1827–78

Lent

58 INNSBRUCK 776 778

15th century German
adapted HEINRICH ISAAC c. 1450–1527
arranged JOHANN SEBASTIAN BACH 1685–1750

1. O thou who dost accord us
    The highest prize and guerdon,
       Thou hope of all our race,
  Jesu, do thou afford us
    The gift we ask of pardon
       For all who humbly seek thy face.

2. With whispered accusation
    Our conscience tells of sinning
       In thought, and word, and deed;
  Thine is our restoration,
    The work of grace beginning
       For souls from every burden freed.

Lent

3 For who, if thou reject us,
    Shall raise the fainting spirit?
        'Tis thine alone to spare:
  If thou to life elect us,
    With cleansèd hearts to near it,
        Shall be our task, our lowly prayer.

4 O Trinity most glorious,
    Thy pardon free bestowing,
        Defend us evermore;
  That in thy courts victorious,
    Thy love more truly knowing,
        We may with all thy saints adore.

Summi largitor praemii 6th century
tr. JOHN WILLIAMS HEWETT 1824–86 and others.

Passiontide and Holy Week

59 HERZLIEBSTER JESU   11 11 11 5   JOHANN CRÜGER 1598–1662
after Ps. 23 in the Genevan *Psalter* 1543
arranged JOHANN SEBASTIAN BACH 1685–1750

1 Ah, holy Jesu, how hast thou offended,
  That man to judge thee hath in hate pretended?
  By foes derided, by thine own rejected,
        O most afflicted.

2 Who was the guilty? Who brought this upon thee?
  Alas! my treason, Jesu, hath undone thee.
  'Twas I, Lord Jesu, I it was denied thee:
        I crucified thee.

3 Lo, the good Shepherd for the sheep is offered;
  The slave hath sinnèd, and the Son hath suffered;
  For man's atonement, while he nothing heedeth,
        God intercedeth.

Passiontide and Holy Week

4 For me, kind Jesu, was thy incarnation,
    Thy mortal sorrow, and thy life's oblation;
    Thy death of anguish and thy bitter Passion,
        For my salvation.

5 Therefore, kind Jesu, since I cannot pay thee,
    I do adore thee, and will ever pray thee,
    Think on thy pity and thy love unswerving,
        Not my deserving.

Herzliebster Jesu
JOHANN HEERMAN 1585–1647
tr. ROBERT BRIDGES 1844–1930

Passiontide and Holy Week

60 VALET WILL ICH DIR GEBEN   Melchior Teschner 1584–1635
76 76 D   arranged Johann Sebastian Bach 1685–1750

This hymn is most suitable for Palm Sunday

All glory, laud and honour
To thee, Redeemer, King,
To whom the lips of children
Made sweet hosannas ring.

1 Thou art the King of Israel,
　Thou David's royal Son,
　Who in the Lord's name comest,
　The King and blessèd One.

2 The company of angels
　Are praising thee on high,
　And mortal men and all things
　Created make reply.

3 The people of the Hebrews
　With palms before thee went;
　Our praise and prayer and anthems
　Before thee we present.

Passiontide and Holy Week

4 In hast'ning to thy Passion,
    They raised their hymns of praise;
  In reigning 'midst thy glory,
    Our melody we raise.

5 Thou didst accept their praises,
    Accept the prayers we bring,
  Who in all good delightest,
    Thou good and gracious King.

Gloria, laus, et honor
ST THEODULPH OF ORLÉANS died 821
tr. JOHN MASON NEALE 1818–66

Passiontide and Holy Week

61 STABAT MATER   887   Mainz *Gesangbuch* 1661
adapted SAMUEL WEBBE the elder 1740–1816

1. At the Cross her station keeping
 Stood the mournful Mother weeping,
 Close to Jesus to the last;

2. Through her heart, his sorrow sharing,
 All his bitter anguish bearing,
 Now at length the sword has passed.

3. Oh, how sad and sore distress'd
 Was that Mother highly blest
 Of the sole-begotten One,

4. Christ above in torment hangs;
 She beneath beholds the pangs
 Of her dying glorious Son.

Passiontide and Holy Week

5 Is there one who would not weep,
   Whelmed in miseries so deep,
   Christ's dear Mother to behold?

6 Can the human heart refrain
   From partaking in her pain,
   In that Mother's pain untold?

7 Bruised, derided, cursed, defil'd,
   She beheld her tender Child
   All with bloody scourges rent;

8 For the sins of his own nation,
   Saw him hang in desolation,
   Till his Spirit forth he sent.

9 O thou Mother! fount of love!
   Touch my spirit from above,
   Make my heart with thine accord:

10 Make me feel as thou hast felt;
   Make my soul to glow and melt
   With the love of Christ my Lord.

continued overleaf

Passiontide and Holy Week

11 Holy Mother, pierce me through;
In my heart each wound renew
Of my Saviour crucified:

12 Let me share with thee his pain
Who for all my sins was slain,
Who for me in torments died.

13 Let me mingle tears with thee,
Mourning him who mourned for me,
All the days that I may live:

14 By the Cross with thee to stay;
There with thee to weep and pray;
Is all I ask of thee to give.

Passiontide and Holy Week

15 Virgin of all virgins best,
    Listen to my fond request:
    Let me share thy grief divine;

16 Let me, to my latest breath,
    In my body bear the death
    Of that dying Son of thine.

17 Wounded with his every wound,
    Steep my soul till it hath swooned
    In his very Blood away;

18 Be to me, O Virgin, nigh,
    Lest in flames I burn and die,
    In his awful judgment day.

19 Christ, when thou shalt call me hence,
    Be thy Mother my defence,
    Be thy Cross my victory.

20 While my body here decays,
    May my soul thy goodness praise,
    Safe in Paradise with thee.

Stabat Mater
attributed JACOPONE DA TODI O.F.M. died 1306
tr. EDWARD CASWALL Cong. Orat. 1814–78

Passiontide and Holy Week

62 CROSS OF JESUS 87 87 JOHN STAINER 1840–1901

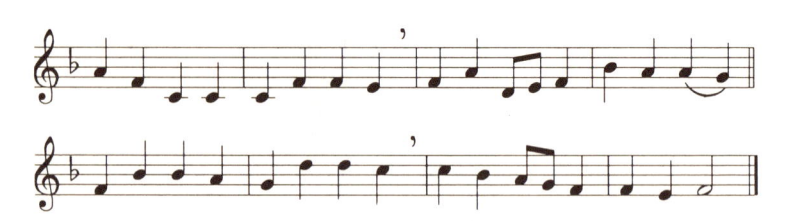

1. Cross of Jesus, Cross of sorrow,
   Where the Blood of Christ was shed,
   Perfect Man on thee was tortured,
   Perfect God on thee has bled!

2. Here the King of all the ages,
   Throned in light ere worlds could be,
   Robed in mortal flesh is dying,
   Crucified by sin for me.

3. O mysterious condescending!
   O abandonment sublime!
   Very God himself is bearing
   All the sufferings of time!

4. Evermore for human failure
   By his Passion we can plead;
   But, as full of mortal anguish,
   Surely he will know our need.

5. From the 'Holy, holy, holy',
   We adore thee, O most high!
   Down to earth's blaspheming voices,
   And the shout of 'Crucify!'

6. Cross of Jesus, Cross of sorrow,
   Where the Blood of Christ was shed,
   Perfect Man on thee was tortured,
   Perfect God on thee has bled!

WILLIAM SPARROW-SIMPSON 1860–1952

Passiontide and Holy Week

63 ST MARTIN   66 66   Caspar Ett's *Cantica Sacra* 1840

An alternative tune will be found at Hymn 241.

1 Jesu, meek and lowly,
  Saviour, pure and holy,
  On thy love relying,
  Come I to thee flying.

2 Prince of life and power,
  My salvation's tower,
  On the Cross I view thee,
  Calling sinners to thee.

3 There behold me gazing
  At the sight amazing;
  Bending low before thee,
  Helpless I adore thee.

4 See the red wounds streaming,
  With Christ's life-blood gleaming:
  Blood for sinners flowing,
  Pardon free bestowing.

5 Fountains rich in blessing,
  Christ's fond love expressing,
  Thou my aching sadness
  Turnest into gladness.

6 Lord in mercy guide me,
  Be thou e'er beside me;
  In thy ways direct me,
  'Neath thy wings protect me.

HENRY COLLINS O.C.R. 1827–1919

Passiontide and Holy Week

64 ARFON 77 77 D Welsh variant of a French carol
(O vous dont les tendres ans) adapted RICHARD RUNCIMAN TERRY 1865–1938

1. Man of sorrows, wrapt in grief,
   Bow thine ear to our relief;
   Thou for us the path hast trod
   Of the dreadful wrath of God;
   Thou the cup of fire hast drained
   Till its light alone remained.
   Lamb of love! we look to thee:
   Hear our mournful litany.

2. By the garden, fraught with woe,
   Whither thou full oft wouldst go!
   By thine agony of prayer
   In the desolation there;
   By the dire and deep distress
   Of that mystery fathomless—
   Lord, our tears in mercy see:
   Hearken to our litany.

Passiontide and Holy Week

3 By the chalice brimming o'er
  With disgrace and torment sore;
  By those lips which fain would pray
  That it might but pass away;
  By the heart which drank it dry,
  Lest a rebel race should die—
  Be thy pity, Lord, our plea:
  Hear our solemn litany.

4 Man of sorrows! let thy grief
  Purchase for us our relief:
  Lord of mercy! bow thine ear,
  Slow to anger, swift to hear:
  By the Cross's royal road
  Lead us to the throne of God,
  There for aye to sing to thee
  Heaven's triumphant litany.

MATTHEW BRIDGES 1800–94

Passiontide and Holy Week

65 LOVE UNKNOWN 66 66 44 44 JOHN IRELAND 1879–1962

1 My song is love unknown,
　　My Saviour's love to me,
　Love to the loveless shown,
　　That they might lovely be.
　　　O, who am I,
　　　　That for my sake
　　　　My Lord should take
　　　Frail flesh, and die?

2 He came from his blest throne,
　　Salvation to bestow:
　But men made strange, and none
　　The longed-for Christ would know.
　　　But O, my Friend,
　　　　My Friend indeed,
　　　　Who at my need
　　　His life did spend!

Passiontide and Holy Week

3 Sometimes they strew his way,
   And his sweet praises sing;
Resounding all the day
   Hosannas to their King.
     Then 'Crucify!'
       Is all their breath,
      And for his death
     They thirst and cry.

4 They rise, and needs will have
   My dear Lord made away;
A murderer they save,
   The Prince of Life they slay.
     Yet cheerful he
       To suffering goes,
      That he his foes
     From thence might free.

5 In life, no house, no home,
   My Lord on earth might have;
In death no friendly tomb
   But what a stranger gave.
     What may I say?
       Heav'n was his home;
      But mine the tomb
     Wherein he lay.

6 Here might I stay and sing,
   No story so divine;
Never was love, dear King,
   Never was grief like thine.
     This is my Friend,
       In whose sweet praise
      I all my days
     Could gladly spend.

SAMUEL CROSSMAN 1624–83

Passiontide and Holy Week

66

FIRST TUNE

OLD HALL GREEN LM JOHN CROOKALL 1821–87

SECOND TUNE

ST CROSS LM JOHN BACCHUS DYKES 1823–76

Passiontide and Holy Week

1 O come and mourn with me awhile;
   See, Mary calls us to her side;
   O come and let us mourn with her;
     Jesus, our love, is crucified.

2 Have we no tears to shed for him,
   While soldiers scoff and crowds deride?
   Ah! look how patiently he hangs;

3 How fast his feet and hands are nailed,
   His blessèd tongue with thirst is tied;
   His failing eyes are blind with blood;

4 Seven times he spoke, seven words of love,
   And all three hours his silence cried
   For mercy on the souls of men;

5 O break, O break, hard heart of mine.
   Thy weak self-love and guilty pride
   His Pilate and his Judas were;

6 A broken heart, a fount of tears,
   Ask, and they will not be denied;
   A broken heart love's cradle is;

7 O love of God! O sin of man!
   In this dread act your strength is tied;
   And victory remains with love;
     Jesus, our love, is crucified.

      FREDERICK WILLIAM FABER Cong. Orat. 1814–63 *

Passiontide and Holy Week

67 PASSION CHORALE   secular song by HANS LEO HASSLER 1564–1612
76 76 D   arranged JOHANN SEBASTIAN BACH 1685–1750

1. O sacred head, sore wounded,
    Defiled and put to scorn;
  O kingly head, surrounded
    With mocking crown of thorn:
  What sorrow mars thy grandeur?
    Can death thy bloom deflower?
  O countenance whose splendour
    The hosts of heaven adore.

2. Thy beauty, long-desirèd,
    Hath vanished from our sight;
  Thy power is all expirèd,
    And quenched the Light of light.
  Ah me! for whom thou diest,
    Hide not so far thy grace:
  Show me, O Love most highest,
    The brightness of thy face.

Passiontide and Holy Week

3 I pray thee, Jesus, own me,
　　Me, Shepherd good, for thine;
　Who to thy fold hast won me,
　　And fed with truth divine.
　Though guilty, me refuse not,
　　Incline thy face to me,
　This comfort that I lose not,
　　On earth to comfort thee.

4 In thy most bitter Passion
　　My heart to share doth cry,
　With thee for my salvation
　　Upon the Cross to die.
　Ah, keep my heart thus movèd
　　To stand thy Cross beneath,
　To mourn thee, well belovèd,
　　Yet thank thee for thy death.

5 My days are few, O fail not,
　　With thine immortal power,
　To hold me that I quail not
　　In death's most fearful hour:
　That I may fight befriended,
　　And see in my last strife
　To me thine arms extended
　　Upon the Cross of life.

　　　　based on *Salve caput cruentatum* 14th century
O Haupt voll Blut und Wunden PAUL GERHARDT 1607–76
　　　　　　　　　　tr. ROBERT BRIDGES 1844–1930

Passiontide and Holy Week

68 WINCHESTER NEW   LM   *Musicalisches Hand-Buch* Hamburg 1690
adapted WILLIAM HENRY HAVERGAL 1793–1870

This hymn is most suitable for Palm Sunday.

1. Ride on, ride on in majesty!
   Hark, all the tribes hosanna cry;
   Thy humble beast pursues his road
   With palms and scattered garments strowed.

2. Ride on, ride on in majesty!
   In lowly pomp ride on to die:
   O Christ, thy triumphs now begin
   O'er captive death and conquered sin.

3. Ride on, ride on in majesty!
   The wingèd squadrons of the sky
   Look down with sad and wondering eyes
   To see the approaching sacrifice.

Passiontide and Holy Week

4 Ride on, ride on in majesty!
 Thy last and fiercest strife is nigh;
 The Father, on his sapphire throne,
 Expects his own anointed Son.

5 Ride on, ride on in majesty!
 In lowly pomp ride on to die;
 Bow thy meek head to mortal pain,
 Then take, O God, thy power, and reign.

HENRY HART MILMAN 1791–1868

Passiontide and Holy Week

69 BROMPTON ROAD   87 87 87   Edward d'Evry died 1951

An alternative tune will be found at Hymn 120.

1. Sing, my tongue, the glorious battle,
  Sing the ending of the fray;
 Now above the Cross, the trophy,
  Sound the loud triumphant lay:
 Tell how Christ, the world's Redeemer,
  As a victim won the day.

2. Tell how, when at length the fullness
  Of th'appointed time was come,
 He, the Word, was born of woman,
  Left for us his Father's home,
 Showed to men the perfect Manhood,
  Shone as light amidst the gloom.

Passiontide and Holy Week

3 Thus, with thirty years accomplished,
    Went he forth from Nazareth,
Destined, dedicate, and willing,
    Wrought his work, and met his death;
Like a lamb he humbly yielded
    On the Cross his dying breath.

4 Faithful Cross, thou sign of triumph,
    Now for man the noblest Tree,
None in foliage, none in blossom,
    None in fruit thy peer may be;
Symbol of the world's redemption,
    For the weight that hung on thee!

5 Unto God be praise and glory:
    To the Father and the Son,
To the eternal Spirit, honour
    Now and evermore be done;
Praise and glory in the highest,
    While the timeless ages run.

Pange lingua gloriosi proelium certaminis
VENANTIUS FORTUNATUS 530–609
tr. PERCY DEARMER 1867–1936

Passiontide and Holy Week

70 VEXILLA REGIS Mode I

An alternative tune will be found at Hymn 88.

1. The royal banners forward go,
   The Cross shines forth in mystic glow;
   Where he in flesh, our flesh who made,
   Our sentence bore, our ransom paid.

2. Where deep for us the spear was dyed,
   Life's torrent rushing from his side,
   To wash us in that precious flood,
   Where mingled water flowed, and Blood.

3. Fulfilled is all that David told
   In true prophetic song of old,
   Amid the nations, God, saith he
   Hath reigned and triumphed from the Tree.

Passiontide and Holy Week

4 O Tree of beauty, Tree of light,
　O Tree with royal purple dight,
　Elect on whose triumphal breast
　Those holy limbs should find their rest.

5 On whose dear arms, so widely flung,
　The weight of this world's ransom hung,
　The price which none but he could pay,
　And spoil the spoiler of his prey.

6 O Cross, our one reliance, hail!
　So may this Passiontide avail
　To give fresh merit to the saint
　And pardon to the penitent.

7 To thee, eternal Three in One,
　Let homage meet by all be done;
　As by thy Cross thou dost restore,
　Preserve and govern evermore.

Vexilla Regis prodeunt
VENANTIUS FORTUNATUS 530–609
tr. JOHN MASON NEALE 1818–66 and others

Passiontide and Holy Week

71 HORSLEY   CM   WILLIAM HORSLEY 1774–1858

1. There is a green hill far away,
   Without a city wall,
   Where the dear Lord was crucified
   Who died to save us all.

2. We may not know, we cannot tell,
   What pains he had to bear,
   But we believe it was for us
   He hung and suffered there.

3. He died that we might be forgiven,
   He died to make us good;
   That we might go at last to heaven,
   Saved by his Precious Blood.

4. There was no other good enough
   To pay the price of sin;
   He only could unlock the gate
   Of heaven, and let us in.

5. O, dearly, dearly has he loved,
   And we must love him too,
   And trust in his redeeming Blood,
   And try his works to do.

CECIL FRANCES ALEXANDER 1818–95

Passiontide and Holy Week

72 ROCKINGHAM LM *Second Supplement to Psalmody* c. 1780
adapted Edward Miller 1731–1807

1. When I survey the wondrous Cross,
   On which the Prince of glory died,
   My richest gain I count but loss,
   And pour contempt on all my pride.

2. Forbid it, Lord, that I should boast
   Save in the death of Christ my God;
   All the vain things that charm me most,
   I sacrifice them to his Blood.

3. See from his head, his hands, his feet,
   Sorrow and love flow mingled down;
   Did e'er such love and sorrow meet,
   Or thorns compose so rich a crown?

4. His dying crimson like a robe,
   Spreads o'er his body on the Tree;
   Then am I dead to all the globe,
   And all the globe is dead to me.

5. Were the whole realm of nature mine,
   That were a present far too small;
   Love so amazing, so divine,
   Demands my soul, my life, my all.

Isaac Watts 1674–1748

Easter

73 SALZBURG 77 77 D   JAKOB HINTZE 1622–1702
arranged JOHANN SEBASTIAN BACH 1685–1750

1. At the Lamb's high feast we sing
Praise to our victorious King,
Who hath washed us in the tide
Flowing from his piercèd side.
Praise we him whose love divine
Gives the guests his Blood for wine,
Gives his Body for the feast,
Love the Victim, Love the Priest.

2. Where the Paschal Blood is poured,
Death's dark angel sheathes his sword;
Israel's hosts triumphant go
Through the wave that drowns the foe.
Christ, the Lamb, whose Blood was shed,
Paschal Victim, Paschal Bread;
With sincerity and love
Eat we manna from above.

Easter

3 Mighty Victim from on high,
  Powers of hell beneath thee lie;
  Death is broken in the fight;
  Thou hast brought us life and light.
  Now thy banner thou dost wave;
  Conquering Satan and the grave;
  Angels join his praise to tell—
  See o'erthrown the prince of hell.

4 Paschal triumph, Paschal joy,
  Only sin can this destroy;
  From sin's death do thou set free,
  Souls re-born, dear Lord, in thee.
  Hymns of glory, songs of praise,
  Father, unto thee we raise.
  Risen Lord, all praise to thee,
  Ever with the Spirit be.

Ad coenam Agni providi 7th century
tr. ROBERT CAMPBELL 1814–68

Easter

74 SURREXIT   ANTHONY GREGORY MURRAY O.S.B. 1905–92
888 + alleluias

Al-le-lu-ia, al-le-lu-ia!

1. Battle is o'er, hell's armies flee;
   Raise we the cry of victory
   With abounding joy resounding:
      Alleluia, alleluia!

2. Christ, who endured the shameful Tree,
   O'er death triumphant welcome we.
   Our adoring praise outpouring:

3. On the third morn from death rose he,
   Clothed with what light in heaven shall be,
   Our unswerving faith deserving:

4. Hell's gloomy gates yield up their key,
   Paradise door thrown wide we see;
   Never-tiring be our choiring:

5. Lord, by the stripes men laid on thee,
   Grant us to live from death set free,
   This our greeting still repeating:
      Alleluia, alleluia!

Finita iam sunt proelia 17th century
tr. RONALD ARBUTHNOTT KNOX 1888–1957

Easter

75 ORIENTIBUS PARTIBUS
77 77 + alleluia

Office de la Circoncision Sens
13th century

Al-le-lu - ia!

1. Christ the Lord is risen again!
   Christ hath broken every chain!
   Hark, the angels shout for joy,
   Singing evermore on high,
      Alleluia!

2. He who gave for us his life,
   Who for us endured the strife,
   Is our Paschal Lamb today!
   We too sing for joy, and say,

3. He who bore all pain and loss
   Comfortless upon the Cross,
   Lives for glory now on high,
   Pleads for us, and hears our cry,

4. He whose path no records tell,
   Who descended into hell;
   Who the strong man armed hath bound,
   Now in highest heaven is crowned.

5. Now he bids us tell abroad
   How the lost may be restored,
   How the penitent forgiven,
   How we too may enter heaven.

6. Thou, our Paschal Lamb indeed,
   Christ, today thy people feed;
   Take our sins and guilt away,
   That we all may sing for ay,
      Alleluia!

Christus ist erstanden
MICHAEL WEISSE c. 1480–1534
tr. CATHERINE WINKWORTH 1827–78

Easter

76 ST GEORGE'S WINDSOR   77 77 D   GEORGE JOB ELVEY 1816–93

An alternative tune will be found at Hymn 79.

1   Christ the Lord is ris'n today,
Christians, haste your vows to pay;
Offer ye your praises meet
At the Paschal Victim's feet;
For the sheep the Lamb hath bled,
Sinless in the sinner's stead.
Christ the Lord is ris'n on high;
Now he lives, no more to die.

2   Christ, the Victim undefiled,
Man to God hath reconciled;
When in strange and awful strife
Met together death and life;
Christians, on this happy day
Haste with joy your vows to pay.
Christ the Lord is ris'n on high;
Now he lives, no more to die.

Easter

3 Say, O wond'ring Mary, say,
What thou sawest on thy way;
'I beheld, where Christ had lain,
Empty tomb and angels twain;
I beheld the glory bright
Of the rising Lord of Light:
Christ my hope is ris'n again;
Now he lives, and lives to reign.'

4 Christ, who once for sinners bled,
Now the first-born from the dead,
Throned in endless might and power,
Lives and reigns for evermore.
Hail, eternal hope on high!
Hail, thou King of victory!
Hail, thou Prince of Life adored!
Help and save us, gracious Lord.

Victimae paschali laudes
WIPO OF BURGUNDY 11th century
tr. JANE LEESON 1807–82

Easter

77 AVE VIRGO VIRGINUM   medieval German in Johann Leisentritt's
76 76 D   *Catholicum Hymnologium Germanicum* 1584

1 Come, ye faithful, raise the strain
Of triumphant gladness;
God hath brought his Israel
Into joy from sadness;
Loosed from Pharaoh's bitter yoke
Jacob's sons and daughters;
Led them with unmoistened feet
Through the Red Sea waters.

2 'Tis the spring of souls today;
Christ hath burst his prison,
And from three days' sleep in death
As a sun hath risen;
All the winter of our sins,
Long and dark, is flying
From his light, to whom we give
Laud and praise undying.

Easter

3 Now the queen of seasons, bright
　　With the day of splendour,
　　With the royal feast of feasts,
　　Comes its joy to render;
　　Comes to glad Jerusalem,
　　Who with true affection
　　Welcomes in unwearied strains
　　Jesu's resurrection.

4 Neither might the gates of death,
　　Nor the tomb's dark portal,
　　Nor the watchers, nor the seal,
　　Hold thee as a mortal;
　　But today amidst the twelve
　　Thou didst stand, bestowing
　　That thy peace which evermore
　　Passeth human knowing.

　　　　　　　　Greek ST JOHN DAMASCENE 8th century
　　　　　　　　　　tr. JOHN MASON NEALE 1818–66

Easter

78 VULPIUS 888 + alleluias Melchior Vulpius's *Gesangbuch* 1609
(Gelobt sei Gott)

Al - le - lu - ia, _____ al - le - lu - ia, _____ al - le - lu - ia!

1. Good Christian men, rejoice and sing!
   Now is the triumph of our King:
   To all the world glad news we bring:
   Alleluia!

2. The Lord of Life is risen for ay;
   Bring flowers of song to strew his way;
   Let all mankind rejoice and say:

3. Praise we in songs of victory
   That Love, that Life which cannot die,
   And sing with hearts uplifted high:

4. Thy name we bless, O risen Lord,
   And sing today with one accord
   The Life laid down, the Life restored:
   Alleluia!

CYRIL ALINGTON 1872–1955

Easter

79 EASTER HYMN   77 77 + alleluias   *Lyra Davidica* 1708
adapted *The Compleat Psalmodist* 1749

1. Jesus Christ is risen to-day, Alleluia!
   Our triumphant holy day, Alleluia!
   Who did once, upon the Cross, Alleluia!
   Suffer to redeem our loss. Alleluia!

2. Hymns of praise then let us sing, Alleluia!
   Unto Christ, our heavenly King, Alleluia!
   Who endured the Cross and grave, Alleluia!
   Sinners to redeem and save. Alleluia!

3. But the pains which he endured, Alleluia!
   Our salvation have procured; Alleluia!
   Now above the sky he's King, Alleluia!
   Where the angels ever sing. Alleluia!

based on *Surrexit Christus hodie* 14th century
The Compleat Psalmodist 1749 and
Supplement to the New Version 1816

Easter

80 SAVANNAH (Herrnhut)
77 77

Herrnhut *Choralbuch* c. 1740
in John Wesley's *Foundery Collection* 1742

1. Love's redeeming work is done;
   Fought the fight, the battle won:
   Lo, our Sun's eclipse is o'er!
   Lo, he sets in blood no more!

2. Vain the stone, the watch, the seal,
   Christ has burst the gates of hell;
   Death in vain forbids his rise;
   Christ has opened Paradise.

3. Lives again our glorious King;
   Where, O death, is now thy sting?
   Dying once, he all doth save;
   Where thy victory, O grave?

4. Soar we now where Christ has led,
   Following our exalted Head;
   Made like him, like him we rise;
   Ours the Cross, the grave, the skies.

5. Hail the Lord of earth and heaven!
   Praise to thee by both be given:
   Thee we greet triumphant now;
   Hail, the Resurrection thou!

CHARLES WESLEY 1707–88

Easter

81 NOEL NOUVELET 11 10 10 11 traditional French carol

1. Now the green blade riseth from the buried grain,
   Wheat that in dark earth many days has lain;
   Love lives again, that with the dead had been:
   Love is come again,
   Like wheat that springeth green.

2. In the grave they laid him, Love whom men had slain,
   Thinking that never he would wake again,
   Laid in the earth like grain that sleeps unseen:

3. Forth he came at Easter, like the risen grain,
   He that for three days in the grave had lain,
   Quick from the dead, my risen Lord is seen:

4. When our hearts are wintry, grieving, or in pain,
   Thy touch can call us back to life again,
   Fields of our hearts that dead and bare have been:

JOHN MACLEOD CAMPBELL CRUM 1872–1958

Easter

82 ELLACOMBE 76 76 D

Würtemburg *Gesangbuch* 1784
adapted Mainz *Gesangbuch* 1833

1. The Day of Resurrection!
      Earth, tell it out abroad;
   The Passover of gladness,
      The Passover of God!
   From death to life eternal,
      From earth unto the sky,
   Our Christ hath brought us over
      With hymns of victory.

2. Our hearts be pure from evil,
      That we may see aright
   The Lord in rays eternal
      Of resurrection-light;
   And, listening to his accents,
      May hear so calm and plain
   His own 'All hail,' and, hearing,
      May raise the victor strain.

3. Now let the heavens be joyful,
      And earth her song begin,
   The round world keep high triumph,
      And all that is therein;
   Let all things seen and unseen
      Their notes of gladness blend,
   For Christ the Lord hath risen,
      Our Joy that hath no end.

Greek St John Damascene c. 750
tr. John Mason Neale 1818–66

Easter

83 VICTORY 888 + alleluia WILLIAM HENRY MONK 1823–89
after PALESTRINA *Magnificat III toni*

Al - le - lu - ia!

An alternative tune will be found at Hymn 78.

1 The strife is o'er, the battle done;
   Now is the Victor's triumph won;
   O let the song of praise be sung:
   Alleluia!

2 Death's mightiest powers have done their worst,
   And Jesus hath his foes dispersed;
   Let shouts of praise and joy outburst:

3 On the third morn he rose again
   Glorious in majesty to reign;
   O let us swell the joyful strain:

4 He broke the age-bound chains of hell;
   The bars from heaven's high portals fell;
   Let hymns of praise his triumph tell:

5 Lord, by the stripes which wounded thee
   From death's dread sting thy servants free,
   That we may live, and sing to thee:
   Alleluia!

Finita jam sunt proelia 17th century
tr. FRANCIS POTT 1832–1909

Easter

84 THIS JOYFUL EASTERTIDE   *David's Psalmen* Amsterdam 1685
67 67 + refrain

1 This joyful Eastertide,
   Away with sin and sorrow.
  My Love, the Crucified,
   Hath sprung to life this morrow:
     Had Christ, that once was slain,
       Ne'er burst his three-day prison,
     Our faith had been in vain:
       But now hath Christ arisen.

2 My flesh in hope shall rest,
   And for a season slumber:
  Till trump from east to west
   Shall wake the dead in number:

3 Death's flood hath lost his chill,
   Since Jesus crossed the river:
  Lover of souls, from ill
   My passing soul deliver:

GEORGE RATCLIFFE WOODWARD 1848–1934

Easter

85 ST FULBERT CM HENRY JOHN GAUNTLETT 1805–76

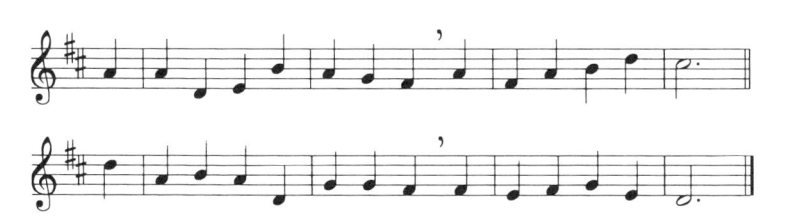

1. Ye choirs of New Jerusalem,
   Your sweetest notes employ,
   The Paschal victory to hymn
   In strains of holy joy.

2. How Judah's Lion burst his chains,
   And crushed the serpent's head;
   And brought with him, from death's domains,
   The long-imprisoned dead.

3. From hell's devouring jaws the prey
   Alone our Leader bore;
   His ransomed hosts pursue their way
   Where he hath gone before.

4. Triumphant in his glory now
   His sceptre ruleth all,
   Earth, heaven and hell before him bow,
   And at his footstool fall.

5. While joyful thus his praise we sing,
   His mercy we implore,
   Into his palace bright to bring
   And keep us evermore.

6. All glory to the Father be,
   All glory to the Son,
   All glory, Holy Ghost, to thee,
   While endless ages run.

Chorus novae Jerusalem
ST FULBERT OF CHARTRES died 1028
tr. ROBERT CAMPBELL 1814–68

Easter

86 O FILII ET FILIAE   *Airs sur les hymnes sacrez* Paris 1623
    888 + alleluias   arranged SAMUEL WEBBE the elder 1740–1816

Alleluia, alleluia, alleluia.

1 Ye sons and daughters of the Lord,
   The King of glory, King adored,
   This day himself from death restored.
     Alleluia.

2 All in the early morning grey
   Went holy women on their way,
   To see the tomb where Jesus lay.

3 Of spices pure a precious store
   In their pure hands those women bore,
   To anoint the sacred body o'er.

Easter

4 Then straightway one in white they see,
   Who saith, 'Ye seek the Lord: but he
   Is risen, and gone to Galilee.'

5 This told they Peter, told they John;
   Who forthwith to the tomb are gone,
   But Peter is by John outrun.

6 That self-same night, while out of fear
   The doors were shut, their Lord most dear
   To his apostles did appear.

7 But Thomas, when of this he heard,
   Was doubtful of his brethren's word;
   Wherefore again there comes the Lord.

8 'Thomas, behold my side,' saith he;
   'My hands, my feet, my body see,
   And doubt not, but believe in me.'

9 When Thomas saw that wounded side,
   The truth no longer he denied;
   'Thou art my Lord and God!' he cried.

10 Oh, blest are they who have not seen
   Their Lord, and yet believe in him,
   Eternal life awaiteth them,

11 Now let us praise the Lord most high,
   And strive his name to magnify
   On this great day, through earth and sky:

12 Whose mercy ever runneth o'er;
   Whom men and angel hosts adore;
   To him be glory evermore.
     Alleluia.

Alleluia, alleluia, alleluia.

O filii et filiae
JEAN TISSERAND O.F.M. died 1494
tr. EDWARD CASWALL Cong. Orat. 1814–78

Ascension

87 LLANFAIR 77 77 + alleluias ROBERT WILLIAMS 1781–1821

1 Hail the day that sees him rise, Alleluia!
Glorious to his native skies; Alleluia!
Christ, awhile to mortals given, Alleluia!
Enters now the highest heaven! Alleluia!

2 There the glorious triumph waits; Alleluia!
Lift your heads, eternal gates! Alleluia!
Christ hath vanquished death and sin; Alleluia!
Take the King of Glory in. Alleluia!

3 See! the heaven its Lord receives, Alleluia!
Yet he loves the earth he leaves; Alleluia!
Though returning to his throne, Alleluia!
Still he calls mankind his own. Alleluia!

4 See! he lifts his hands above; Alleluia!
See! he shows the prints of love: Alleluia!
Hark! his gracious lips bestow. Alleluia!
Blessings on his Church below. Alleluia!

Ascension

5 Still for us he intercedes; Alleluia!
   His prevailing death he pleads; Alleluia!
   Near himself prepares our place, Alleluia!
   Harbinger of human race. Alleluia!

6 Lord, though parted from our sight, Alleluia!
   Far above yon azure height, Alleluia!
   Grant our hearts may thither rise, Alleluia!
   Seeking thee beyond the skies. Alleluia!

7 There we shall with thee remain, Alleluia!
   Partners of thine endless reign; Alleluia!
   There thy face unclouded see, Alleluia!
   Find our heaven of heavens in thee. Alleluia!

CHARLES WESLEY 1707–88
and THOMAS COTTERILL 1779–1823

Ascension

88 GONFALON ROYAL   LM   Percy Buck 1871–1947

1. O Christ our joy, to whom is given
   A throne o'er all the thrones of heaven,
   In thee, whose hand all things obey,
   The world's vain pleasures pass away.

2. So, suppliants here, we seek to win
   Thy pardon for thy people's sin,
   That, by thine all-prevailing grace,
   Uplifted, we may seek thy face.

3. And when, all heaven beneath thee bowed,
   Thou com'st to judgement throned in cloud,
   Then from our guilt wash out the stain
   And give us our lost crowns again.

Ascension

4 Be thou our joy and strong defence,
  Who art our future recompense:
  So shall the light that springs from thee
  Be ours through all eternity.

5 O risen Christ, ascended Lord,
  All praise to thee let earth accord,
  Who art, while endless ages run,
  With Father and with Spirit One.

>   *Tu Christe nostrum gaudium* c. 5th century
>   *tr.* LAURENCE HOUSMAN 1865–1959

Ascension

89 LUX EOI   87 87 D   Arthur Sullivan 1842–1900

1. See the Conqueror mounts in triumph,
   See the King in royal state
 Riding on the clouds his chariot
   To his heavenly palace gate;
 Hark! the choirs of angel voices
   Joyful alleluias sing,
 And the portals high are lifted
   To receive their heavenly King.

2. Who is this that comes in glory,
   With the trump of jubilee?
 Lord of battles, God of armies,
   He has gained the victory;
 He who on the Cross did suffer,
   He who from the grave arose,
 He has vanquished sin and Satan,
   He by death has spoiled his foes.

Ascension

3 Thou hast raised our human nature
        In the clouds to God's right hand;
    There we sit in heavenly places,
        There with thee in glory stand;
    Jesus reigns, adored by angels;
        Man with God is on the throne;
    Mighty Lord, in thine ascension
        We by faith behold our own.

4 Glory be to God the Father;
        Glory be to God the Son,
    Dying, risen, ascending for us,
        Who the heavenly realm has won;
    Glory to the Holy Spirit;
        To one God in Persons three;
    Glory both in earth and heaven,
        Glory, endless glory be.

CHRISTOPHER WORDSWORTH 1807–95

Ascension

90 ST MAGNUS   CM   JEREMIAH CLARKE c. 1673–1707

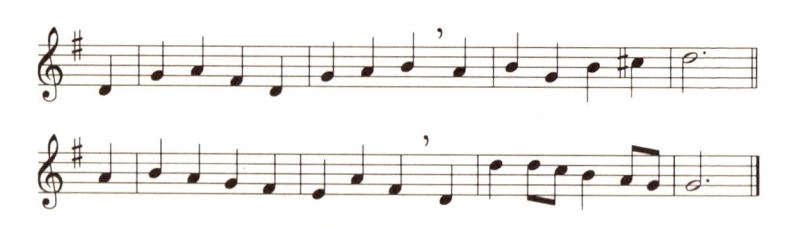

1. The head that once was crowned with thorns
    Is crowned with glory now:
   A royal diadem adorns
    The mighty Victor's brow.

2. The highest place that heaven affords
    Is his, is his by right,
   The King of kings and Lord of lords,
    And heaven's eternal Light;

3. The joy of all who dwell above,
    The joy of all below,
   To whom he manifests his love,
    And grants his name to know.

4. To them the Cross, with all its shame,
    With all its grace is given:
   Their name an everlasting name,
    Their joy the joy of heaven.

5. They suffer with their Lord below,
    They reign with him above,
   Their profit and their joy to know
    The mystery of his love.

6. The Cross he bore is life and health,
    Though shame and death to him;
   His people's hope, his people's wealth,
    Their everlasting theme.

THOMAS KELLY 1769–1854

Pentecost

91 MOUNT EPHRAIM   SM   BENJAMIN MILGROVE 1713–1810

An alternative tune will be found at Hymn 100.

1. Breathe on me, Breath of God,
   Fill me with life anew,
   That I may love what thou dost love,
   And do what thou wouldst do.

2. Breathe on me, Breath of God,
   Until my heart is pure,
   Until with thee I will one will,
   To do and to endure.

3. Breathe on me, Breath of God,
   Till I am wholly thine,
   Until this earthly part of me
   Glows with thy fire divine.

4. Breathe on me, Breath of God,
   So shall I never die,
   But live with thee the perfect life
   Of thine eternity.

EDWIN HATCH 1835–89

Pentecost

92 DOWN AMPNEY   66 11 D   RALPH VAUGHAN WILLIAMS 1872–1958

1. Come down, O Love divine,
   Seek thou this soul of mine,
   And visit it with thine own ardour glowing;
   O Comforter, draw near,
   Within my heart appear,
   And kindle it, thy holy flame bestowing.

2. O let it freely burn,
   Till earthly passions turn
   To dust and ashes in its heat consuming;
   And let thy glorious light
   Shine ever on my sight,
   And clothe me round, the while my path illuming.

Pentecost

3 Let holy charity
    Mine outward vesture be,
    And lowliness become mine inner clothing;
    True lowliness of heart,
    Which takes the humbler part,
    And o'er its own shortcomings weeps with loathing.

4 And so the yearning strong,
    With which the soul will long,
    Shall far outpass the power of human telling;
    For none can guess its grace,
    Till he become the place
    Wherein the Holy Spirit makes his dwelling.

Discendi, Amor santo
BIANCO DA SIENA died 1434
tr. RICHARD FREDERICK LITTLEDALE 1833–90

Pentecost

93 TALLIS'S ORDINAL   CM   Thomas Tallis c. 1510–85

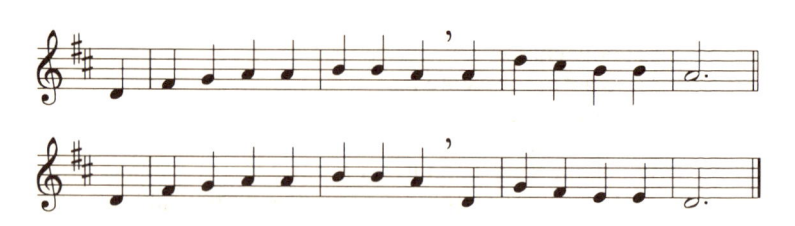

1. Come, Holy Ghost, Creator, come
   From thy bright heavenly throne,
   Come take possession of our souls,
   And make them all thy own.

2. Thou who art called the Paraclete,
   Best gift of God above,
   The living spring, the living fire,
   Sweet unction and true love.

3. Thou who art sev'nfold in thy grace,
   Finger of God's right hand;
   His promise, teaching little ones
   To speak and understand.

4. O guide our minds with thy blest light,
   With love our hearts inflame;
   And with thy strength, which ne'er decays,
   Confirm our mortal frame.

Pentecost

5 Far from us drive our deadly foe;
    True peace unto us bring;
  And through all perils lead us safe
    Beneath thy sacred wing.

6 Through thee may we the Father know,
    Through thee th' eternal Son,
  And thee the Spirit of them both,
    Thrice-blessèd Three in One.

7 All glory to the Father be,
    With his co-equal Son;
  The same to thee, great Paraclete,
    While endless ages run.

Veni Creator Spiritus
attributed RABANUS MAURUS 776–856
tr. ANONYMOUS

Pentecost

94 VENI SANCTE SPIRITUS   SAMUEL WEBBE the elder 1740–1816
777 D

1. Come, thou holy Paraclete,
   And from thy celestial seat
      Send thy light and brilliancy:
   Father of the poor, draw near;
   Giver of all gifts, be here;
      Come, the soul's true radiancy:

2. Come, of comforters the best,
   Of the soul the sweetest guest,
      Come in toil refreshingly:
   Thou in labour rest most sweet;
   Thou art shadow from the heat;
      Comfort in adversity.

3. O thou Light, most pure and blest,
   Shine within the inmost breast
      Of thy faithful company.
   Where thou art not, man hath nought:
   Every holy deed and thought
      Comes from thy divinity.

4. Heal our wounds, our strength renew;
   On our dryness pour thy dew;
      Wash the stains of guilt away:
   Bend the stubborn heart and will;
   Melt the frozen, warm the chill;
      Guide the steps that go astray.

5. Fill thy faithful, who confide
   In thy power to guard and guide,
      With thy sevenfold mystery.
   Here thy grace and virtue send:
   Grant salvation in the end,
      And in heaven felicity.

Veni, Sancte Spiritus
attributed STEPHEN LANGTON died 1228
vv. 1, 2, 3, 5 *tr.* JOHN MASON NEALE 1818–66
v. 4 *tr.* EDWARD CASWALL Cong. Orat. 1814–78

Pentecost

95 MARCHING   87 87   MARTIN SHAW 1875–1958

An alternative tune will be found at Hymn 268.

1. Holy Spirit, come, confirm us
   In the truth that Christ makes known;
   We have faith and understanding
   Through your helping gifts alone.

2. Holy Spirit, come, console us,
   Come as Advocate to plead,
   Loving Spirit from the Father,
   Grant in Christ the help we need.

3. Holy Spirit, come, renew us,
   Come yourself to make us live:
   Holy through your loving presence,
   Holy through the gifts you give.

4. Holy Spirit, come, possess us,
   You the Love of Three in One,
   Holy Spirit of the Father,
   Holy Spirit of the Son.

BRIAN FOLEY born 1919

Trinity

96 NICAEA 11 12 12 10 JOHN BACCHUS DYKES 1823–76

1. Holy, Holy, Holy! Lord God Almighty!
    Early in the morning our song shall rise to thee:
   Holy, Holy, Holy! Merciful and mighty!
    God in three Persons, blessèd Trinity!

2. Holy, Holy, Holy! all the saints adore thee,
    Casting down their golden crowns around the glassy sea,
   Cherubim and seraphim falling down before thee,
    Which wert, and art, and evermore shalt be.

3. Holy, Holy, Holy! though the darkness hide thee,
    Though the eye of sinful man thy glory may not see,
   Only thou art holy; there is none beside thee,
    Perfect in power, in love, and purity.

4. Holy, Holy, Holy! Lord God Almighty!
    All thy works shall praise thy name, in earth and sky and sea;
   Holy, Holy, Holy! Merciful and mighty!
    God in three Persons, blessèd Trinity!

REGINALD HEBER 1783–1826

Trinity

97 ST PATRICK'S BREASTPLATE   traditional Irish melodies
Irregular   arranged CHARLES VILLIERS STANFORD 1852–1924

1 I bind unto myself today The strong name of the Trinity, By invocation of the same, The Three in One and One in Three.

2 I bind this day to me for ever, By power of faith, Christ's incarnation; His baptism in the Jordan river; His death on Cross for my salvation,

Trinity

His burst-ing from the spi-cèd tomb; His rid-ing up the heaven-ly way; His com - ing at the day of doom: I bind un-to my-self to-day.

3 I bind un-to my-self to-day The power of God to hold and lead, His eye to watch, His might to stay, His ear to heark-en to my need;

Trinity

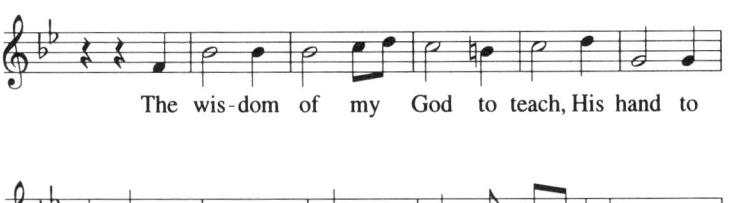

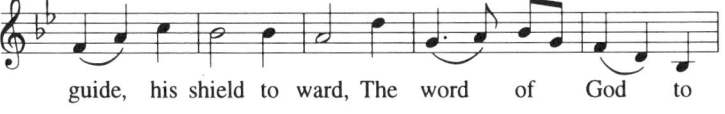

The wis-dom of my God to teach, His hand to guide, his shield to ward, The word of God to give me speech, His heaven-ly host to be my guard.

GARTAN   88 88

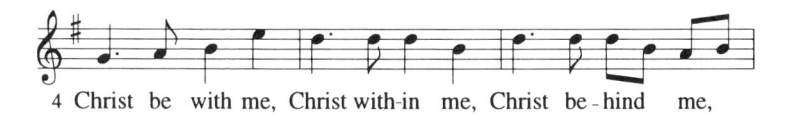

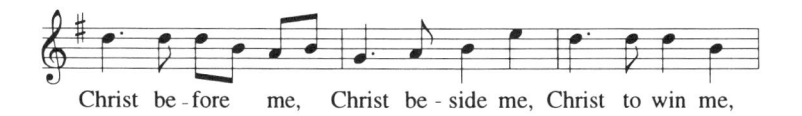

4 Christ be with me, Christ with-in me, Christ be-hind me, Christ be-fore me, Christ be-side me, Christ to win me,

Trinity

Christ to comfort and restore me. Christ beneath me

Christ above me, Christ in quiet Christ in danger,

Christ in hearts of all that love me,

Christ in mouth of friend and stranger.

5 I bind unto myself the name, The strong name

Trinity

... of the Trinity, By invocation
of the same, The Three in One and One in Three,
Of whom all nature hath creation, Eternal
Father, Spirit, Word: Praise to the Lord of
my salvation, Salvation is of Christ the
Lord. Amen.

attributed St Patrick 372–466
tr. Cecil Frances Alexander 1818–95

Trinity

98 SONG 22   10 10 10 10   ORLANDO GIBBONS 1583–1625

1 Love of the Father, love of God the Son,
  From whom all came, in whom was all begun;
  Who formest heavenly beauty out of strife,
  Creation's whole desire and breath of life.

2 Spirit all-holy, thou supreme in might,
  Thou dost give peace, thy presence maketh right;
  Thou with thy favour all things dost enfold,
  With thine all-kindness free from harm wilt hold.

Trinity

3 Hope of all comfort, splendour of all aid,
   That dost not fail nor leave the heart afraid:
   To all that cry thou dost all help accord,
   The angels' armour, and the saints' reward.

4 Purest and highest, wisest and most just,
   There is no truth save only in thy trust;
   Thou dost the mind from earthly dreams recall,
   And bring through Christ to him for whom are all.

5 Eternal glory, all men thee adore,
   Who art and shalt be worshipped evermore:
   Us whom thou madest, comfort with thy might,
   And lead us to enjoy thy heavenly light.

Amor Patris et Filii 12th century
tr. ROBERT BRIDGES 1844–1930

Trinity

99 BANGOR   CM   William Tans'ur's *A Compleat Melody* 1734

An alternative tune will be found at Hymn 54.

1. Most ancient of all mysteries,
   Before thy throne we lie;
   Have mercy now, most merciful,
   Most Holy Trinity.

2. When heaven and earth were yet unmade,
   When time was yet unknown,
   Thou, in thy bliss and majesty,
   Didst live and love alone.

3. Thou wert not born; there was no fount
   From which thy Being flowed;
   There is no end, which thou canst reach:
   But thou art simply God.

4. How wonderful creation is,
   The work that thou didst bless;
   And oh, what then must thou be like,
   Eternal Loveliness!

5. Most ancient of all mysteries,
   Still at thy throne we lie;
   Have mercy now, most merciful,
   Most Holy Trinity.

FREDERICK WILLIAM FABER Cong. Orat. 1814–63

Transfiguration

100 CARLISLE SM CHARLES LOCKHART 1745–1815

1 'Tis good, Lord, to be here!
  Thy glory fills the night;
  Thy face and garments, like the sun,
  Shine with unborrowed light.

2 'Tis good, Lord, to be here,
  Thy beauty to behold,
  Where Moses and Elijah stand,
  Thy messengers of old.

3 Fulfiller of the past,
  Promise of things to be,
  We hail thy Body glorified,
  And our redemption see.

4 Before we taste of death,
  We see thy kingdom come;
  Before us keep the vision bright,
  And make this hill our home.

5 'Tis good, Lord, to be here!
  Yet we may not remain;
  But since thou bid'st us leave the mount,
  Come with us to the plain.

JOSEPH ARMITAGE ROBINSON 1858–1933

Offertory at Mass

101 PEARSALL 76 76 D ROBERT LUCAS DE PEARSALL 1795–1856

1. Accept, Almighty Father,
   This gift of bread and wine
   Which now thy Church doth offer
   To thee, O God benign,
   In humble reparation
   For sins and failings dread,
   To win life everlasting
   For living and for dead.

2. O God, by this commingling
   Of water and of wine,
   May he who took our nature
   Give us his life divine.
   Come, thou who makest holy,
   And bless this sacrifice;
   Then shall our gift be pleasing
   To thee above the skies.

ANONYMOUS

Offertory at Mass

102 BRESLAU LM

Locheim *Gesangbuch* c.1452
arranged Felix Mendelssohn 1809–47

1. Accept, O Father, in thy love,
   These humble gifts of bread and wine,
   That with ourselves we offer thee,
   Returning gifts already thine.

2. Behold this host and chalice, Lord,
   To thee in heaven the gifts we raise;
   Through them may we our homage pay,
   Our adoration, and our praise.

3. No earthly claim to grace is ours,
   Save what thy sacrifice has won;
   Grant then thy grace, fulfil our needs,
   And may thy will in ours be done.

J. Clifford Evers born 1916

Offertory at Mass

103 LIEBSTER JESU 78 78 88 JOHANN RUDOLF AHLE 1625–73
arranged JOHANN SEBASTIAN BACH 1685–1750

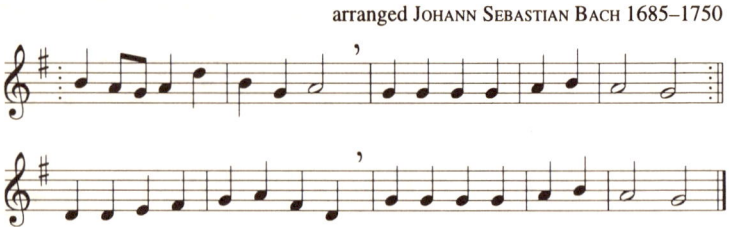

1 Dearest Jesu, we are here,
At thy call thy presence owning;
Pleading now in holy fear
That thy sacrifice atoning:
Word Incarnate, much in wonder
On this mystery deep we ponder.

2 Under forms of bread and wine
Simple hearts in faith adore thee:
Born of Mary, Son divine,
Low we bow the knee before thee:
In this life, oh, ne'er forsake us,
But to bliss hereafter take us.

Liebster Jesu
TOBIAS CLAUSNITZER 1619–1684
tr. GEORGE RATCLIFFE WOODWARD 1848–1934 and others

Offertory at Mass

104 WOODLANDS   10 10 10 10   WALTER GREATOREX 1877–1949

1. 'Lift up your hearts!' We lift them, Lord, to thee;
   Here at thy feet none other may we see:
   'Lift up your hearts!' E'en so, with one accord,
   We lift them up, we lift them to the Lord.

2. Above the level of the former years,
   The mire of sin, the slough of guilty fears,
   The mist of doubt, the blight of love's decay,
   O Lord of Light, lift all our hearts to-day!

3. Lift every gift that thou thyself hast given;
   Low lies the best till lifted up to heaven:
   Low lie the bounding heart, the teeming brain,
   Till, sent from God, they mount to God again.

4. Then, as the trumpet-call, in after years,
   'Lift up your hearts!' rings pealing in our ears,
   Still shall those hearts respond, with full accord,
   'We lift them up, we lift them to the Lord!'

HENRY MONTAGU BUTLER 1833–1918

Offertory at Mass

105 GOTT DES HIMMELS   87 87 87   Heinrich Albert 1604–51

An alternative tune will be found at Hymn 278.

1. Lord, accept the gifts we offer
    At this Eucharistic Feast,
  Bread and wine to be transformed now
    Through the action of thy priest.
  Take us, too, O Lord, transform us;
    Be thy grace in us increased.

2. May our souls be pure and spotless
    As the host of wheat so fine;
  May all stain of sin be crushed out,
    Like the grape that forms the wine,
  As we, too, become partakers
    In this sacrifice divine.

3. Take our gifts, Almighty Father,
    Living God, eternal, true,
  Which we give through Christ, our Saviour,
    Pleading here for us anew.
  Grant salvation to all present
    And our faith and love renew.

Sister M. Teresine O.S.F.

Offertory at Mass

106 FREU' DICH SEHR   87 87 D   attributed Loys Bourgeois c. 1510–61
Ps. 42 in the Genevan *Psalter* 1551
arranged Johann Sebastian Bach 1685–1750

An alternative tune will be found at Hymn 112.

1 Lord, we gather at your altar
   Off'ring sacrifice of praise,
   Just as Abraham and Moses
   Offered in those ancient days;
   But we offer now, O Father,
   Not the blood of goat or ram;
   Here the Son of God we offer
   As our sacrificial Lamb.

2 For the guilt of Adam's children
   Who but Jesus can atone,
   Who appease a God offended
   But the Son of God alone?
   So, with Christ, ourselves we offer
   To our Father throned above,
   As the sacrifice of Calvary
   We renew with grateful love.

                                  J. Clifford Evers born 1916

Offertory at Mass

107 RHUDDLAN   Edward James's *Musical Relicks of Welsh Bards* 1800
        87 87 87   arranged *English Hymnal* 1906

1. Loving Father, from thy bounty
Choicest gifts unnumbered flow:
All the blessings of salvation,
Which to Christ thy Son we owe,
All the gifts that by thy bidding
Nature's hands on us bestow!

2. Here thy grateful children gather,
Offering gifts of bread and wine;
These we give to thee in homage,
Of our love the loving sign,
And restore to thee creation,
Given to man, yet ever thine!

JAMES QUINN S.J. born 1919

Offertory at Mass

108 IRISH CM Powell's *Collection of Hymns* Dublin 1749

1. O God, we give ourselves today
With this pure host to thee,
The selfsame gift which thy dear Son
Gave once on Calvary.

2. Entire and whole, our life and love
With heart and soul and mind,
For all our sins and faults and needs,
Thy Church and all mankind.

3. With humble and with contrite heart
This bread and wine we give,
Because thy Son once gave himself
And died that we might live.

4. Though lowly now, soon by thy word
These offered gifts will be
The very body of our Lord,
His soul and deity.

5. His very body, offered up,
A gift beyond all price,
He gives to us, that we may give
In loving sacrifice.

6. O Lord, who took our human life,
As water mixed with wine,
Grant through this sacrifice that we
May share thy life divine.

ANTHONY NYE S.J.

Offertory at Mass

109 VON GOTT WILL ICH NICHT LASSEN 16th century Franco-German
76 76 D adapted 1563 as chorale

An alternative tune will be found at Hymn 67.

1 O King of might and splendour,
      Creator most adored,
   This sacrifice we render
      To thee as sovereign Lord.
   May these our gifts be pleasing
      Unto thy majesty,
   Mankind from sin releasing
      Who have offended thee.

2 Thy Body thou hast given,
      Thy Blood thou hast outpoured,
   That sin might be forgiven,
      O Jesu, loving Lord.
   As now with love most tender
      Thy death we celebrate,
   Our lives in self-surrender
      To thee we consecrate.

Rex summae maiestatis Ratisbon 19th century
tr. ANTHONY GREGORY MURRAY O.S.B. 1905–92

Offertory at Mass

110 LOBE DEN HERREN   14 14 4 7 8   Stralsund *Gesangbuch* 1665

1. Praise to the Lord, the Almighty, the King of creation!
   O my soul, praise him, for he is thy health and salvation.
   All ye who hear,
   Now to his temple draw near,
   Joining in glad adoration.

2. Praise to the Lord, let us offer
   our gifts at his altar;
   Let not our sins and transgressions
   now cause us to falter.
   Christ, the High Priest,
   Bids us all join in his feast,
   Victims with him on the altar.

3. Praise to the Lord, who o'er all
   things so wondrously reigneth,
   Shelters thee under his wings,
   yea, so gently sustaineth:
   Hast thou not seen?
   All that is needful hath been
   Granted in what he ordaineth.

4. Praise to the Lord, who doth prosper
   thy work and defend thee;
   Surely his goodness and mercy
   here daily attend thee:
   Ponder anew
   What the Almighty can do,
   If with his love he befriend thee.

5. Praise to the Lord! Oh, let all
   that is in me adore him!
   All that hath life and breath, come
   now with praises before him!
   Let the Amen
   Sound from his people again,
   Gladly for aye we adore him.

Lobe den Herren
JOACHIM NEANDER 1650–80
tr. CATHERINE WINKWORTH 1827–78

Offertory at Mass

111 REDHEAD No. 46   87 87   RICHARD REDHEAD 1820–1901

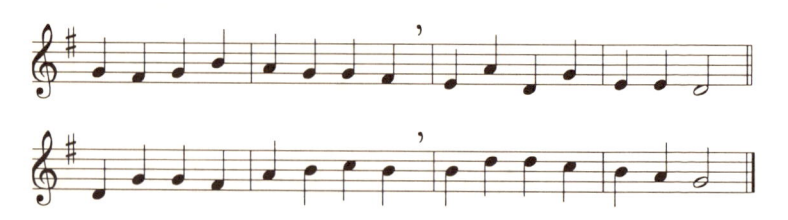

An alternative tune will be found at Hymn 148.

1. See us, Lord, about thine altar;
   Though so many, we are one:
   Many souls by love united
   In the heart of Christ thy Son.

2. Hear our prayers, O loving Father,
   Hear in them thy Son, our Lord:
   Hear him speak our love and worship
   As we sing with one accord.

3. Once were seen the Blood and water:
   Now he seems but bread and wine.
   Then in human form he suffered,
   Now his form is but a sign.

4. Hear us yet: so much is needful
   In our frail, disordered life;
   Stay with us and tend our weakness
   Till that day of no more strife.

5. Members of his mystic body
   Now we know our prayer is heard,
   Heard by thee, because thy children
   Have received the eternal Word.

JOHN GREALLY

Blessed Sacrament

112 HYFRYDOL 87 87 D Richard Huw Pritchard 1811–87

1. Alleluia, sing to Jesus,
   His the sceptre, his the throne;
   Alleluia, his the triumph,
   His the victory alone:
   Hark the songs of peaceful Sion
   Thunder like a mighty flood;
   Jesus, out of every nation,
   Hath redeemed us by his Blood.

2. Alleluia, not as orphans
   Are we left in sorrow now;
   Alleluia, he is near us,
   Faith believes, nor questions how;
   Though the cloud from sight received him
   When the forty days were o'er,
   Shall our hearts forget his promise,
   'I am with you evermore'?

3. Alleluia, Bread of angels,
   Thou on earth our Food, our stay;
   Alleluia, here the sinful
   Flee to thee from day to day;
   Intercessor, Friend of sinners,
   Earth's Redeemer, plead for me,
   Where the songs of all the sinless
   Sweep across the crystal sea.

4. Alleluia, King eternal,
   Thee the Lord of lords we own;
   Alleluia, born of Mary,
   Earth thy footstool, heaven thy throne:
   Thou within the veil hast entered,
   Robed in flesh, our great High Priest;
   Thou on earth both Priest and Victim
   In the Eucharistic Feast.

William Chatterton Dix 1837–98

Blessed Sacrament

113 UNDE ET MEMORES   WILLIAM HENRY MONK 1823–89
10 10 10 10 10

An alternative tune will be found at Hymn 126.

1 And now, O Father, mindful of the love
    That bought us, once for all, on Calvary's Tree,
And having with us him that pleads above,
    We here present, we here spread forth to thee
That only Offering perfect in thine eyes,
The one true, pure, immortal Sacrifice.

2 Look, Father, look on his anointed face,
    And only look on us as found in him;
Look not on our misusings of thy grace,
    Our prayer so languid, and our faith so dim;
For lo, between our sins and their reward
We set the Passion of thy Son our Lord.

Blessed Sacrament

3 And then for those, our dearest and our best,
    By this prevailing presence we appeal;
O fold them closer to thy mercy's breast,
    O do thine utmost for their souls' true weal;
From tainting mischief keep them white and clear
And crown thy gifts with grace to persevere.

4 And so we come: O draw us to thy feet
    Most patient Saviour, who canst love us still;
And by this Food, so aweful and so sweet,
    Deliver us from every touch of ill:
In thine own service make us glad and free,
And grant us nevermore to part from thee.

WILLIAM BRIGHT 1824–1901

Blessed Sacrament

114 SCHMÜCKE DICH   88 88 D   Johann Crüger's
Geistliche Kirchen-Melodien 1649

1 Deck thyself, my soul, with gladness,
    Leave the gloomy haunts of sadness,
    Come into the daylight's splendour,
    There with joy thy praises render
    Unto him whose grace unbounded
    Hath this wondrous banquet founded;
    High o'er all the heavens he reigneth,
    Yet to dwell with thee he deigneth.

Blessed Sacrament

2 Sun, who all my life dost brighten;
  Light, who dost my soul enlighten;
  Joy, the sweetest man e'er knoweth;
  Fount, whence all my being floweth;
  At thy feet I cry, my Maker,
  Let me be a fit partaker
  Of this blessèd Food from heaven,
  For our good, thy glory, given.

3 Jesus, Bread of Life, I pray thee,
  Let me gladly here obey thee;
  Never to my hurt invited,
  Be thy love with love requited:
  From this banquet let me measure,
  Lord, how vast and deep its treasure;
  Through the gifts thou here dost give me,
  As thy guest in heaven receive me.

Schmücke dich, O liebe Seele
JOHANN FRANCK 1618–77
tr. CATHERINE WINKWORTH 1827–78

Blessed Sacrament

115 FIRST TUNE

ELLERS   10 10 10 10   EDWARD JOHN HOPKINS 1818–1901

SECOND TUNE

SONG 24   10 10 10 10   ORLANDO GIBBONS 1583–1625

Blessed Sacrament

1 Draw nigh, and take the Body of the Lord,
  And drink the holy Blood for you outpoured,
  Saved by that Body, hallowed by that Blood,
  Whereby refreshed we render thanks to God.

2 Salvation's giver, Christ the only Son,
  Who by his Cross and Blood the victory won.
  Offered was he for greatest and for least:
  Himself the Victim and himself the Priest.

3 Victims were offered by the law of old,
  That, in a type, celestial mysteries told.
  He, Ransomer from death and Light from shade,
  Giveth his holy grace his saints to aid.

4 Approach ye then with faithful hearts sincere
  And take the safeguard of salvation here.
  He that his saints in this world rules and shields,
  To all believers life eternal yields.

5 With heavenly Bread he makes the hungry whole,
  Gives living waters to the thirsty soul;
  Alpha and Omega, to whom shall bow
  All men at judgement day, is with us now.

Sancti, venite, Corpus Christi sumite
Antiphonary of Bennchar (Bangor, Ireland) c. 690
tr. JOHN MASON NEALE 1818–66 *

Blessed Sacrament

116 RENDEZ À DIEU   98 98 D   Ps. 118 in the Genevan *Psalter* 1543

1 Father, we thank thee who hast planted
    Thy holy name within our hearts.
  Knowledge and faith and life immortal
    Jesus thy Son to us imparts.
  Thou, Lord, didst make all for thy pleasure,
    Didst give us Food for all our days,
  Giving in Christ the Bread eternal;
    Thine is the power, be thine the praise.

Blessed Sacrament

2 Watch o'er thy Church, O Lord, in mercy,
   Save it from evil, guard it still,
Perfect it in thy love, unite it,
   Cleansed and conformed unto thy will.
As grain, once scattered on the hillsides,
   Was in this broken Bread made one,
So from all lands thy Church be gathered
   Into thy kingdom by thy Son.

                   Greek, from the *Didache* 1st century
                   tr. FRANCIS BLAND TUCKER 1895–1984

Blessed Sacrament

117 ADORO TE — Paris *Processionale* 1697

1. Godhead here in hiding, whom I do adore,
   Masked by these bare shadows, shape and nothing more,
   See, Lord, at thy service low lies here a heart
   Lost, all lost in wonder at the God thou art.

2. Seeing, touching, tasting are in thee deceived;
   How says trusty hearing? That shall be believed;
   What God's Son hath told me, take for truth I do;
   Truth himself speaks truly, or there's nothing true.

3. On the Cross thy Godhead made no sign to men;
   Here thy very Manhood steals from human ken;
   Both are my confession, both are my belief,
   And I pray the prayer of the dying thief.

Blessed Sacrament

4 I am not like Thomas, wounds I cannot see,
But can plainly call thee Lord and God as he;
This faith each day deeper be my holding of,
Daily make me harder hope and dearer love.

5 O thou our reminder of Christ crucified,
Living Bread, the life of us for whom he died,
Lend this life to me then; feed and feast my mind,
There be thou the sweetness man was meant to find.

6 Jesu, whom I look at shrouded here below,
I beseech thee send me what I long for so,
Some day to gaze on thee face to face in light
And be blest for ever with thy glory's sight.

Adoro te devote
attributed ST THOMAS AQUINAS 1227–74
tr. GERARD MANLEY HOPKINS S.J. 1844–89

Blessed Sacrament

118 CORPUS CHRISTI Henri Friedrich Hémy's *Crown of Jesus Music* 1864
88 88 88

1. Jesus, my Lord, my God, my all,
   How can I love thee as I ought?
   And how revere this wondrous gift,
   So far surpassing hope or thought?
   Sweet Sacrament, we thee adore;
   Oh, make us love thee more and more.

2. Had I but Mary's sinless heart
   To love thee with, my dearest King,
   Oh, with what bursts of fervent praise
   Thy goodness, Jesus, would I sing!

3. Ah, see! within a creature's hand
   The vast Creator deigns to be,
   Reposing, infant-like, as though
   On Joseph's arm, or Mary's knee.

Blessed Sacrament

4 Thy Body, Soul, and Godhead, all;
    O mystery of love divine!
  I cannot compass all I have,
    For all thou hast and art are mine.

5 Sound, sound his praises higher still,
    And come, ye angels, to our aid;
  'Tis God, 'tis God, the very God,
    Whose power both man and angels made.

              FREDERICK WILLIAM FABER Cong. Orat. 1814–63

Blessed Sacrament

119   SAFFRON WALDEN   86 86   ARTHUR HENRY BROWN 1830–1926

1. Just as I am, without one plea
But that thy Blood was shed for me,
And that thou bidd'st me come to thee,
   O Lamb of God, I come.

2. Just as I am, though tossed about
With many a conflict, many a doubt,
Fightings within, and fears without,

3. Just as I am, poor, wretched, blind;
Sight, riches, healing of the mind,
Yea all I need, in thee to find,

4. Just as I am, thou wilt receive,
Wilt welcome, pardon, cleanse, relieve:
Because thy promise I believe,

5. Just as I am (thy love unknown
Has broken every barrier down),
Now to be thine, yea thine alone,

6. Just as I am, of that free love
The breadth, length, depth and height to prove,
Here for a season then above,
   O Lamb of God, I come.

CHARLOTTE ELLIOTT 1789–1871

Blessed Sacrament

120 PICARDY   87 87 87   17th century French carol
in *Chansons populaires des Provinces de France*
Paris 1860

1. Let all mortal flesh keep silence, and with fear and trembling stand;
Ponder nothing earthly-minded, for with blessing in his hand,
Christ our God to earth descendeth, our full homage to demand.

2. King of kings, yet born of Mary, as of old on earth he stood,
Lord of lords, in human vesture—in the Body and the Blood—
He will give to all the faithful his own self for heavenly Food.

3. Rank on rank the host of heaven spreads its vanguard on the way,
As the Light of Light descendeth from the realms of endless day,
That the powers of hell may vanish as the darkness clears away.

4. At his feet the six-winged seraph; cherubim with sleepless eye,
Veil their faces to the Presence, as with ceaseless voice they cry,
Alleluia, Alleluia, Alleluia, Lord most high.

Greek and Syriac
Cherubic Hymn *Liturgy of St James* 4th century
tr. GERARD MOULTRIE 1829–85

Blessed Sacrament

121 ST HELEN   87 87 87   GEORGE MARTIN 1844–1916

1. Lord, enthroned in heav'nly splendour,
   First-begotten from the dead,
   Thou alone, our strong defender,
   Liftest up thy people's head.
   Alleluia! Alleluia!
   Jesu, true and living Bread.

2. Here our humblest homage pay we;
   Here in loving reverence bow;
   Here for faith's discernment pray we,
   Lest we fail to know thee now.
   Alleluia! Alleluia!
   Thou art here, we ask not how.

3. Though the lowliest form doth veil thee
   As of old in Bethlehem,
   Here as there thine angels hail thee,
   Branch and Flower of Jesse's stem.
   Alleluia! Alleluia!
   We in worship join with them.

Blessed Sacrament

4 Paschal Lamb, thine offering, finished
    Once for all when thou wast slain,
In its fulness undiminished
    Shall for evermore remain,
        Alleluia! Alleluia!
      Cleansing souls from every stain.

5 Life-imparting heav'nly Manna,
    Stricken Rock with streaming side,
Heaven and earth with loud hosanna
    Worship thee, the Lamb who died,
        Alleluia! Alleluia!
      Ris'n, ascended, glorified!

GEORGE HUGH BOURNE 1840–1925

Blessed Sacrament

122 TYNEMOUTH 88 88 88   Henri Friedrich Hémy 1818–1888

1. O Bread of heaven, beneath this veil
   Thou dost my very God conceal:
   My Jesus, dearest treasure, hail;
   I love thee and adoring kneel;
   Each loving soul by thee is fed
   With thine own self in form of bread.

2. O Food of life, thou who dost give
   The pledge of immortality;
   I live; no, 'tis not I that live;
   God gives me life, God lives in me:
   He feeds my soul, he guides my ways,
   And every grief with joy repays.

Blessed Sacrament

3 O Bond of love, that dost unite
    The servant to his living Lord;
Could I dare live, and not requite
    Such love—then death were meet reward:
I cannot live unless to prove
Some love for such unmeasured love.

4 Belovèd Lord in heav'n above,
    There, Jesus, thou awaitest me;
To gaze on thee with changeless love;
    Yes, thus, I hope, thus shall it be:
For how can he deny me heav'n
Who here on earth himself hath giv'n?

St Alphonsus Liguori 1696–1787
tr. Edmund Vaughan C.Ss.R. 1827–1908

Blessed Sacrament

123 IN ALLEN MEINEN THATEN
776 D

Davidisches Harfen-und-Psalterspiel
1749

1. O Food of men wayfaring,
   The Bread of angels sharing,
     O Manna from on high!
   We hunger; Lord, supply us,
   Nor thy delights deny us,
     Whose hearts to thee draw nigh.

2. O Stream of love past telling,
   O purest Fountain, welling
     From out the Saviour's side!
   We faint with thirst; revive us,
   Of thine abundance give us,
     And all we need provide.

Blessed Sacrament

3 O Jesu, by thee bidden,
   We here adore thee, hidden
     'Neath forms of bread and wine.
   Grant when the veil is riven,
   We may behold, in heaven,
     Thy countenance divine.

O esca viatorum 17th century
tr. ATHELSTAN RILEY 1858–1945

Blessed Sacrament

124 AQUINAS   11 11 11 11   RICHARD RUNCIMAN TERRY 1865–1938

1. O Godhead hid, devoutly I adore thee,
   Who truly art within the forms before me;
   To thee my heart I bow with bended knee,
   As failing quite in contemplating thee.

2. Sight, touch, and taste in thee are each deceivèd;
   The ear alone most safely is believèd:
   I believe all the Son of God has spoken,
   Than Truth's own word there is no truer token.

3. God only on the Cross lay hid from view;
   But here lies hid at once the Manhood too:
   And I, in both professing my belief,
   Make the same prayer as the repentant thief.

Blessed Sacrament

4 Thy wounds, as Thomas saw, I do not see;
  Yet thee confess my Lord and God to be;
  Make me believe thee ever more and more;
  In thee my hope, in thee my love to store.

5 O thou memorial of our Lord's own dying!
  O Bread that living art and vivifying!
  Make ever thou my soul on thee to live;
  Ever a taste of heavenly sweetness give.

6 O loving Pelican! O Jesus, Lord!
  Unclean I am, but cleanse me in thy Blood,
  Of which a single drop for sinners spilt,
  Is ransom for a world's entire guilt.

7 Jesu! whom for the present veiled I see,
  What I so thirst for, oh vouchsafe to me:
  That I may see thy countenance unfolding,
  And may be blest thy glory in beholding.

Adoro te devote
attributed St Thomas Aquinas 1227–74
tr. Edward Caswall Cong. Orat. 1814–78

Blessed Sacrament

125 MUNICH 76 76 D Meiningen *Gesangbuch* 1693
arranged Felix Mendelssohn 1809–47

An alternative tune will be found at Hymn 101.

1 O Jesus Christ, remember,
  When thou shalt come again,
 Upon the clouds of heaven,
  With all thy shining train:
 When every eye shall see thee
  In Deity revealed,
 Who now upon this altar
  In silence art concealed.

Blessed Sacrament

2 Remember, then, O Saviour,
   I supplicate of thee,
That here I bowed before thee,
   Upon my bended knee;
That here I owned thy presence,
   And did not thee deny;
And glorified thy greatness
   Though hid from human eye.

3 Accept, divine Redeemer,
   The homage of my praise;
Be thou the light and honour
   And glory of my days.
Be thou my consolation
   When death is drawing nigh;
Be thou my only treasure
   Through all eternity.

                    EDWARD CASWALL Cong. Orat. 1814–78

Blessed Sacrament

126 SONG 1   10 10 10 10 10 10   ORLANDO GIBBONS 1583–1625

1. O thou, who at thy Eucharist didst pray
    That all thy Church might be for ever one,
   Grant us at every Eucharist to say
    With longing heart and soul, 'Thy will be done.'
   Oh, may we all one Bread, one Body be,
   One through this Sacrament of unity.

2. For all thy Church, O Lord, we intercede;
    Make thou our sad divisions soon to cease;
   Draw us the nearer each to each, we plead,
    By drawing all to thee, O Prince of Peace:
   Thus may we all one Bread, one Body be,
   One through this Sacrament of unity.

Blessed Sacrament

3 We pray thee too for wanderers from thy fold;
    O bring them back, good Shepherd of the sheep,
Back to the faith which saints believed of old,
    Back to the Church which still that faith doth keep:
Soon may we all one Bread, one Body be,
One through this Sacrament of unity.

4 So, Lord, at length when sacraments shall cease,
    May we be one with all thy Church above,
One with thy saints in one unbroken peace,
    One with thy saints in one unbounded love:
More blessèd still, in peace and love to be
One with the Trinity in Unity.

based on John 17:11
WILLIAM TURTON 1856–1938

Blessed Sacrament

127 NEANDER (Unser Herrscher)   87 87 87   JOACHIM NEANDER 1650–80
adapted Darmstadt *Gesangbuch* 1698

An alternative tune will be found at Hymn 278.

1 Of the glorious Body telling,
   O my tongue, its mysteries sing,
And the Blood, all price excelling,
   Which the world's eternal King,
In a noble womb once dwelling,
   Shed for this world's ransoming.

2 Giv'n for us, for us descending,
   Of a virgin to proceed,
Man with man in converse blending,
   Scattered he the gospel seed,
Till his sojourn drew to ending,
   Which he closed in wondrous deed.

3 At the last great supper lying
   Circled by his brethren's band,
Meekly with the law complying,
   First he finished its command,
Then, immortal food supplying,
   Gave himself with his own hand.

Blessed Sacrament

4 Word-made-flesh, by word he maketh
    Bread his very Flesh to be;
  Man in wine Christ's Blood partaketh:
    And if senses fail to see,
  Faith alone the true heart waketh
    To behold the mystery.

PART 2 *Tantum ergo*

5 Therefore we, before him bending,
    This great Sacrament revere;
  Types and shadows have their ending,
    For the newer rite is here;
  Faith, our outward sense befriending,
    Makes the inward vision clear.

6 Glory let us give, and blessing
    To the Father and the Son;
  Honour, might, and praise addressing,
    While eternal ages run;
  Ever too his love confessing,
    Who from both, with both is one.

Pange lingua gloriosi corporis mysterium
ST THOMAS AQUINAS 1227–74
tr. JOHN MASON NEALE 1818–66 and others

Blessed Sacrament

128 ALBANO   CM   Vincent Novello 1781–1861

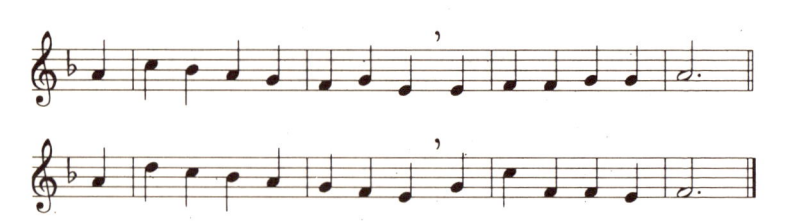

1 Once, only once, and once for all,
   His precious life he gave;
  Before the Cross in faith we fall,
   And own it strong to save.

2 'One offering, single and complete',
   With lips and hearts we say;
  But what he never can repeat
   He shows forth day by day.

3 For as the priest of Aaron's line
   Within the holiest stood,
  And sprinkled all the mercy-shrine
   With sacrificial blood;

4 So he, who once atonement wrought,
   Our Priest of endless power,
  Presents himself for those he bought
   In that dark noontide hour.

5 His Manhood pleads where now it lives
   On heaven's eternal throne,
  And where in mystic rite he gives
   Its presence to his own.

6 And so we show thy death, O Lord,
   Till thou again appear,
  And feel, when we approach thy board,
   We have an altar here.

William Bright 1824–1901

Blessed Sacrament

129 ANIMA CHRISTI   10 10 10 10   WILLIAM MAHER S.J. 1823–77

1. Soul of my Saviour, sanctify my breast;
   Body of Christ, be thou my saving guest;
   Blood of my Saviour, bathe me in thy tide,
   Wash me with water flowing from thy side.

2. Strength and protection may thy Passion be;
   O blessèd Jesus, hear and answer me;
   Deep in thy wounds, Lord, hide and shelter me;
   So shall I never, never part from thee.

3. Guard and defend me from the foe malign;
   In death's dread moments make me only thine;
   Call me, and bid me come to thee on high,
   When I may praise thee with thy saints for aye.

Anima Christi
attributed POPE JOHN XXII 1249–1334
tr. ANONYMOUS

Blessed Sacrament

130 DIVINE MYSTERIES   66 66 886   FRANCIS STANFIELD 1835–1914

1. Sweet Sacrament divine,
   Hid in thine earthly home,
   Lo, round thy lowly shrine,
   With suppliant hearts we come;
   Jesus, to thee our voice we raise
   In songs of love and heartfelt praise:
   Sweet Sacrament divine.

2. Sweet Sacrament of peace,
   Dear home for every heart,
   Where restless yearnings cease
   And sorrows all depart;
   There in thine ear all trustfully
   We tell our tale of misery:
   Sweet Sacrament of peace.

Blessed Sacrament

3 Sweet Sacrament of rest,
    Ark from the ocean's roar,
Within thy shelter blest
    Soon may we reach the shore;
Save us, for still the tempest raves,
Save, lest we sink beneath the waves:
    Sweet Sacrament of rest.

4 Sweet Sacrament divine,
    Earth's light and jubilee,
In thy far depths doth shine
    Thy Godhead's majesty;
Sweet light, so shine on us, we pray,
That earthly joys may fade away:
    Sweet Sacrament divine.

FRANCIS STANFIELD 1835–1914

Blessed Sacrament

131 WAREHAM LM

WILLIAM KNAPP 1698–1768

1. The heavenly Word proceeding forth,
    Yet leaving not his Father's side,
   And going to his work on earth,
    Had reached at length life's eventide.

2. Soon by his own false friend betrayed,
    Giv'n to his foes, to death went he;
   His own true self, in form of bread,
    He gave his friends, their life to be.

3. A double gift his love did plan,
    His Flesh to feed, his Blood to cheer,
   That flesh and blood, the whole of man,
    Might find its own fulfilment here.

4. The manger, Christ their equal made;
    That upper room, their souls' repast;
   The Cross, their ransom dearly paid,
    And heav'n, their high reward at last.

Blessed Sacrament

PART 2   *O salutaris hostia*

5 O saving Victim, opening wide
    The gate of heav'n to man below;
  Our foes press hard on every side,
    Thine aid supply, thy strength bestow.

6 All praise and thanks to thee ascend
    For evermore, blest One in Three;
  O grant us life that shall not end,
    In our true native land with thee.

Verbum supernum prodiens
ST THOMAS AQUINAS 1227–74
vv. 1, 5, 6 *tr.* JOHN MASON NEALE 1818–66 and others
vv. 2–4 *tr.* RONALD ARBUTHNOTT KNOX 1888–1957

Blessed Sacrament

132 UFFINGHAM   LM   Jeremiah Clarke c. 1673–1707

An alternative tune will be found at Hymn 72.

1. With all the powers my poor soul hath
   Of humble love and loyal faith;
   Thus low, my God, I bow to thee,
   Whom too much love bowed lower for me.

2. Down, down, proud sense, discourses die,
   And all adore faith's mystery!
   Faith is my skill, faith can believe
   As far as love new laws can give.

3. Faith is my force, faith strength affords
   To keep pace with those powerful words:
   And words more sure, more sweet than they,
   Love could not think, truth could not say.

Blessed Sacrament

4 O dear memorial of that death,
   Which still survives, and gives us breath,
   Live ever, Bread of Life, and be
   My Food, my joy, my all to me.

5 O soft, self-wounding Pelican!
   Whose breast weeps balm for wounded man,
   That Blood, whose least drops sovereign be
   To wash my words of sin from me.

6 Come, glorious Lord, my hopes increase,
   And fill my portion in thy peace:
   Come hidden life, and that long day
   For which I languish, come away.

7 When this dry soul those eyes shall see,
   And drink the unsealèd source of thee;
   When glory's sun faith's shade shall chase,
   Then for thy veil, give me thy face.

Adoro te devote
attributed St Thomas Aquinas 1227–74
tr. Richard Crashaw 1613–50
and adapted John Austin 1613–89

Sacred Heart

133 ST BERNARD   CM   *Tochter Sion* Cologne 1741
adapted JOHN RICHARDSON 1816–79

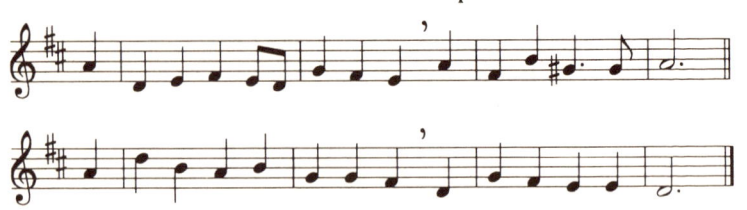

1. All ye who seek a comfort sure
   In trouble and distress,
Whatever sorrow vex the mind,
   Or guilt the soul oppress,

2. Jesus, who gave himself for you
   Upon the Cross to die,
Opens to you his Sacred Heart;
   Oh, to that Heart draw nigh.

3. Ye hear how kindly he invites;
   Ye hear his words so blest—
'All ye that labour, come to me,
   And I will give you rest.'

4. What meeker than the Saviour's Heart
   As on the Cross he lay;
It did his murderers forgive
   And for their pardon pray.

5. O Heart, thou joy of saints on high!
   Thou hope of sinners here,
Attracted by those loving words,
   To thee I lift my prayer.

6. Wash thou my wounds in that dear Blood
   Which forth from thee doth flow;
New grace, new hope inspire, a new
   And better heart bestow.

Quicumque certum quaeritis 18th century
tr. EDWARD CASWALL Cong. Orat. 1814–78

Sacred Heart

134 SONG 13   77 77   ORLANDO GIBBONS 1583–1625

1. Jesu, grant me this, I pray,
    Ever in thy Heart to stay;
  Let me evermore abide
    Hidden in thy wounded side.

2. If the evil one prepare,
    Or the world, a tempting snare,
  I am safe when I abide
    In thy Heart and wounded side.

3. If the flesh, more dangerous still,
    Tempt my soul to deeds of ill,
  Naught I fear when I abide
    In thy Heart and wounded side.

4. Death will come one day to me;
    Jesu, cast me not from thee;
  Dying let me still abide
    In thy Heart and wounded side.

Dignare me, O Jesu rogo te 17th century
tr. HENRY WILLIAMS BAKER 1821–77

Sacred Heart

135 LAURENCE   4 6 88 4   Richard Runciman Terry 1865–1938

1. O Sacred Heart,
   Our home lies deep in thee;
   On earth thou art an exile's rest,
   In heaven the glory of the blest,
   O Sacred Heart.

2. O Sacred Heart,
   Thou fount of contrite tears;
   Where'er those living waters flow,
   New life to sinners they bestow,
   O Sacred Heart.

3. O Sacred Heart,
   Bless our dear native land;
   May England's sons in truth e'er stand,
   With faith's bright banner still in hand,
   O Sacred Heart.

Sacred Heart

4 O Sacred Heart,
 Our trust is all in thee;
 For though earth's night be dark and drear,
 Thou breathest rest where thou art near,
 O Sacred Heart.

5 O Sacred Heart,
 When shades of death shall fall,
 Receive us 'neath thy gentle care,
 And save us from the tempter's snare,
 O Sacred Heart.

6 O Sacred Heart,
 Lead exiled children home,
 Where we may ever rest near thee,
 In peace and joy eternally,
 O Sacred Heart.

FRANCIS STANFIELD 1835–1914

Sacred Heart

136 NARENZA SM
(Ave Maria klare)

Johann Leisentritt's
Catholicum Hymnologium Germanicum 1584
adapted WILLIAM HENRY HAVERGAL 1793–1870

1. To Christ, the Prince of Peace,
   And Son of God most high,
   The father of the world to come,
   Sing we with holy joy.

2. Deep in his Heart for us,
   The wound of love he bore;
   That love wherewith he still inflames
   The hearts that him adore.

3. O Jesu, victim blest,
   What else but love divine,
   Could thee constrain to open thus
   That Sacred Heart of thine?

4. O fount of endless life,
   O spring of water clear,
   O flame celestial, cleansing all
   Who unto thee draw near!

5. Hide us in thy dear Heart,
   For thither do we fly;
   There seek thy grace through life, in death
   Thine immortality.

6. Praise to the Father be,
   And sole-begotten Son;
   Praise, holy Paraclete, to thee
   While endless ages run.

Summi parentis filio
Catholicum Hymnologium Germanicum 1584
tr. EDWARD CASWALL Cong. Orat. 1814–78

Sacred Heart

137 COR JESU   76 76 + refrain   WILLIAM MAHER S.J. 1823–77

1. To Jesus' Heart, all burning
   With fervent love for men,
   My heart with fondest yearning
   Shall raise its joyful strain.
   While ages course along,
   Blest be with loudest song
   The Sacred Heart of Jesus
   By every heart and tongue.

2. O Heart, for me on fire
   With love no man can speak,
   My yet untold desire
   God gives me for thy sake.

3. Too true, I have forsaken
   Thy love for wilful sin;
   Yet now let me be taken
   Back by thy grace again.

4. As thou art meek and lowly,
   And ever pure of heart,
   So may my heart be wholly
   Of thine the counterpart.

5. When life away is flying,
   And earth's false glare is done;
   Still, Sacred Heart, in dying
   I'll say I'm all thine own.

Dem Herzen Jesu singe
ALOYS SCHLÖR 1805–52
tr. ALBANY JAMES CHRISTIE S.J. 1817–91

Precious Blood

138 WESTMINSTER OLD   77 77 D   JOHN RICHARDSON 1816–79

1. By the blood that flowed from thee
In thy grievous agony;
By the traitor's guileful kiss,
Filling up thy bitterness;
    Jesus, Saviour, hear our cry;
    Thou wert suff'ring once as we:
    Now enthroned in majesty
    Countless angels sing to thee.

2. By the cords that, round thee cast,
Bound thee to the pillar fast;
By the scourge so meekly borne;
By the purple robe of scorn;

3. By the thorns that crowned thy head;
By the sceptre of a reed;
By thy foes on bending knee,
Mocking at thy royalty;

4. By the people's cruel jeers;
By the holy women's tears;
By thy footsteps, faint and slow,
Weighed beneath thy Cross of woe;

5. By thy weeping Mother's woe;
By the sword that pierced her through,
When in anguish standing by,
On the Cross she saw thee die;

CECILIA MARY CADDELL

Precious Blood

139 WEM IN LEIDENSTAGEN (Caswall)   FRIEDRICH FILITZ 1804–76
     65 65

1. Glory be to Jesus,
   Who in bitter pains
   Poured for me the life-blood
   From his sacred veins.

2. Grace and life eternal
   In that Blood I find;
   Blest be his compassion,
   Infinitely kind.

3. Blest through endless ages
   Be the precious stream,
   Which from endless torment
   Doth the world redeem.

4. Abel's blood for vengeance
   Pleaded to the skies;
   But the Blood of Jesus
   For our pardon cries.

5. Oft as it is sprinkled
   On our guilty hearts,
   Satan in confusion
   Terror-struck departs.

6. Oft as earth exulting,
   Wafts its praise on high,
   Hell with horror trembles,
   Heav'n is filled with joy.

7. Lift ye, then, your voices;
   Swell the mighty flood;
   Louder still and louder,
   Praise the Precious Blood.

Viva, viva Gesù 18th century
tr. EDWARD CASWALL Cong. Orat. 1814–78

Precious Blood

140 CORNWALL   886 886   Samuel Sebastian Wesley 1810–76

1. Hail, Jesus, hail! who for my sake
 Sweet blood from Mary's veins didst take
    And shed it all for me:
 Oh, blessèd be my Saviour's Blood,
 My light, my life, my only good,
    To all eternity.

2. To endless ages let us praise
 The Precious Blood, whose price could raise
    The world from wrath and sin;
 Whose streams our inward thirst appease
 And heal the sinner's worst disease,
    If he but bathe therein.

Precious Blood

3 Oh, sweetest Blood, that can implore
   Pardon of God, and heav'n restore,
      The heav'n which sin had lost;
   While Abel's blood for vengeance pleads,
   What Jesus shed still intercedes
      For those who wrong him most.

4 Ah, there is joy amid the saints,
   And hell's despairing courage faints
      When this sweet song we raise:
   Oh, louder then, and louder still,
   Earth with one mighty chorus fill,
      The Precious Blood to praise.

Viva, viva Gesù 18th century
tr. FREDERICK WILLIAM FABER Cong. Orat. 1814–63

Christ the King

141 DIADEMATA DSM   GEORGE ELVEY 1816–93

1. Crown him with many crowns,
    The Lamb upon his throne;
   Hark, how the heavenly anthem drowns
    All music but its own:
   Awake, my soul, and sing
    Of him who died for thee,
   And hail him as thy matchless King
    Through all eternity.

2. Crown him the Virgin's Son,
    The God incarnate born,
   Whose arm those crimson trophies won
    Which now his brow adorn;
   Fruit of the mystic Rose,
    As of that Rose the stem;
   The Root, whence mercy ever flows,
    The Babe of Bethlehem.

Christ the King

3 Crown him the Lord of love:
    Behold his hands and side,
Those wounds yet visible above
    In beauty glorified:
No angel in the sky
    Can fully bear that sight,
But downward bends his burning eye
    At mysteries so bright.

4 Crown him the Lord of peace,
    Whose power a sceptre sways
From pole to pole, that wars may cease,
    Absorbed in prayer and praise;
His reign shall know no end,
    And round his piercèd feet
Fair flowers of Paradise extend
    Their fragrance ever sweet.

5 Crown him the Lord of heaven,
    One with the Father known,
And the blest Spirit through him given
    From yonder triune throne:
All hail, Redeemer, hail,
    For thou hast died for me,
Thy praise shall never, never fail
    Throughout eternity.

MATTHEW BRIDGES 1800–94

Christy the King

142 KING DIVINE 77 77 + refrain Charles Rigby 1901–62

1. Hail Redeemer, King divine!
   Priest and Lamb, the throne is thine,
   King, whose reign shall never cease,
   Prince of everlasting peace.
   Angels, saints and nations sing:
   'Praised be Jesus Christ, our King;
   Lord of life, earth, sky and sea,
   King of love on Calvary.'

2. King whose name creation thrills,
   Rule our minds, our hearts, our wills,
   Till in peace each nation rings
   With thy praises, King of kings.

3. King most holy, King of truth,
   Guide the lowly, guide the youth;
   Christ, thou King of glory bright,
   Be to us eternal light.

4. Shepherd-King, o'er mountains steep,
   Homeward bring the wandering sheep;
   Shelter in one royal fold
   States and kingdoms, new and old.

Patrick Brennan C.Ss.R. 1877–1952

Christ the King

143 DEUS TUORUM MILITUM LM Grenoble *Antiphonale* 1753

1. To Christ the Lord of worlds we sing,
   The nations' universal King.
   Hail, conquering Christ, whose reign alone
   Over our hearts and souls we own.

2. Christ, who art known the Prince of Peace,
   Bid all rebellious tumults cease;
   Call home thy straying sheep, and hold
   For ever in one faithful fold.

3. For this, thine arms, on Calvary,
   Were stretched across th' empurpled tree,
   And the sharp spear that through thee ran
   Laid bare the Heart that burned for man.

4. For this, in forms of bread and wine
   Lies hid the plenitude divine,
   And from thy wounded body runs
   The stream of life to all thy sons.

5. May those who rule o'er men below
   Thee for their greater Sovereign know,
   And human wisdom, arts, and laws
   In thee repose as in their cause.

6. Let kingly signs of pomp and state
   Unto thy name be dedicate,
   City and hearth and household be
   Under thy gentle sceptre free.

7. Praise be to Christ, whose name and throne
   O'er every throne and name we own;
   And equal praises still repeat
   The Father and the Paraclete.

Te saeculorum Principem
tr. WALTER SHEWRING 1906–90

Blessed Virgin Mary

144 QUEEN OF THE ANGELS   66 11 66 11 + refrain   traditional

1 Bring flowers of the rarest,
  Bring blossoms the fairest,
  From garden and woodland and hillside and dale,
  Our full hearts are swelling,
  Our glad voices telling
  The praise of the loveliest Flower of the Vale.
    O Mary, we crown thee with blossoms today,
    Queen of the angels and Queen of the May.
    O Mary, we crown thee with blossoms today,
    Queen of the angels and Queen of the May.

Blessed Virgin Mary

2   Their lady they name thee,
    Their mistress proclaim thee,
    Oh, grant that thy children on earth be as true;
    As long as the bowers
    Are radiant with flowers,
    As long as the azure shall keep its bright hue.

3   Sing gaily in chorus,
    The bright angels o'er us
    Re-echo the strains we begin upon earth;
    Their harps are repeating
    The notes of our greeting,
    For Mary herself is the cause of our mirth.

                                                ANONYMOUS

Blessed Virgin Mary

145 DAILY DAILY
87 87 87 87

19th century English form of *Maria zu lieben*
Paderborn *Gesangbuch* 1765

1. Daily, daily, sing to Mary,
    Sing my soul, her praises due;
   All her feasts, her actions worship,
    With the heart's devotion true.
   Lost in wond'ring contemplation
    Be her majesty confessed:
   Call her Mother, call her Virgin,
    Happy Mother, Virgin blest.

2. She is mighty to deliver;
    Call her, trust her lovingly:
   When the tempest rages round thee,
    She will calm the troubled sea,
   Gifts of heaven she has given,
    Noble Lady! to our race:
   She, the Queen, who decks her subjects
    With the light of God's own grace.

Blessed Virgin Mary

3 Sing, my tongue, the Virgin's trophies,
    Who for us her Maker bore;
For the curse of old inflicted,
    Peace and blessings to restore.
Sing in songs of praise unending,
    Sing the world's majestic Queen;
Weary not nor faint in telling
    All the gifts she gives to men.

4 All my senses, heart, affections,
    Strive to sound her glory forth:
Spread abroad the sweet memorials
    Of the Virgin's priceless worth.
Where the voice of music thrilling,
    Where the tongues of eloquence,
That can utter hymns beseeming
    All her matchless excellence?

5 All our joys do flow from Mary,
    All then join her praise to sing:
Trembling sing the Virgin Mother,
    Mother of our Lord and King.
While we sing her awful glory,
    Far above our fancy's reach,
Let our hearts be quick to offer
    Love the heart alone can teach.

Omni die dic Mariae
attributed ST BERNARD OF CLUNY 12th century
tr. HENRY BITTLESTON 1818–86

Blessed Virgin Mary

146 SALVE REGINA COELITUM traditional American
84 84 + refrain

1. Hail, holy Queen enthroned above, O Maria!
   Hail, Mother of mercy and of love, O Maria!
   Triumph all ye cherubim,
   Sing with us, ye seraphim,
   Heav'n and earth resound the hymn:
   Salve, Salve, Salve Regina.

2. Our life, our sweetness here below, O Maria!
   Our hope in sorrow and in woe, O Maria!

Blessed Virgin Mary

3 To thee we cry, poor sons of Eve, O Maria!
   To thee we sigh, we mourn, we grieve, O Maria!

4 Turn then most gracious advocate, O Maria!
   T'ward us thine eyes compassionate, O Maria!

5 When this our exile is complete, O Maria!
   Show us thy Son, our Jesus sweet, O Maria!

based on *Salve Regina*
traditional American

Blessed Virgin Mary

147 STELLA   88 88 88 88   traditional melody in Henri Friedrich Hémy's *Easy Hymn-Tunes for Catholic Schools* 1851

1. Hail, Queen of heav'n, the ocean star,
    Guide of the wand'rer here below:
   Thrown on life's surge, we claim thy care—
    Save us from peril and from woe.
        Mother of Christ, Star of the Sea,
        Pray for the wanderer, pray for me.

2. O gentle, chaste, and spotless Maid,
    We sinners make our prayers through thee;
   Remind thy Son that he has paid
    The price of our iniquity.
        Virgin most pure, Star of the Sea,
        Pray for the sinner, pray for me.

Blessed Virgin Mary

3 Sojourners in this vale of tears,
    To thee, blest advocate, we cry;
Pity our sorrows, calm our fears,
    And soothe with hope our misery.
        Refuge in grief, Star of the Sea,
        Pray for the mourner, pray for me.

4 And while to him who reigns above,
    In Godhead One, in Persons Three,
The source of life, of grace, of love,
    Homage we pay on bended knee;
        Do thou, bright Queen, Star of the Sea,
        Pray for thy children, pray for me.

based on *Salve Regina*
JOHN LINGARD 1771–1851

Blessed Virgin Mary

148   DRAKES BOUGHTON   87 87   EDWARD ELGAR 1857–1935

1. Hear thy children, gentlest Mother,
    Prayerful hearts to thee arise;
   Hear us while our evening Ave
    Soars beyond the starry skies.

2. Dark'ning shadows fall around us,
    Stars their silent watches keep;
   Hush the heart oppressed with sorrow,
    Dry the tears of those who weep.

3. Hear, sweet Mother, hear the weary,
    Borne upon life's troubled sea;
   Gentle guiding Star of Ocean,
    Lead thy children home to thee.

4. Still watch o'er us, dearest Mother,
    From thy beauteous throne above;
   Guard us from all harm and danger,
    'Neath thy sheltering wings of love.

FRANCIS STANFIELD 1835–1914

Blessed Virgin Mary

149 FARLEY CASTLE (Lawes' Psalm 72)   HENRY LAWES 1596–1662
10 10 10 10

1. Her Virgin eyes saw God incarnate born,
   When she to Bethl'em came that happy morn;
   How high her raptures then began to swell,
   None but her own omniscient Son can tell.

2. As Eve when she her fontal sin reviewed,
   Wept for herself and all she should include,
   Blest Mary with man's Saviour in embrace
   Joyed for herself and for all human race.

3. All saints are by her Son's dear influence blest,
   She kept the very Fountain at her breast;
   The Son adored and nursed by the sweet Maid
   A thousandfold of love for love repaid.

4. Heav'n with transcendent joys her entrance graced,
   Next to his throne her Son his Mother placed;
   And here below, now she's of heaven possessed,
   All generations are to call her blest.

THOMAS KEN 1637–1711

Blessed Virgin Mary

150 BLAENWERN   87 87 D   William Rowlands 1860–1937

1 Holy light on earth's horizon,
  Star of hope to fallen man,
  Light amid a world of shadows,
  Dawn of God's redemptive plan.
  Chosen from eternal ages,
  Thou alone of all our race,
  By thy Son's atoning merits
  Wast conceived in perfect grace.

Blessed Virgin Mary

2 Mother of the world's Redeemer,
  Promised from the dawn of time:
  How could one so highly favoured
  Share the guilt of Adam's crime?
  Sun and moon and stars adorn thee,
  Sinless Eve, triumphant sign;
  Thou art she who crushed the serpent,
  Mary, pledge of life divine.

3 Earth below and highest heaven
  Praise the splendour of thy state,
  Thou who now art crowned in glory
  Wast conceived immaculate.
  Hail, beloved of the Father,
  Mother of his only Son,
  Mystic bride of Love eternal,
  Hail, thou fair and spotless one!

Alma lux 17th century
tr. EDWARD CASWALL Cong. Orat. 1814–78

Blessed Virgin Mary

151 ABBOT'S LEIGH   87 87 D   Cyril Taylor 1907–91

1 Holy Mary, we implore thee,
   By thy purity divine;
Help us, bending here before thee,
   Help us truly to be thine.
      Thou, unfolding wide the portals
         Of the kingdom in the skies,
      Holy Virgin, hast to mortals
         Shown the land of Paradise.

Blessed Virgin Mary

2 Thou, when deepest night infernal
    Had for ages shrouded man,
  Gavest us that Light eternal
    Promised since the world began.
        God in thee hath showered plenty
          On the hungry and the weak;
        Sending back the mighty empty,
          Setting up on high the meek.

3 Teach, oh teach us, holy Mother,
    How to conquer every sin,
  How to love and help each other,
    How the prize of life to win.
        Thou to whom a Child was given,
          Greater than the sons of men,
        Coming down from highest heaven,
          To create this world again.

4 Oh, by that Almighty Maker,
    Whom thyself a Virgin bore;
  Oh, by thy supreme Creator,
    Linked with thee for evermore;
        By the hope thy name inspires,
          By our doom, reversed through thee:
        Help us, Queen of angel choirs,
          Now and through eternity.

                            based on *Ave maris stella*
                          EDWARD CASWALL Cong. Orat. 1814–78

Blessed Virgin Mary

152 VIERGE SAINTE   87 99 + refrain

Paul Décha
arranged Stephen Dean

1. Holy Virgin, by God's decree,
   You were called eternally;
   That he could give his Son to our race.
   Mary, we praise you, hail full of grace.
   Ave, ave, ave Maria.

2. By your faith and loving accord,
   As the handmaid of the Lord,
   You undertook God's plan to embrace.
   Mary, we thank you, hail full of grace.

3. Refuge for your children so weak,
   Sure protection all can seek.
   Problems of life you help us to face.
   Mary, we trust you, hail full of grace.

4. To our needy world of today
   Love and beauty you portray,
   Showing the path to Christ we must trace.
   Mary, our Mother, hail, full of grace.

Jean-Paul Lécot
tr. W. Raymond Lawrence

Blessed Virgin Mary

153 TURRIS DAVIDICA   76 76 D   HENRI FRIEDRICH HÉMY 1818–88

An alternative tune will be found at Hymn 3.

1. I'll sing a hymn to Mary,
    The Mother of my God,
   The Virgin of all virgins,
    Of David's royal blood,
   O teach me, holy Mary,
    A loving song to frame,
   When wicked men blaspheme thee,
    To love and bless thy name.

2. O noble Tower of David,
    Of gold and ivory,
   The Ark of God's own promise,
    The gate of Heav'n to me.
   To live and not to love thee
    Would fill my soul with shame;
   When wicked men blaspheme thee,
    I'll love and bless thy name.

3. The saints are high in glory,
    With golden crowns so bright;
   But brighter far is Mary,
    Upon her throne of light.
   O that which God did give thee
    Let mortal ne'er disclaim,
   When wicked men blaspheme thee,
    I'll love and bless thy name.

4. But in the crown of Mary
    There lies a wondrous gem,
   As Queen of all the angels,
    Which Mary shares with them.
   'No sin hath e'er defiled thee',
    So doth our faith proclaim,
   When wicked men blaspheme thee,
    I'll love and bless thy name.

JOHN WYSE 1825–98

Blessed Virgin Mary

154 LOURDES HYMN   65 65 + refrain   traditional Pyreneean

1. Immaculate Mary!
     Our hearts are on fire,
   That title so wondrous
     Fills all our desire.
       Ave, Ave, Ave Maria!
       Ave, Ave, Ave Maria!

2. We pray for God's glory,
     May his kingdom come!
   We pray for his Vicar,
     Our Father, and Rome.

3. We pray for our Mother
     The Church upon earth,
   And bless, sweetest Lady
     The land of our birth.

4. O Mary! O Mother!
     Reign o'er us once more,
   Be England thy dowry
     As in days of yore.

5. We pray for all sinners,
     And souls that now stray
   From Jesus and Mary,
     In heresy's way.

Blessed Virgin Mary

6 For poor, sick, afflicted,
      Thy mercy we crave;
   And comfort the dying—
      Thou light of the grave.

7 There is no need, Mary,
      Nor ever has been,
   Which thou canst not succour,
      Immaculate Queen.

8 In grief and temptation,
      In joy or in pain,
   We'll ask thee, our Mother,
      Nor seek thee in vain.

9 O bless us, dear Lady,
      With blessings from heaven,
   And to our petitions
      Let answer be given.

10 In death's solemn moment
      Our Mother be nigh,
   As children of Mary—
      O teach us to die.

11 And crown thy sweet mercy
      With this special grace,
   To behold soon in heaven
      God's ravishing face.

12 Now to God be all glory
      And worship for aye,
   And to God's Virgin Mother,
      An endless Ave.

ANONYMOUS

Blessed Virgin Mary

155 UNE VAINE CRAINTE   65 65 D   traditional French carol

1. Maiden, yet a Mother,
    Daughter of thy Son,
   High beyond all other—
    Lowlier is none;
   Thou the consummation
    Planned by God's decree,
   When our lost creation
    Nobler rose in thee!

2. Thus his place preparèd,
    He who all things made
   'Mid his creatures tarried,
    In thy bosom laid;
   There his love he nourished—
    Warmth that gave increase
   To the Root whence flourished
    Our eternal peace.

Blessed Virgin Mary

3 Nor alone thou hearest
    When thy name we hail;
Often thou art nearest
    When our voices fail;
Mirrored in thy fashion
    All creation's good,
Mercy, might, compassion
    Grace thy womanhood.

4 Lady, lest our vision,
    Striving heavenward, fail,
Still let thy petition
    With thy Son prevail,
Unto whom all merit,
    Power and majesty
With the Holy Spirit
    And the Father be.

Vergine Madre
DANTE ALIGHIERI 1265–1321
tr. RONALD ARBUTHNOTT KNOX 1888–1957

Blessed Virgin Mary

156 LIEBSTER IMMANUEL 11 10 11 10 *Himmelslust* Jena 1679
arranged JOHANN SEBASTIAN BACH 1685–1750

1. Mary Immaculate, star of the morning,
   Chosen before the creation began,
   Chosen to bring, for thy bridal adorning,
   Woe to the serpent and rescue to man.

2. Here, in an orbit of shadow and sadness
   Veiling thy splendour, thy course thou hast run;
   Now thou art throned in all glory and gladness,
   Crowned by the hand of thy Saviour and Son.

3. Sinners, we worship thy sinless perfection;
   Fallen and weak, for thy pity we plead:
   Grant us the shield of thy sovereign protection,
   Measure thine aid by the depth of our need.

Blessed Virgin Mary

4 Frail is our nature, and strict our probation,
    Watchful the foe that would lure us to wrong;
  Succour our souls in the hour of temptation,
    Mary Immaculate, tender and strong.

5 See how the wiles of the serpent assail us,
    See how we waver and flinch in the fight;
  Let thine immaculate merit avail us,
    Make of our weakness a proof of thy might.

6 Bend from thy throne at the voice of our crying,
    Bend to this earth which thy footsteps have trod;
  Stretch out thine arms to us living and dying,
    Mary Immaculate, Mother of God.

F.W. WEATHERELL

Blessed Virgin Mary

157 ST URSULA 86 86 75 75   Frederick Westlake 1840–98

1. O Mother blest, whom God bestows
   On sinners and on just,
   What joy, what hope thou givest those
   Who in thy mercy trust.
   Thou art clement, thou art chaste,
   Mary, thou art fair;
   Of all mothers sweetest, best;
   None with thee compare.

2. O heavenly Mother, mistress sweet!
   It never yet was told
   That suppliant sinner left thy feet
   Unpitied, unconsoled.

Blessed Virgin Mary

3 O Mother, pitiful and mild,
    Cease not to pray for me;
  For I do love thee as a child,
    And sigh for love of thee.

4 Most powerful Mother, all men know
    Thy Son denies thee nought;
  Thou askest, wishest it, and lo!
    His power thy will hath wrought.

5 O Mother blest, for me obtain,
    Ungrateful though I be,
  To love that God who first could deign
    To show such love for me.

Sei pura, sei pia
St Alphonsus Liguori 1696–1787
tr. Edmund Vaughan C.Ss.R. 1827–1908

Blessed Virgin Mary

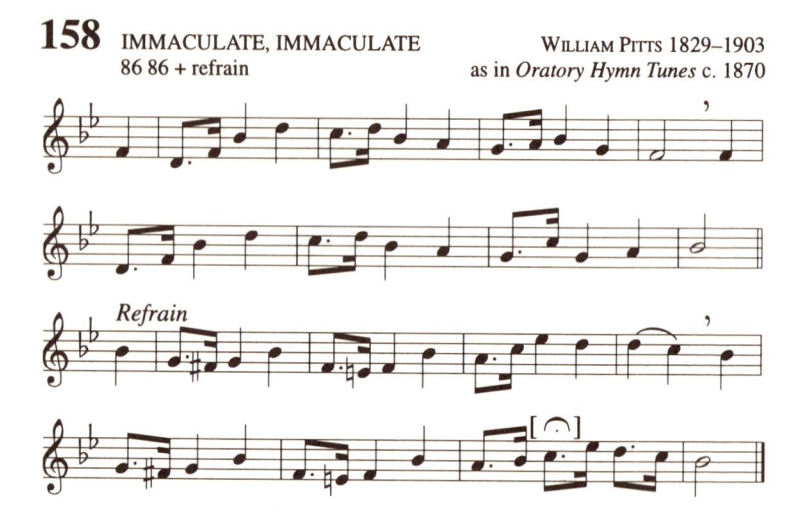

158 IMMACULATE, IMMACULATE WILLIAM PITTS 1829–1903
86 86 + refrain as in *Oratory Hymn Tunes* c. 1870

1. O Mother! I could weep for mirth,
   Joy fills my heart so fast;
   My soul today is heaven on earth,
   Oh could the transport last!
   I think of thee, and what thou art,
   Thy majesty, thy state;
   And I keep singing in my heart—
   Immaculate! Immaculate!

2. When Jesus looks upon thy face,
   His heart with rapture glows,
   And in the Church, by his sweet grace,
   Thy blessèd worship grows.

3. The angels answer with their songs,
   Bright choirs in gleaming rows;
   And saints flock round thy feet in throngs,
   And heaven with bliss o'erflows.

Blessed Virgin Mary

4 And I would rather, Mother dear!
    Thou shouldst be what thou art,
Than sit where thou dost, oh, so near
    Unto the Sacred Heart.

5 Yes, I would forfeit all for thee,
    Rather than thou shouldst miss
One jewel from thy majesty,
    One glory from thy bliss.

6 Conceived, conceived Immaculate!
    Oh what a joy for thee!
Conceived, conceived Immaculate!
    Oh greater joy for me!

7 Immaculate Conception! far
    Above all graces blest!
Thou shinest like a royal star
    On God's eternal breast!

8 It is this thought today that lifts
    My happy heart to heaven:
That for our sakes thy choicest gifts
    To thee, dear Queen, were given.

9 God prosper thee, my Mother dear;
    God prosper thee, my Queen;
God prosper his own glory here,
    As it hath ever been!

                    Frederick William Faber Cong. Orat. 1814–63

Blessed Virgin Mary

159 MARIA ZU LIEBEN   11 11 11 11   Paderborn *Gesangbuch* 1765
arranged *Westminster Hymnal* 1912

1. O purest of creatures! sweet Mother, sweet Maid;
   The one spotless womb wherein Jesus was laid.
   Dark night hath come down on us, Mother, and we
   Look out for thy shining, sweet Star of the Sea.

2. Deep night hath come down on this rough-spoken world,
   And the banners of darkness are boldly unfurled;
   And the tempest-tossed Church—all her eyes are on thee,
   They look to thy shining, sweet Star of the Sea.

3. He gazed on thy soul; it was spotless and fair;
   For the empire of sin—it had never been there;
   None ever had owned thee, dear Mother, but he,
   And he blessed thy clear shining, sweet Star of the Sea.

4. Earth gave him one lodging; 'twas deep in thy breast,
   And God found a home where the sinner finds rest;
   His home and his hiding-place, both were in thee;
   He was won by thy shining, sweet Star of the Sea.

5. Oh, blissful and calm was the wonderful rest
   That thou gavest thy God in thy virginal breast;
   For the heaven he left he found heaven in thee,
   And he shone in thy shining, sweet Star of the Sea.

FREDERICK WILLIAM FABER Cong. Orat. 1814–63

Blessed Virgin Mary

160 ST MARTIN   66 66   Caspar Ett's *Cantica Sacra* 1840

1. Star of sea and ocean,
   Gateway to man's haven,
   Mother of our maker,
   Hear our prayer, O Maiden.

2. Welcoming the Ave
   Of God's simple greeting,
   You have borne a Saviour
   Far beyond all dreaming.

3. Loose the bonds that hold us
   Bound in sin's own blindness,
   That with eyes now open'd
   God's own light may guide us.

4. Show yourself our Mother:
   He will hear your pleading
   Whom your womb has sheltered
   And whose hand brings healing.

5. Gentlest of all virgins,
   That our love be faithful
   Keep us from all evil,
   Gentle, strong and grateful.

6. Guard us through life's dangers,
   Never turn and leave us,
   May our hope find harbour
   In the calm of Jesus.

7. Sing to God our Father
   Through the Son who saves us,
   Joyful in the Spirit,
   Everlasting praises.

Ave maris stella c. 9th century
tr. RALPH WRIGHT O.S.B. born 1938

Blessed Virgin Mary

161 EISENACH   LM   JOHANN HERMANN SCHEIN 1586–1630
arranged JOHANN SEBASTIAN BACH 1685–1750

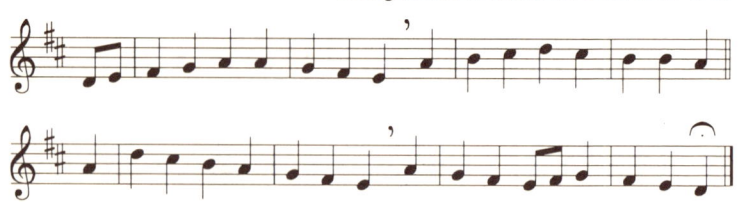

1. The God whom earth, and sea, and sky
   Adore and laud and magnify,
   Who o'er their threefold fabric reigns,
   The Virgin's spotless womb contains.

2. The God whose will by moon and sun
   And all things in due course is done,
   Is borne upon a Maiden's breast
   By fullest heav'nly grace possest.

3. How blest that Mother, in whose shrine
   The great Artificer divine,
   Whose hand contains the earth and sky,
   Vouchsafed, as in his ark, to lie!

4. Blest, in the message Gabriel brought;
   Blest, by the work the Spirit wrought;
   From whom the great Desire of earth
   Took human flesh and human birth.

5. All honour, laud and glory be,
   O Jesu, Virgin-born, to thee!
   All glory, as is ever meet,
   To Father and to Paraclete.

Quem terra, pontus, sidera
ascribed VENANTIUS FORTUNATUS 530–609
tr. JOHN MASON NEALE 1818–66

Blessed Virgin Mary

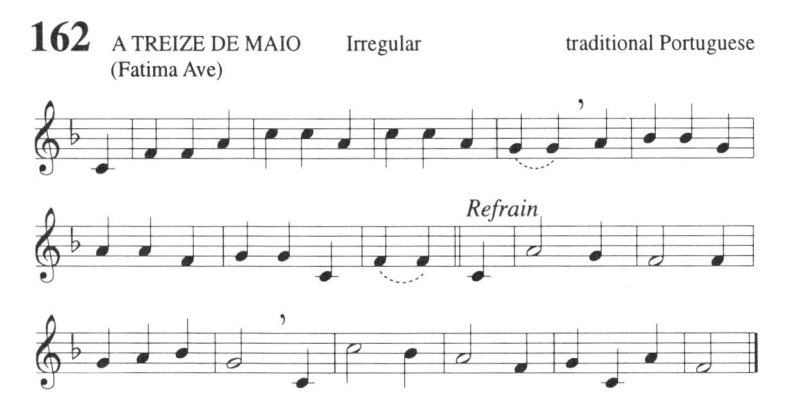

162 A TREIZE DE MAIO Irregular traditional Portuguese
(Fatima Ave)

1. The thirteenth of May
   In the Cova d'Iria
   Appeared, oh so brilliant,
   The Virgin Maria.
   Ave, ave, ave Maria.
   Ave, ave, ave Maria.

2. The Virgin Maria
   Encircled with light,
   Our own dearest Mother
   And heaven's delight.

3. To three little shepherds
   Our Lady appeared.
   The light of her grace
   To her Son souls endeared.

4. With war and its evils
   The whole world was seething,
   And countless of thousands
   Were mourning and weeping.

5. To save all poor souls
   Who had wandered astray,
   With words of sweet comfort
   She asked us to pray.

6. By honouring Mary
   And loving her Son,
   The peace of the world
   Will most surely be won.

traditional Fatima hymn

Blessed Virgin Mary

163 MON DIEU, PRÊTE MOI L'OREILLE
Irregular
Ps. 86 in the Genevan *Psalter* 1542

1. Virgin-born, we bow before thee: Bless-èd was the womb that bore thee: Mary, Mother meek and mild, Bless-èd was she in her Child. Bless-èd was the breast that fed thee; Bless-èd was the hand that led thee; Bless-èd was the parent's eye That watched thy slumb'ring infancy.

2. Bless-èd she by all creation, Who brought forth the world's salvation, And bless-èd they, for ever blest, Who love thee most and serve thee best. Virgin-born, we bow before thee; Bless-èd was the womb that bore thee; Mary, Mother meek and mild, Bless-èd was she in her Child.

REGINALD HEBER 1783–1826

Blessed Virgin Mary

164 NUN KOMM DER HEIDEN HEILAND 7777 Johann Walter's
Gesangbüchlein 1524

An alternative tune will be found at Hymn 75.

1 Virgin, wholly marvellous,
Who didst bear God's Son for us,
Worthless is my tongue and weak
Of thy purity to speak.

2 Who can praise thee as he ought?
Gifts, with every blessing fraught,
Gifts that bring the gifted life,
Thou didst grant us, Maiden-Wife.

3 God became thy lowly Son,
Made himself thy little one,
Raising men to tell thy worth
High in heaven as here on earth.

4 Heaven and earth, and all that is,
Thrill today with ecstasies,
Chanting glory unto thee,
Singing praise with festal glee.

5 Cherubim with fourfold face
Are no peers of thine in grace;
And the six-winged seraphim
Shine, amid thy splendour, dim.

6 Purer art thou than are all
Heavenly hosts angelical,
Who delight with pomp and state
On thy beauteous Child to wait.

Syriac ST EPHREM SYRUS c. 307–73
tr. JOHN ATKINSON S.J. 1866–1921

Blessed Virgin Mary

165 FIRST TUNE

REGENT SQUARE   87 87 87   HENRY SMART 1813–79

1 Ye who own the faith of Jesus,
     Sing the wonders that were done
  When the love of God the Father
     O'er our sin the victory won,
  When he made the Virgin Mary
     Mother of his only Son.

2 Blessèd were the chosen people
     Out of whom the Lord did come,
  Blessèd was the land of promise
     Fashioned for his earthly home;
  But more blessèd far the Mother
     She who bare him in her womb.

3 Wherefore let all faithful people
     Tell the honour of her name,
  Let the Church in her foreshadowed
     Part in her thanksgiving claim;
  What Christ's Mother sang in gladness
     Let Christ's people sing the same.

Blessed Virgin Mary

SECOND TUNE

DAILY DAILY
87 87 87 87 + refrain

19th century English form of *Maria zu lieben*
Paderborn *Gesanguch* 1765

Refrain
Hail Mary, hail Mary, hail Mary full of grace.

4 May the Mother's intercessions
   On our homes a blessing win,
That the children all be prospered,
   Strong and fair and pure within,
Following our Lord's own footsteps,
   Firm in faith and free from sin.

5 For the sick and for the agèd,
   For our dear ones far away,
For the hearts that mourn in secret,
   All who need our prayers today,
For the faithful gone before us,
   May the holy Virgin pray.

6 Praise, O Mary, praise the Father,
   Praise thy Saviour and thy Son,
Praise the everlasting Spirit,
   Who hath made thee ark and throne;
O'er all creatures high exalted,
   Lowly praise the Three in One.

VICTOR STUCKEY STRATTON COLES 1845–1929

Saints

166 SINE NOMINE
10 10 10 + alleluias

Ralph Vaughan Williams 1872–1958

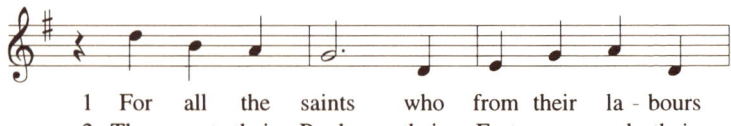

1. For all the saints who from their la-bours rest, Who thee by faith be-fore the world con-fessed, Thy name, O
2. Thou wast their Rock, their Fort-ress, and their Might; Thou, Lord, their Cap-tain in the well-fought fight;
3. O may thy sol-diers, faith-ful, true, and bold, Fight as the saints who no-bly fought of old,

7. But lo! there breaks a yet more glo-rious day; The saints tri-um-phant rise in bright ar-ray; The King of
8. From earth's wide bounds, from o-cean's far-thest coast, Through gates of pearl streams in the count-less host, Sing-ing to

And win with

Thou, in the

Saints

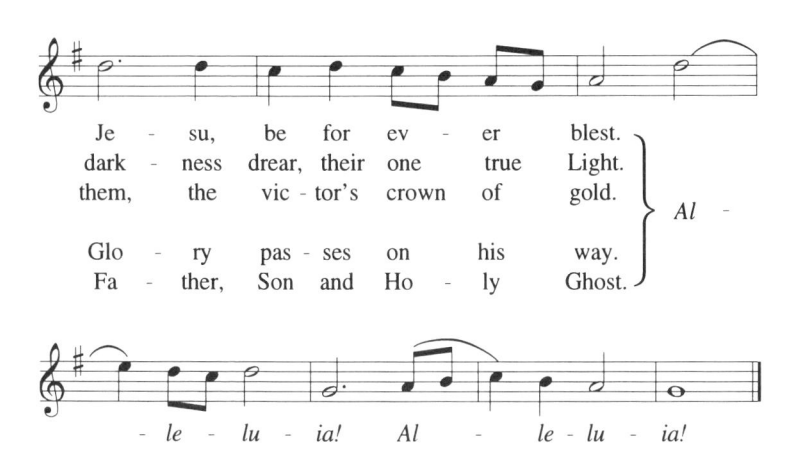

Je - su, be for ev - er blest.
dark - ness drear, their one true Light.
them, the vic - tor's crown of gold.

Glo - ry pas - ses on his way.
Fa - ther, Son and Ho - ly Ghost.

Al - le - lu - ia! Al - le - lu - ia!

turn for verses 4–6

Saints

4. O blest communion, fellowship divine!
   We feebly struggle, they in glory shine;
   Yet all are one in thee, for all are thine.
   Alleluia! Alleluia!

5. And when the strife is fierce, the warfare long,
   Steals on the ear the distant triumph-song,
   And hearts are brave again, and arms are strong.
   Alleluia! Alleluia!

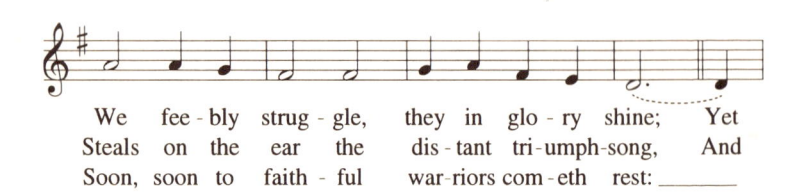

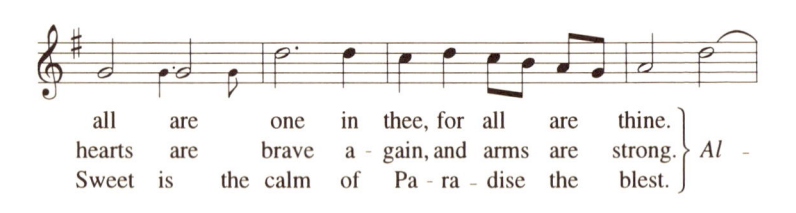

6. The golden evening brightens in the west;
   Soon, soon to faithful warriors cometh rest:
   Sweet is the calm of Paradise the blest.
   Alleluia! Alleluia!

turn back for vv. 7–8

WILLIAM WALSHAM HOW 1823–97

Saints

167 SONG 67 CM ORLANDO GIBBONS 1583–1625

An alternative tune will be found at Hymn 247 (second tune).

1. Give me the wings of faith to rise
   Within the veil, and see
   The saints above, how great their joys,
   How bright their glories be.

2. Once they were mourning here below,
   And wet their couch with tears;
   They wrestled hard, as we do now,
   With sins and doubts and fears.

3. I ask them whence their victory came;
   They, with united breath,
   Ascribe their conquest to the Lamb,
   Their triumph to his death.

4. They marked the footsteps that he trod,
   His zeal inspired their breast,
   And, following their incarnate God,
   Possess the promised rest.

5. Our glorious Leader claims our praise
   For his own pattern given;
   While the long cloud of witnesses
   Show the same path to heaven.

ISAAC WATTS 1674–1748

Saints

168 BROCKHAM LM Jeremiah Clarke c. 1673–1707

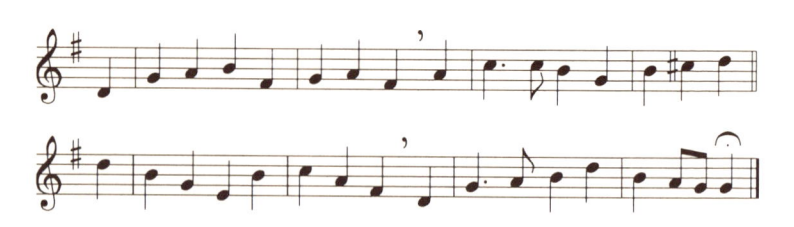

1. Let all on earth their voices raise,
   Re-echoing heaven's triumphant praise,
   To him who gave the apostles grace
   To run on earth their glorious race.

2. Thou at whose word they bore the light
   Of gospel truth o'er heathen night,
   To us that heavenly light impart,
   To glad our eyes and cheer our heart.

3. Thou at whose will to them was given
   To bind and loose in earth and heaven,
   Our chains unbind, our sins undo,
   And in our hearts thy grace renew.

4. Thou in whose might they spoke the word
   Which cured disease and health restored,
   To us its healing power prolong,
   Support the weak, confirm the strong.

5. And when the thrones are set on high
   And judgment's awful hour draws nigh,
   Then, Lord, with them pronounce us blest,
   And take us to thine endless rest.

Exsultet caelum laudibus 11th century
tr. Richard Mant 1776–1848
and others

Saints

169 REGNATOR ORBIS   10 10 10 10   Paris *Antiphonale* 1681

1. O what their joy and their glory must be,
   Those endless sabbaths the blessèd ones see!
   Crown for the valiant; to weary ones rest;
   God shall be all, and in all ever blest.

2. Truly 'Jerusalem' name we that shore,
   'Vision of peace', that brings joy evermore!
   Wish and fulfilment can severed be ne'er,
   Nor the thing prayed for come short of the prayer.

3. We, where no trouble distraction can bring,
   Safely the anthems of Sion shall sing;
   While for thy grace, Lord, their voices of praise
   Thy blessèd people shall evermore raise.

4. Now in the meanwhile, with hearts raised on high,
   We for that country must yearn and must sigh,
   Seeking Jerusalem, dear native land,
   Through our long exile on Babylon's strand.

5. Low before him with our praises we fall,
   Of whom, and in whom, and through whom are all;
   Of whom, the Father; and through whom, the Son;
   In whom, the Spirit, with these ever One.

O quanta qualia
PETER ABELARD 1079–1142
tr. JOHN MASON NEALE 1818–66

Saints

170 ALL SAINTS (Zeuch mich)
87 87 77

Darmstadt *Gesangbuch* 1698
adapted WILLIAM HENRY MONK 1823–89

1 Who are these, like stars appearing,
   These before God's throne who stand?
 Each a golden crown is wearing;
   Who are all this glorious band?
 Alleluia, hark! they sing,
 Praising loud their heavenly King.

2 Who are these of dazzling brightness,
   These in God's own truth arrayed,
 Clad in robes of purest whiteness,
   Robes whose lustre ne'er shall fade,
 Ne'er be touched by time's rude hand—
 Whence comes all this glorious band?

3 These are they who have contended
   For their Saviour's honour long,
 Wrestling on till life was ended,
   Following not the sinful throng;
 These, who well the fight sustained,
 Triumph through the Lamb have gained.

Saints

4 These are they whose hearts were riven,
    Sore with woe and anguish tried,
Who in prayer full oft have striven
    With the God they glorified;
Now, their painful conflict o'er,
God has bid them weep no more.

5 These like priests have watched and waited,
    Offering up to Christ their will,
Soul and body consecrated,
    Day and night to serve him still:
Now, in God's most holy place
Blest they stand before his face.

Wer sind die von Gottes Throne
HEINRICH THEOBALD SCHENK 1656–1727
tr. FRANCES ELIZABETH COX 1812–97

Saints

171 MARIA JUNG UND ZART   66 66   Cologne *Gesangbuch* 1623
adapted *Harmonicum Sacrarum Cantilenum* 1642

St Joseph

1. Hail, holy Joseph, hail!
    Husband of Mary, hail!
 Chaste as the lily flower
    In Eden's peaceful vale.

2. Hail, holy Joseph, hail!
    Father of Christ esteemed,
 Father be thou to those
    Thy foster Son redeemed.

3. Hail, holy Joseph, hail!
    Prince of the house of God,
 May his blest graces be
    By thy sweet hands bestowed.

4. Hail, holy Joseph, hail!
    Comrade of angels, hail!
 Cheer thou the hearts that faint,
    And guide the steps that fail.

5. Hail, holy Joseph, hail!
    God's choice wert thou alone;
 To thee the Word made flesh
    Was subject as a son.

6. Mother of Jesu, bless,
    And bless, ye saints on high,
 All meek and simple souls,
    That to Saint Joseph cry.

FREDERICK WILLIAM FABER Cong. Orat. 1814–63

Saints

172 ANNUE CHRISTI   12 12 12 12   Cluny *Antiphonale* 1686

Saints Peter & Paul

1. The beauteous light of God's eternal majesty
   Streams down in golden rays to grace this holy day
   Which crowned the princes of the apostles' glorious choir,
   And unto guilty mortals showed the heavenward way.

2. The teacher of the world and keeper of heaven's gate,
   Rome's founders twain and rulers too of every land,
   Triumphant over death by sword and shameful cross,
   With laurel crowned are gathered to the eternal band.

3. O happy Rome! who in thy martyr princes' blood,
   A twofold stream, art washed and doubly sanctified.
   All earthly beauty thou alone outshinest far,
   Empurpled by their outpoured life-blood's glorious tide.

4. All honour, power, and everlasting jubilee
   To him who all things made and governs here below,
   To God, in Essence one, and yet in Persons three,
   Both now and ever, while unending ages flow.

Decora lux 5th century
tr. Mgr Canon Hall

Saints

173 MONKS GATE 65 65 66 66   English folk tune 'Our Captain Calls'
adapted RALPH VAUGHAN WILLIAMS 1872–1958

St Peter

1. Wouldst thou a patron see
    Thy cause defending?
   Christ's chief apostle be
    All thy befriending.
    Key-bearer, we implore,
     Grace by thy prayers restore;
    Grant us through heaven's door
     Entrance hereafter.

2. Thou didst thy Master grieve,
    Yet pardon borrow;
   May we our faults retrieve
    With daily sorrow.

3. As once an angel freed
    The chains that bound thee,
   Loose thou the souls in need
    Thou seest round thee.

Saints

4 Firm rock (our Saviour saith),
    Pillar unyielding,
  Strengthen the Church, her faith
    From error shielding.

5 In death's tremendous hour
    On thee relying,
  His rage we'll overpower,
    Valiant in dying.

Si vis patronum quaere 18th century
tr. RONALD ARBUTHNOTT KNOX 1888–1957

Saints

174 SWAVESEY 87 87 D JOHN CROOKALL 1821–87

St George

1. Leader now on earth no longer,
   Soldier of the eternal King,
 Victor in the fight for heaven,
   We thy loving praises sing.
   Great Saint George, our patron, help us,
     In the conflict be thou nigh;
   Help us in that daily battle,
     Where each one must win or die.

2. Praise him who in deadly battle
     Never shrank from foeman's sword,
 Proof against all earthly weapon,
     Gave his life for Christ the Lord.

Saints

3 Who, when earthly war was over,
    Fought, but not for earth's renown;
  Fought, and won a nobler glory—
    Won the martyr's purple crown.

4 Help us when temptation presses;
    We have still our crown to win;
  Help us when our soul is weary,
    Fighting with the powers of sin.

5 Clothe us in thy shining armour,
    Place thy good sword in our hand;
  Teach us how to wield it, fighting
    Onward towards the heavenly land.

JOSEPH REEKS 1849–1900

Saints

175 OMNI DIE   87 87   David Gregor Corner's *Gesangbuch* 1631
arranged WILLIAM SMITH ROCKSTRO 1823–95

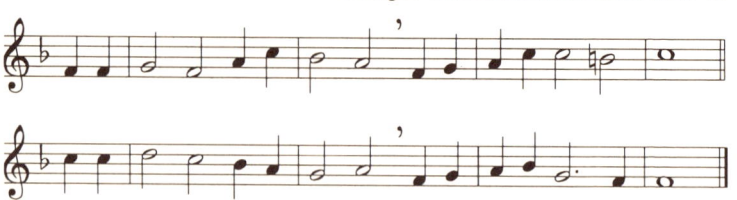

An alternative tune will be found at Hymn 42.

St Andrew

1 Great Saint Andrew, friend of Jesus,
    Lover of his glorious Cross,
 Early by his voice effective
    Called from ease to pain and loss.

2 Strong Saint Andrew, Simon's brother,
    Who with haste fraternal flew,
 Fain with him to share the treasure
    Which at Jesus' lips he drew.

3 Blest Saint Andrew, Jesus' herald,
    True apostle, martyr bold,
 Who, by deeds his words confirming,
    Sealed with blood the truth he told.

Saints

4 Ne'er to king was crown so beauteous,
　　Ne'er was prize to heart so dear,
　As to him the Cross of Jesus
　　When its promised joys drew near.

5 Loved Saint Andrew, Scotland's patron,
　　Watch thy land with heedful eye,
　Rally round the Cross of Jesus
　　All her storied chivalry!

6 To the Father, Son, and Spirit,
　　Fount of sanctity and love,
　Give we glory, now and ever,
　　With the saints who reign above.

FREDERICK OAKELEY 1802–80

Saints

176 ST DAVID ANTHONY GREGORY MURRAY O.S.B. 1905–92
11 10 11 10 11 10 11 9

Saints

St David

1. O great Saint David, still we hear thee call us,
    Unto a life that knows no fear of death;
 Yea, down the ages, will thy words enthral us,
    Strong happy words: 'Be joyful, keep the faith.'
      On Cambria's sons stretch out thy hands in blessing;
      For our dear land thy help we now implore.
      Lead us to God, with humble hearts confessing
      Jesus, Lord and King for evermore.

2. Christ was the centre rock of all thy teaching,
    God's holy will—the splendour of its theme.
 His grace informed, his love inflamed thy preaching.
    Christ's sway on earth, the substance of thy dream.

3. In early childhood, choosing Jesus only,
    Thy fervour showed his yoke was light and sweet;
 And thus for thee, life's journey was not lonely—
    The path made plain by prints of wounded feet.

4. O glorious saint, we wander in the dark;
    With thee we seek our trusted guide in Rome.
 Help him to steer on earth Saint Peter's barque,
    That we may safely reach our heavenly home.

FRANCIS MOSTYN 1860–1939

Saints

177 ST PATRICK   11 11 11 11   traditional

St Patrick

1. Hail, glorious Saint Patrick, dear saint of our isle,
   On us thy poor children bestow a sweet smile:
   And now thou art high in the mansions above,
   On Erin's green valleys look down in thy love,
   On Erin's green valleys look down in thy love.

2. Hail, glorious Saint Patrick! thy words were once strong
   Against Satan's wiles and an infidel throng;
   Not less is thy might where in heaven thou art;
   Oh, come to our aid, in our battle take part,
   Oh, come to our aid, in our battle take part.

Saints

3 In the war against sin, in the fight for the faith,
  Dear saint, may thy children resist unto death;
  May their strength be in meekness, in penance, in prayer,
  Their banner the Cross which they glory to bear,
  Their banner the Cross which they glory to bear.

4 Thy people, now exiles on many a shore,
  Shall love and revere thee till time be no more;
  And the fire thou hast kindled shall ever burn bright,
  Its warmth undiminished, undying its light,
  Its warmth undiminished, undying its light.

5 Ever bless and defend the sweet land of our birth,
  Where the shamrock still blooms as when thou wert on earth,
  And our hearts shall yet burn, wheresoever we roam,
  For God and Saint Patrick, and our native home,
  For God and Saint Patrick, and our native home.

SISTER AGNES

Angels

178 COELITES PLAUDANT   11 11 11 5   Rouen *Antiphonale* 1728

1. Christ, the fair glory of the holy angels,
   Thou who hast made us, thou who o'er us rulest,
   Grant of thy mercy unto us thy servants
       Steps up to heaven.

2. Send thy archangel, Michael, to our succour;
   Peacemaker blessèd, may he banish from us
   Striving and hatred, so that for the peaceful
       All things may prosper.

3. Send thy archangel, Gabriel, the mighty;
   Herald of heaven, may he from us mortals
   Spurn the old serpent, watching o'er the temples
       Where thou art worshipped.

Angels

4 Send thy archangel, Raphael, the restorer
　Of the misguided ways of men who wander,
　Who at thy bidding strengthens soul and body
　　　With thine anointing.

5 May the blest Mother of our God and Saviour,
　May the assembly of the saints in glory,
　May the celestial companies of angels
　　　Ever assist us.

6 Father Almighty, Son and Holy Spirit,
　God ever blessèd, be thou our preserver;
　Thine is the glory which the angels worship,
　　　Veiling their faces.

Christe sanctorum decus angelorum 9th century
tr. ATHELSTAN RILEY 1858–1945

Angels

179 PILGRIMS 11 10 11 10 + refrain HENRY SMART 1813–79

1. Hark! hark, my soul! Angelic songs are swelling
    O'er earth's green fields and ocean's wave-beat shore;
   How sweet the truth those blessèd strains are telling
    Of that new life when sin shall be no more!
     Angels of Jesus, angels of light,
     Singing to welcome the pilgrims of the night!

2. Onward we go, for still we hear them singing,
    Come, weary souls, for Jesus bids you come:
   And through the dark, its echoes sweetly ringing,
    The music of the gospel leads us home.

Angels

3 Far, far away, like bells at evening pealing,
    The voice of Jesus sounds o'er land and sea,
  And laden souls, by thousands meekly stealing,
    Kind Shepherd, turn their weary steps to thee.

4 Rest comes at length; though life be long and dreary,
    The day must dawn, and darksome night be past;
  All journeys end in welcomes to the weary,
    And heaven, the heart's true home, will come at last.

5 Angels! sing on, your faithful watches keeping,
    Sing us sweet fragments of the songs above;
  While we toil on, and soothe ourselves with weeping,
    Till life's long night shall break in endless love.

FREDERICK WILLIAM FABER Cong. Orat. 1814–63

Angels

180 ANGELUS (Du meiner Seelen) LM Georg Joseph
in *Heilige Seelenlust* Breslau 1657
adapted *Cantica Spiritualia* Munich 1847

1. They come, God's messengers of love,
   They come from realms of peace above,
   From homes of never-fading light,
   From blissful mansions ever bright.

2. They come to watch around us here,
   To soothe our sorrow, calm our fear:
   Ye heavenly guides, speed not away,
   God willeth you with us to stay.

3. But chiefly at its journey's end
   'Tis yours the spirit to befriend,
   And whisper to the faithful heart,
   'O Christian soul, in peace depart.'

4. Blest Jesu, thou whose groans and tears
   Have sanctified frail nature's fears,
   To earth in bitter sorrow weighed,
   Thou didst not scorn thine angel's aid.

5. An angel guard to us supply,
   When on the bed of death we lie;
   And by thine own almighty power
   O shield us in the last dread hour.

Robert Campbell 1814–68

Departed

181 BURFORD   CM   John Chetham's *Book of Psalmody* 1718

An alternative tune will be found at Hymn 244.

1. Help, Lord, the souls that thou hast made,
    The souls to thee so dear,
   In prison for the debt unpaid
    Of sins committed here.

2. Those holy souls, they suffer on,
    Resigned in heart and will,
   Until thy high behest is done,
    And justice has its fill.

3. For daily falls, for pardoned crime,
    They joy to undergo
   The shadow of thy Cross sublime,
    The remnant of thy woe.

4. Oh, by their patience of delay,
    Their hope amid their pain,
   Their sacred zeal to burn away
    Disfigurement and stain;

5. Oh, by their fire of love, not less
    In keenness than the flame;
   Oh, by their very helplessness,
    Oh, by thy own great name:

6. Good Jesu help, sweet Jesu aid
    The souls to thee most dear,
   In prison for the debt unpaid
    Of sins committed here.

The Venerable JOHN HENRY NEWMAN Cong. Orat. 1801–90

Departed

182 OLD 124th   10 10 10 10 10   attributed Loys Bourgeois c. 1510–61
Ps. 124 in the Genevan *Psalter* 1551

1. Merciful Saviour, hear our humble prayer,
   For all thy servants passed beyond life's care;
   Though sin has touched them, yet their weakness spare.
   O grant them pardon, Jesus Saviour blest,
   And give their spirits light and endless rest.

2. Jesus, all holy, merciful and just,
   Do thou remember man was made from dust;
   Unto thy mercy we these souls entrust.

3. O gentle Saviour, Lamb for sinners slain,
   Look on thy brothers, cleanse their hearts of stain:
   Thy Cross has won them everlasting gain.

4. Lord, at thy Passion love did conquer fear;
   Now share that triumph with these souls so dear:
   Banish their sorrows, let thy light appear.

MELVIN FARRELL

Church

183 SAWSTON 88 88 + refrain traditional

1. Faith of our fathers, living still
   In spite of dungeon, fire and sword:
   Oh how our hearts beat high with joy
   Whene'er we hear that glorious word!
   Faith of our fathers! Holy Faith!
   We will be true to thee till death.

2. Our fathers, chained in prisons dark,
   Were still in heart and conscience free:
   How sweet would be their children's fate,
   If they, like them, could die for thee!

3. Faith of our fathers! Mary's prayers
   Shall win our country back to thee:
   And through the truth that comes from God,
   England shall then indeed be free.

4. Faith of our fathers! we will love
   Both friend and foe in all our strife;
   And preach thee too, as love knows how,
   By kindly words and virtuous life.

FREDERICK WILLIAM FABER Cong. Orat. 1814–63

Church

184 WISEMAN   88 88 + refrain   C.A. Cox 1853–1916

Refrain

God bless our Pope, God bless our Pope, God bless our Pope, the great, the good.

1. Full in the panting heart of Rome,
   Beneath the apostle's crowning dome,
   From pilgrims' lips that kiss the ground,
   Breathes in all tongues one only sound:
   'God bless our Pope, the great, the good.'

2. The golden roof, the marble walls,
   The Vatican's majestic halls,
   The note redouble, till it fills
   With echoes sweet the seven hills:

Church

3 Then surging through each hallowed gate.
  Where martyrs glory, in peace, await,
  It sweeps beyond the solemn plain,
  Peals over Alps, across the main:

4 From torrid south to frozen north,
  That wave harmonious stretches forth,
  Yet strikes no chord more true to Rome's,
  Than rings within our hearts and homes:
    'God bless our Pope, the great, the good.'

NICHOLAS WISEMAN 1802–65

Church

185 WOLVERCOTE   86 86 D   WILLIAM HAROLD FERGUSON 1874–1950

1. Long live the Pope! His praises sound
     Again and yet again.
   His rule is over space and time;
     His throne the hearts of men.
   All hail, the shepherd King of Rome,
     The theme of loving song:
   Let all the earth his glory ring
     And heav'n the strain prolong.

2. His signet is the Fisherman's;
     No sceptre does he bear;
   In meek and lowly majesty,
     He rules from Peter's chair.
   And yet from every tribe and tongue,
     From every clime and zone,
   All with united voices sing
     The glory of his throne.

Church

3 Then raise the chant, with heart and voice,
    In church, and school, and home:
  'Long live the shepherd of the Flock,
    Long live the Pope of Rome.'
  Almighty Father, bless his work,
    Protect him in his ways,
  Receive his prayers, fulfil his hopes,
    And grant him length of days.

HUGH HENRY

Church

186 O MENSCH BEWEIN' 887 887 D MATTHAÜS GREITER c. 1490–1550
as in the Genevan *Psalter* 1551

1 O English hearts, what heart can know
How spent with labours long ago
  Was England's Church that bore you?
The paths you tread, in lane or street,
Long since were trodden by the feet
  Of saints that went before you;
When priests, like sudden angels, came
To light in distant shires the flame
  That faith's dull embers cherished,
When Mass and shrift were sought for still
In silent farm, on lonely hill,
  Ere ancient memories perished.

Church

2 Their kindred and their homes forgot,
  The traitor's name, the wanderer's lot
    For all their portion choosing;
  God's hungry sheep they toiled to save,
  The peace that only exile gave
    For love of Christ refusing:
  Till, late or early, go they must
  (Who not in princes put their trust)
    Where earthly justice waited;
  From rack and dungeon, freed at last,
  The hurdle's way, to death they passed,
    From death to life translated.

3 O saints of English speech and race,
  Caught up to heaven, of heavenly grace
    A double portion send us;
  From faint resolves and mean desires
  And all this languid age inspires
    Of worldly aims, defend us!
  And, if such influence love can earn,
  O bid the faith you loved return,
    The land you loved awaking;
  An England sunk in long despair
  To holier thoughts, sublimer prayer,
    And larger hopes awaking.

                    RONALD ARBUTHNOTT KNOX 1888–1957

Church

187 AURELIA 76 76 D SAMUEL SEBASTIAN WESLEY 1810–76

1. The Church's one foundation
    Is Jesus Christ, her Lord;
   She is his new creation
    By water and the word:
   From heaven he came and sought her
    To be his holy Bride,
   With his own Blood he bought her,
    And for her life he died.

2. Elect from every nation,
    Yet one o'er all the earth,
   Her charter of salvation
    One Lord, one faith, one birth;
   One holy name she blesses,
    Partakes one holy Food,
   And to one hope she presses
    With every grace endued.

Church

3   Though with a scornful wonder
    Men see her sore oppressed,
By schisms rent asunder,
    By heresies distressed,
Yet saints their watch are keeping,
    Their cry goes up 'How long?'
And soon the night of weeping
    Shall be the morn of song.

4   'Mid toil, and tribulation,
    And tumult of her war,
She waits the consummation
    Of peace for evermore;
Till with the vision glorious
    Her longing eyes are blest,
And the great Church victorious
    Shall be the Church at rest.

4   Yet she on earth hath union
    With God the Three in One,
And mystic sweet communion
    With those whose rest is won:
Oh happy ones and holy!
    Lord, give us grace that we
Like them, the meek and lowly,
    On high may dwell with thee.

SAMUEL JOHN STONE 1830–1900

Church

188 THORNBURY   76 76 D   BASIL HARWOOD 1859–1949

1. Thy hand, O God, has guided
   Thy flock, from age to age;
   The wondrous tale is written,
   Full clear, on every page;
   Our fathers owned thy goodness,
   And we their deeds record;
   And both of this bear witness:
   One Church, one Faith, one Lord.

2. Thy heralds brought glad tidings
   To greatest, as to least;
   They bade men rise, and hasten
   To share the great King's feast;
   And this was all their teaching,
   In every deed and word,
   To all alike proclaiming
   One Church, one Faith, one Lord.

Church

3   When shadows thick were falling,
        And all seemed sunk in night,
    Thou, Lord, didst send thy servants,
        Thy chosen sons of light.
    On them and on thy people
        Thy plenteous grace was poured,
    And this was still their message:
        One Church, one Faith, one Lord.

4   And we, shall we be faithless?
        Shall hearts fail, hands hang down?
    Shall we evade the conflict,
        And cast away our crown?
    Not so: in God's deep counsels
        Some better thing is stored;
    We will maintain, unflinching:
        One Church, one Faith, one Lord.

5   Thy mercy will not fail us,
        Nor leave thy work undone;
    With thy right hand to help us,
        The victory shall be won;
    And then, by men and angels,
        Thy name shall be adored,
    And this shall be their anthem:
        One Church, one Faith, one Lord.

EDWARD HAYES PLUMPTRE 1821–91

Morning

189 MORNING HYMN François Hippolite Barthélémon 1741–1808
LM

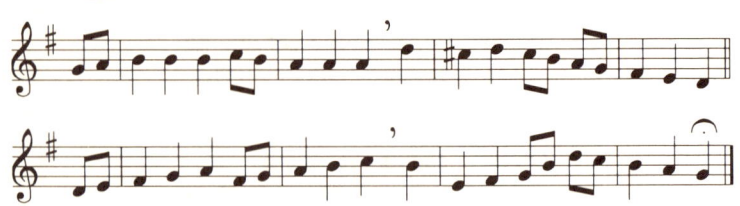

This hymn was originally sung to the tune at Hymn 132.

1 Awake, my soul, and with the sun
  Thy daily stage of duty run,
  Shake off dull sloth, and joyful rise
  To pay thy morning sacrifice.

2 Redeem thy mis-spent time that's past,
  Live this day as if 'twere thy last:
  Improve thy talent with due care,
  For the Great Day thyself prepare.

3 Wake, and lift up thyself, my heart,
  And with the angels bear thy part,
  Who all night long unwearied sing
  High praise to the eternal King.

4 All praise to thee who safe hast kept
  And hast refreshed me while I slept.
  Grant, Lord, when I from death shall wake
  I may of endless light partake.

5 Heav'n is, dear Lord, where'er thou art,
  O never then from me depart;
  For to my soul 'tis hell to be
  But for one moment void of thee.

6 Lord, I my vows to thee renew,
  Disperse my sins like morning dew.
  Guard my first springs of thought and will
  And with thyself my spirit fill.

Thomas Ken 1637–1711

Morning

190 DIVA SERVATRIX 11 11 11 5 Bayeux *Antiphonale* 1739

An alternative tune will be found at Hymn 216.

1 Father, we praise thee, now the night is over,
  Active and watchful, stand we all before thee;
  Singing, we offer prayer and meditation:
    Thus we adore thee.

2 Monarch of all things, fit us for thy mansions;
  Banish our weakness, health and wholeness sending;
  Bring us to heaven, where thy saints united
    Joy without ending.

3 All-holy Father, Son and equal Spirit,
  Trinity blessèd, send us thy salvation;
  Thine is the glory, gleaming and resounding
    Through all creation.

Nocte surgentes c. 10th century
tr. PERCY DEARMER 1867–1936

Morning

191 SONG 34 (Angels' Song)   ORLANDO GIBBONS 1583–1625
LM   rhythm of bar 2 from Song 9

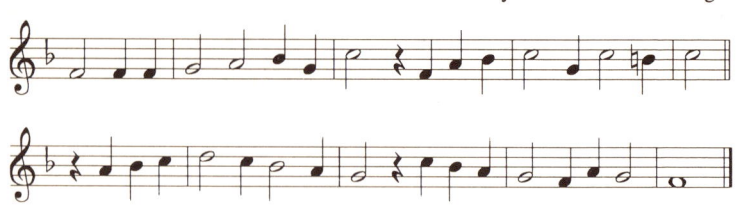

1 Forth in thy name, O Lord, I go,
   My daily labour to pursue;
Thee, only thee, resolved to know,
   In all I think or speak or do.

2 The task thy wisdom hath assigned
   O let me cheerfully fulfil,
In all my works thy presence find,
   And prove thine acceptable will.

3 Preserve me from my calling's snare,
   And hide my simple heart above,
Above the thorns of choking care,
   The gilded baits of worldly love.

Morning

4 Thee may I set at my right hand,
    Whose eyes my inmost substance see,
  And labour on at thy command,
    And offer all my works to thee.

5 Give me to bear thy easy yoke,
    And every moment watch and pray,
  And still to things eternal look,
    And hasten to thy glorious day;

6 For thee delightfully employ
    What e'er thy bounteous grace hath given,
  And run my course with even joy,
    And closely walk with thee to heaven.

CHARLES WESLEY 1707–88

Evening

192 EVENTIDE   11 10 11 10   WILLIAM HENRY MONK 1823–89

1. Abide with me: fast falls the eventide;
   The darkness deepens; Lord, with me abide:
   When other helpers fail, and comforts flee,
   Help of the helpless, O abide with me.

2. Swift to its close ebbs out life's little day;
   Earth's joys grow dim, its glories pass away;
   Change and decay in all around I see;
   O thou who changest not, abide with me.

3. Come not in terrors as the King of kings,
   But kind and good, with healing in thy wings,
   Tears for all woes, a heart for every plea—
   Come, friend of sinners, and thus bide with me.

Evening

4 I need thy presence every passing hour;
  What but thy grace can foil the tempter's power?
  Who like thyself my guide and stay can be?
  Through cloud and sunshine, O abide with me.

5 I fear no foe with thee at hand to bless;
  Ills have no weight, and tears no bitterness.
  Where is death's sting? where, grave, thy victory?
  I triumph still, if thou abide with me.

6 Hold thou thy Cross before my closing eyes;
  Shine through the gloom, and point me to the skies:
  Heaven's morning breaks, and earth's vain shadows flee;
  In life, in death, O Lord, abide with me!

HENRY FRANCIS LYTE 1793–1847

Evening

193 TALLIS'S CANON (The Eighth Tune)   THOMAS TALLIS c. 1505–85
      LM   adapted Thomas Ravenscroft's *Psalmes* 1621

1   Glory to thee, my God, this night
     For all the blessings of the light;
     Keep me, O keep me, King of kings,
     Beneath thy own almighty wings.

2   Forgive me Lord, for thy dear Son,
     The ill that I this day have done,
     That with the world, myself, and thee,
     I, ere I sleep, at peace may be.

3   Teach me to live, that I may dread
     The grave as little as my bed;
     Teach me to die, that so I may
     Rise glorious at the aweful day.

4   When in the night I sleepless lie,
     My soul with heavenly thoughts supply;
     Let no ill dreams disturb my rest,
     No powers of darkness me molest.

5   O may my soul on thee repose,
     And with sweet sleep my eyelids close,
     Sleep that may me more vigorous make
     To serve my God when I awake.

6   Praise God from whom all blessings flow,
     Praise him all creatures here below,
     Praise him above, ye heavenly host,
     Praise Father, Son and Holy Ghost.

THOMAS KEN 1637–1761

Evening

194 SEELENBRAÜTIGAM 55 88 55   ADAM DRESE 1620–1710

1. Round me falls the night;
   Saviour, be my light:
   Through the hours in darkness shrouded
   Let me see thy face unclouded;
     Let thy glory shine
     In this heart of mine.

2. Earthly work is done,
   Earthly sounds are none;
   Rest in sleep and silence seeking,
   Let me hear thee softly speaking;
     In my spirit's ear
     Whisper, 'I am near.'

3. Blessèd, heavenly light,
   Shining through earth's night;
   Voice, that oft of love hast told me;
   Arms, so strong to clasp and hold me;
     Thou thy watch wilt keep,
     Saviour, o'er my sleep.

WILLIAM ROMANIS 1824–99

Evening

195

FIRST TUNE

ABENDS   LM   HERBERT OAKLEY 1830–1903

SECOND TUNE

FULDA   LM   William Gardiner's *Sacred Melodies* 1815

Evening

1 Sun of my soul, thou Saviour dear,
  It is not night if thou be near:
  O may no earth-born cloud arise,
  To hide thee from thy servant's eyes.

2 When the soft dews of kindly sleep
  My wearied eyelids gently steep,
  Be my last thought, how sweet to rest
  For ever on my Saviour's breast.

3 Abide with me from morn till eve,
  For without thee I cannot live;
  Abide with me when night is nigh,
  For without thee I dare not die.

4 If some poor wand'ring child of thine
  Have spurned today the voice divine,
  Now, Lord, the gracious work begin;
  Let him no more lie down in sin.

5 Watch by the sick; enrich the poor
  With blessings from thy boundless store;
  Be every mourner's sleep to-night
  Like infant's slumbers, pure and light.

6 Come near and bless us when we wake,
  Ere through the world our way we take;
  Till in the ocean of thy love
  We lose ourselves in heaven above.

JOHN KEBLE 1792–1866

Evening

196 SUNSET (St Philip) 88 88 88 GEORGE HERBERT 1817–1906

1 Sweet Saviour! bless us ere we go;
　Thy word into our minds instil;
　And make our lukewarm hearts to glow
　　With lowly love and fervent will.
　　　Through life's long day and death's dark night,
　　　O gentle Jesus, be our light.

2 The day is done; its hours have run,
　　And thou hast taken count of all,
　The scanty triumphs grace has won,
　　The broken vow, the frequent fall.

Evening

3 Grant us, dear Lord! from evil ways
    True absolution and release;
  And bless us, more than in past days,
    With purity and inward peace.

4 For all we love—the poor, the sad,
    The sinful—unto thee we call;
  Oh let thy mercy make us glad;
    Thou art our Jesus and our all.

5 Sweet Saviour! bless us; night is come;
    Mary and Joseph near us be!
  Good angels watch about our home,
    And we are one day nearer thee.

                  FREDERICK WILLIAM FABER Cong. Orat. 1814–63

Evening

197 ST CLEMENT 98 98 CLEMENT COTTERILL SCHOLEFIELD 1839–1904

1. The day thou gavest, Lord, is ended,
   The darkness falls at thy behest;
   To thee our morning hymns ascended,
   Thy praise shall sanctify our rest.

2. We thank thee that thy Church unsleeping,
   While earth rolls onward into light,
   Through all the world her watch is keeping,
   And rests not now by day or night.

Evening

3 As o'er each continent and island
    The dawn leads on another day,
  The voice of prayer is never silent,
    Nor dies the strain of praise away.

4 The sun that bids us rest is waking
    Our brethren 'neath the western sky,
  And hour by hour fresh lips are making
    Thy wondrous doings heard on high.

5 So be it, Lord; thy throne shall never
    Like earth's proud empires, pass away;
  Thy kingdom stands, and grows for ever,
    Till all thy creatures own thy sway.

JOHN ELLERTON 1826–93

General

198 LASST UNS ERFREUEN   *Geistliche Kirchengesäng* Cologne 1623
88 44 88 + refrain   arranged RALPH VAUGHAN WILLIAMS 1872–1958

1. All creatures of our God and King,
   Lift up your voice and with us sing
       Alleluia, Alleluia!
   Thou burning sun with golden beam,
   Thou silver moon with softer gleam,
       O praise him, O praise him,
       Alleluia, Alleluia, Alleluia!

2. Thou rushing wind that art so strong,
   Ye clouds that sail in heaven along,
       O praise him, Alleluia!
   Thou rising moon, in praise rejoice,
   Ye lights of evening, find a voice:

General

3 Thou flowing water, pure and clear,
　Make music for thy Lord to hear,
　　　Alleluia, Alleluia!
　Thou fire so masterful and bright,
　That givest man both warmth and light:

4 Dear mother earth, who day by day
　Unfoldest blessings on our way,
　　　O praise him, Alleluia!
　The flowers and fruits that in thee grow,
　Let them his glory also show:

5 Let all things their Creator bless,
　And worship him in humbleness,
　　　O praise him, Alleluia!
　Praise, praise the Father, praise the Son,
　And praise the Spirit, Three in One.

Cantico di fratre sole
St Francis of Assisi 1182–1226
tr. William Draper 1855–1933

General

199 MILES LANE   CM   William Shrubsole 1760–1806

1. All hail the power of Jesu's name!
   Let angels prostrate fall;
   Bring forth the royal diadem
   To crown him Lord of all.

2. Crown him, ye martyrs of your God,
   Who from his altar call;
   Praise him whose way of pain ye trod,
   And crown him Lord of all.

3. Ye souls redeemed of Adam's race,
   Ye ransomed of the fall,
   Hail him who saves you by his grace,
   And crown him Lord of all.

General

4 Hail him, ye heirs of David's line,
    Whom David Lord did call;
  The God incarnate, Man divine,
    And crown him Lord of all.

5 Sinners, whose love can ne'er forget
    The wormwood and the gall,
  Go, spread your trophies at his feet,
    And crown him Lord of all.

6 Let every tribe and every tongue
    To him their hearts enthral;
  And shout in universal song
    To crown him Lord of all.

EDWARD PERRONET 1726–92
and others

General

200 MICHAEL   87 87 33 7   HERBERT HOWELLS 1892–1983

1. All my hope on God is founded;
   He doth still my trust renew.
   Me through change and chance he guideth,
   Only good and only true.
   God unknown,
   He alone
   Calls my heart to be his own.

2. Pride of man and earthly glory,
   Sword and crown betray his trust;
   What with care and toil he buildeth,
   Tower and temple, fall to dust;
   But God's power,
   Hour by hour,
   Is my temple and my tower.

3. God's great goodness ay endureth,
   Deep his wisdom, passing thought:
   Splendour, light and life attend him,
   Beauty springeth out of naught.
   Evermore
   From his store
   New-born worlds rise and adore.

General

4 Daily doth the almighty Giver
    Bounteous gifts on us bestow;
 His desire our soul delighteth,
    Pleasure leads us where we go.
      Love doth stand
      At his hand;
    Joy doth wait on his command.

5 Still from man to God eternal
    Sacrifice of praise be done,
 High above all praises praising
    For the gift of Christ his Son.
      Christ doth call
      One and all:
    Ye who follow shall not fall.

Meine Hoffnung stehet feste
JOACHIM NEANDER 1650–80
freely adapted ROBERT BRIDGES 1844–1930

General

201 OLD HUNDREDTH   LM   Ps. 134 in the Genevan *Psalter* 1551
English form of last line from 1563

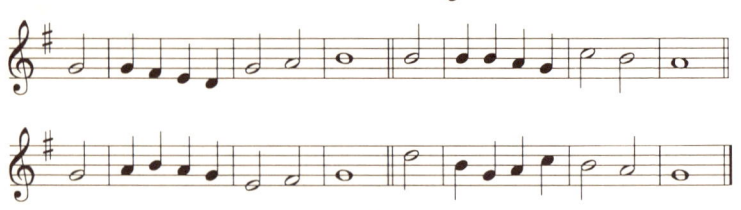

1. All people that on earth do dwell,
   Sing to the Lord with cheerful voice;
   Him serve with fear, his praise forth tell,
   Come ye before him, and rejoice.

2. The Lord, ye know, is God indeed,
   Without our aid he did us make;
   We are his folk, he doth us feed,
   And for his sheep he doth us take.

3. O enter then his gates with praise,
   Approach with joy his courts unto;
   Praise, laud, and bless his name always,
   For it is seemly so to do.

4. For why? the Lord our God is good:
   His mercy is for ever sure;
   His truth at all times firmly stood,
   And shall from age to age endure.

5. To Father, Son, and Holy Ghost,
   The God whom heaven and earth adore,
   From men and from the angel-host
   Be praise and glory evermore.

based on *Psalm 100*
WILLIAM KETHE died 1594

General

202 ALL THINGS BRIGHT AND BEAUTIFUL
76 76 + refrain

WILLIAM HENRY MONK
1823–89

All things bright and beautiful,
All creatures great and small,
All things wise and wonderful,
The Lord God made them all.

1. Each little flower that opens,
   Each little bird that sings,
   He made their glowing colours,
   He made their tiny wings.

2. The purple-headed mountain,
   The river running by,
   The sunset, and the morning
   That brightens up the sky;

3. The cold wind in the winter,
   The pleasant summer sun,
   The ripe fruits in the garden,
   He made them every one;

4. The tall trees in the greenwood,
   The meadows for our play,
   The rushes by the water,
   To gather every day;

5. He gave us eyes to see them,
   And lips that we may tell
   How great is God Almighty,
   Who has made all things well.

CECIL FRANCES ALEXANDER 1818–95

General

203 AMAZING GRACE   CM   American folk tune 'Virginia Harmony' of Scottish origin

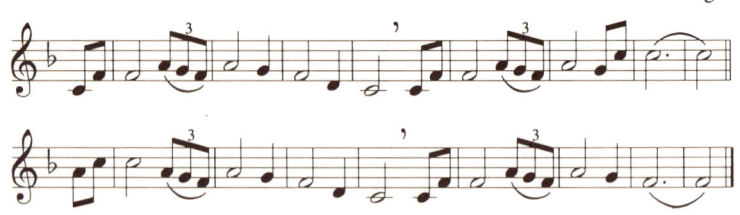

1. Amazing grace! how sweet the sound
   That saved a wretch like me!
   I once was lost, but now am found,
   Was blind, but now I see.

2. 'Twas grace that taught my heart to fear,
   And grace my fears relieved;
   How precious did that grace appear
   The hour I first believed.

3. Through many dangers, toils, and snares
   I have already come;
   'Tis grace hath brought me safe thus far,
   And grace will lead me home.

4. The Lord has promised good to me,
   His word my hope secures;
   He will my shield and portion be
   As long as life endures.

JOHN NEWTON 1725–1807

General

204 JERUSALEM   DLM   CHARLES HUBERT HASTINGS PARRY 1848–1918

Slow, but with animation

And did those feet in an-cient time walk up-on England's moun-tains green? And was the ho-ly Lamb of God on Eng-land's plea-sant pas-tures seen? And did the coun-te-nance di-vine shine forth up-on our cloud-ed hills? And was Je-ru-sa-lem build-ed

General

here among those dark satanic mills? Bring me my bow of burning gold! Bring me my arrows of desire! Bring me my spear! O clouds unfold! Bring me my chariot of fire! I will not cease from mental fight, nor shall my sword sleep in my

General

hand, Till we have built Je - ru - sa - lem in Eng-land's green and plea - sant land.

WILLIAM BLAKE 1757–1827

General

205 ANGEL VOICES   85 85 843   Edwin George Monk 1819–1900

1. Angel-voices ever singing
   Round thy throne of light,
   Angel-harps for ever ringing,
   Rest not day nor night;
   Thousands only live to bless thee
   And confess thee
   Lord of might.

2. Thou who art beyond the farthest
   Mortal eye can scan,
   Can it be that thou regardest
   Songs of sinful man?
   Can we know that thou art near us,
   And wilt hear us?
   Yes, we can.

General

3 For we know that thou rejoicest
    O'er each work of thine;
Thou didst ears and hands and voices
    For thy praise design;
Craftsman's art and music's measure
    For thy pleasure
        All combine.

4 In thy house, great God, we offer
    Of thine own to thee;
And for thine acceptance proffer
    All unworthily
Hearts and minds and hands and voices
    In our choicest
        Psalmody.

5 Honour, glory, might and merit
    Thine shall ever be,
Father, Son and Holy Spirit,
    Blessed Trinity.
Of the best which thou hast given
    Earth and heaven
        Render thee.

FRANCIS POTT 1832–1909

General

206

FIRST TUNE

MARTYRDOM   CM

Hugh Wilson 1766–1824
adapted Robert Smith 1780–1829

SECOND TUNE

ABRIDGE   CM

Isaac Smith died 1805

General

1 As pants the hart for cooling streams
    When heated in the chase,
So longs my soul, O God, for thee,
    And thy refreshing grace.

2 For thee, my God, the living God,
    My thirsty soul doth pine;
O when shall I behold thy face,
    Thou Majesty divine?

3 Why restless, why cast down, my soul?
    Trust God, and he'll employ
His aid for thee, and change these sighs
    To thankful hymns of joy.

4 God of my strength, how long shall I,
    Like one forgotten, mourn?
Forlorn, forsaken, and exposed
    To my oppressors' scorn?

5 Why restless, why cast down, my soul?
    Hope still, and thou shalt sing
The praise of him who is thy God,
    Thy health's eternal spring.

based on *Psalm 42*
New Version Psalter 1696 of NAHUM TATE 1652–1715
and NICHOLAS BRADY 1659–1726

General

207 EVELYNS   65 65 D   William Henry Monk 1823–89

1. At the name of Jesus
   Every knee shall bow,
   Every tongue confess him
   King of glory now;
   'Tis the Father's pleasure
   We should call him Lord,
   Who from the beginning
   Was the mighty Word.

2. At his voice creation
   Sprang at once to sight,
   All the angel faces,
   All the hosts of light,
   Thrones and dominations,
   Stars upon their way,
   All the heavenly orders,
   In their great array.

3. Humbled for a season,
   To receive a name
   From the lips of sinners
   Unto whom he came,
   Faithfully he bore it
   Spotless to the last,
   Brought it back victorious
   When from death he passed:

4. Bore it up triumphant
   With its human light,
   Through all ranks of creatures,
   To the central height,
   To the throne of Godhead,
   To the Father's breast;
   Filled it with the glory
   Of that perfect rest.

5. In your hearts enthrone him;
   There let him subdue
   All that is not holy,
   All that is not true:
   He is God the Saviour,
   He is Christ the Lord,
   Ever to be worshipped,
   Trusted, and adored.

Caroline Noel 1817–77

General

208 FRANCONIA   SM

Johann Balthasar König's
Harmonischer Lieder-Schatz 1738
adapted WILLIAM HENRY HAVERGAL 1793–1870

1. Blest are the pure in heart,
   For they shall see our God,
   The secret of the Lord is theirs,
   Their soul is Christ's abode.

2. The Lord, who left the heavens
   Our life and peace to bring,
   To dwell in lowliness with men,
   Their pattern and their King;

3. Still to the lowly soul
   He doth himself impart,
   And for his cradle and his throne
   Chooseth the pure in heart.

4. Lord, we thy presence seek;
   May ours this blessing be;
   Give us a pure and lowly heart,
   A temple meet for thee.

JOHN KEBLE 1792–1866
and WILLIAM JOHN HALL 1793–1861

General

209 WESTMINSTER ABBEY   87 87 87   Henry Purcell 1659–95
adapted 1843 from 'O God, Thou art my God'

1. Christ is made the sure Foundation,
   Christ the Head and Corner-stone,
   Chosen of the Lord, and precious,
   Binding all the Church in one,
   Holy Sion's help for ever,
   And her confidence alone.

2. All that dedicated city,
   Dearly loved of God on high,
   In exultant jubilation,
   Pours perpetual melody,
   God the One in Three adoring
   In glad hymns eternally.

General

3 To this temple, where we call thee,
    Come, O Lord of Hosts, today;
With thy wonted loving-kindness
    Hear thy servants as they pray;
And thy fullest benediction
    Shed within its walls alway.

4 Here vouchsafe to all thy servants
    What they ask of thee to gain,
What they gain from thee for ever
    With the blessèd to retain,
And hereafter in thy glory
    Evermore with thee to reign.

5 Laud and honour to the Father,
    Laud and honour to the Son;
Laud and honour to the Spirit;
    Ever Three and ever One:
Consubstantial, co-eternal,
    While unending ages run.

Angularis fundamentum c. 7th century
tr. JOHN MASON NEALE 1818–66

General

210 NATIVITY CM   Henry Lahee 1826–1912

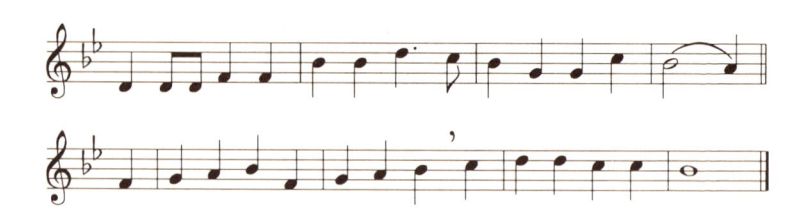

1. Come, let us join our cheerful songs
   With angels round the throne;
   Ten thousand thousand are their tongues,
   But all their joys are one.

2. 'Worthy the Lamb that died,' they cry,
   'To be exalted thus;'
   'Worthy the Lamb,' our lips reply,
   'For he was slain for us.'

3. Jesus is worthy to receive
   Honour and power divine;
   And blessings, more than we can give,
   Be, Lord, for ever thine.

4. Let all that dwell above the sky,
   And air and earth and seas,
   Conspire to lift thy glories high,
   And speak thine endless praise.

5. The whole creation join in one
   To bless the sacred name
   Of him that sits upon the throne,
   And to adore the Lamb.

based on *Revelation 5:11–13*
Isaac Watts 1674–1748

General

211 ST GEORGE'S WINDSOR 77 77 D GEORGE JOB ELVEY 1816–93

1. Come, ye thankful people, come,
   Raise the song of harvest-home:
   All is safely gathered in,
   Ere the winter storms begin;
   God, our Maker, doth provide
   For our wants to be supplied:
   Come to God's own temple, come,
   Raise the song of harvest-home.

2. All this world is God's own field,
   Fruit unto his praise to yield;
   Wheat and tares together sown,
   Unto joy or sorrow grown;
   First the blade, and then the ear,
   Then the full corn shall appear:
   Lord of harvest, grant that we
   Wholesome grain and pure may be.

3. For the Lord our God shall come,
   And shall take his harvest home;
   From his field shall in that day
   All offences purge away;
   Give his angels charge at last
   In the fire the tares to cast;
   But the fruitful ears to store
   In his garner evermore.

4. Even so, Lord, quickly come;
   Bring thy final harvest home:
   Gather thou thy people in,
   Free from sorrow, free from sin;
   There, for ever purified,
   In thy garner to abide:
   Come, with all thine angels, come,
   Raise the glorious harvest-home.

HENRY ALFORD 1810–71

General

212 REPTON 86 88 6   CHARLES HUBERT HASTINGS PARRY 1848–1918
from 'Long since in Egypt's pleasant land' in *Judith*

1. Dear Lord and Father of mankind,
    Forgive our foolish ways!
   Re-clothe us in our rightful mind,
   In purer lives thy service find,
    In deeper reverence praise.

2. In simple trust like theirs who heard,
    Beside the Syrian sea,
   The gracious calling of the Lord,
   Let us, like them, without a word
    Rise up and follow thee.

3. O Sabbath rest by Galilee!
    O calm of hills above,
   Where Jesus knelt to share with thee
   The silence of eternity,
    Interpreted by love!

General

4 With that deep hush subduing all
    Our words and works, that drown
  The tender whisper of thy call,
  As noiseless let thy blessing fall
    As fell thy manna down.

5 Drop thy still dews of quietness,
    Till all our strivings cease;
  Take from our souls the strain and stress,
  And let our ordered lives confess
    The beauty of thy peace.

6 Breathe through the heats of our desire
    Thy coolness and thy balm;
  Let sense be dumb, let flesh retire;
  Speak through the earthquake, wind, and fire,
    O still small voice of calm!

JOHN GREENLEAF WHITTIER 1807–92

General

213 MELITA 88 88 88   JOHN BACCHUS DYKES 1823–76

1. Eternal Father, strong to save,
   Whose arm doth bind the restless wave,
   Who bidd'st the mighty ocean deep
   Its own appointed limits keep;
     O hear us when we cry to thee
     For those in peril on the sea.

2. O Saviour, whose almighty word
   The winds and waves submissive heard,
   Who walkedst on the foaming deep,
   And calm amid its rage didst sleep:
     O hear us when we cry to thee
     For those in peril on the sea.

3. O sacred Spirit, who didst brood
   Upon the chaos dark and rude,
   Who bad'st its angry tumult cease,
   And gavest light and life and peace:
     O hear us when we cry to thee
     For those in peril on the sea.

4. O Trinity of love and power,
   Our brethren shield in danger's hour;
   From rock and tempest, fire and foe,
   Protect them whereso'er they go:
     And ever let there rise to thee
     Glad hymns of praise from land and sea.

WILLIAM WHITING 1825–78

General

214 SUSSEX   87 87

English folk tune
adapted RALPH VAUGHAN WILLIAMS 1872–1958

An alternative tune will be found at Hymn 95.

1 Father, hear the prayer we offer:
　Not for ease that prayer shall be,
　But for strength that we may ever
　Live our lives courageously.

2 Not for ever in green pastures
　Do we ask our way to be;
　But the steep and rugged pathway
　May we tread rejoicingly.

3 Not for ever by still waters
　Would we idly rest and stay;
　But would smite the living fountains
　From the rocks along our way.

4 Be our strength in hours of weakness,
　In our wanderings be our guide;
　Through endeavour, failure, danger,
　Father, be thou at our side.

MARIA WILLIS 1824–1908

General

215 DUNEDIN LM V ERNON G RIFFITHS 1894–1985

An alternative tune will be found at Hymn 191.

1 Father of heaven, whose love profound
A ransom for our souls hath found,
Before thy throne we sinners bend:
To us thy pardoning love extend.

2 Almighty Son, incarnate Word,
Our Prophet, Priest, Redeemer, Lord,
Before thy throne we sinners bend:
To us thy saving grace extend.

3 Eternal Spirit, by whose breath
The soul is raised from sin and death,
Before thy throne we sinners bend:
To us thy quickening power extend.

4 Thrice Holy! Father, Spirit, Son,
Mysterious Godhead, Three in One,
Before thy throne we sinners bend:
Grace, pardon, life to us extend.

E DWARD C OOPER 1770–1833

General

216 CHRISTE SANCTORUM   11 11 11 5   Paris *Antiphonale* 1681

1. Father of mercy, God of consolation,
   Look on your people, gathered here to praise you,
   Pity our weakness, come in power to aid us,
       Source of all blessing.

2. Son of the Father, Lord of all creation,
   Come as our Saviour, Jesus, friend of sinners,
   Grant us forgiveness, lift our downcast spirit,
       Heal us and save us.

3. Life-giving Spirit, be our light in darkness,
   Come to befriend us, help us bear our burdens,
   Give us true courage, breathe your peace around us,
       Stay with us always.

4. God in Three Persons, Father, Son, and Spirit,
   Come to renew us, fill your Church with glory,
   Grant us your healing, pledge of resurrection,
       Foretaste of heaven.

JAMES QUINN S.J. born 1919

General

217
FIRST TUNE

SHIPSTON   87 87   Warwickshire folk tune
adapted RALPH VAUGHAN WILLIAMS 1872–1958

SECOND TUNE

HALTON HOLGATE   87 87   WILLIAM BOYCE 1711–79
arranged SAMUEL SEBASTIAN WESLEY 1810–76

A further alternative tune will be found at Hymn 42.

General

1 Firmly I believe and truly
    God is Three, and God is One;
And I next acknowledge duly
    Manhood taken by the Son.

2 And I trust and hope most fully
    In that Manhood crucified;
And each thought and deed unruly
    Do to death, as he has died.

3 Simply to his grace and wholly
    Light and life and strength belong,
And I love supremely, solely,
    Him the holy, him the strong.

4 And I hold in veneration,
    For the love of him alone,
Holy Church as his creation,
    And her teachings as his own.

5 Adoration ay be given,
    With and through the angelic host,
To the God of earth and heaven,
    Father, Son and Holy Ghost.

from *The Dream of Gerontius*
The Venerable JOHN HENRY NEWMAN Cong. Orat. 1801–90

General

218 ABBOT'S LEIGH   87 87 D   Cyril Taylor 1907–91

An alternative tune will be found at Hymn 259.

1 Glorious things of thee are spoken,
   Sion, city of our God;
He whose word cannot be broken
   Formed thee for his own abode:
On the Rock of Ages founded,
   What can shake thy sure repose?
With salvation's walls surrounded,
   Thou may'st smile at all thy foes.

General

2 See, the streams of living waters,
    Springing from eternal love,
Well supply thy sons and daughters,
    And all fear of want remove:
Who can faint, while such a river
    Ever flows their thirst to assuage?
Grace, which like the Lord the Giver,
    Never fails from age to age.

3 Saviour, if of Sion's city
    I through grace a member am,
Let the world deride or pity,
    I will glory in thy name:
Fading is the worldling's pleasure,
    All his boasted pomp and show;
Solid joys and lasting treasure
    None but Sion's children know.

JOHN NEWTON 1725–1807

General

219 LONDON NEW   CM   Scottish *Psalter* 1635

1. God moves in a mysterious way
      His wonders to perform;
   He plants his footsteps in the sea,
      And rides upon the storm.

2. Deep in unfathomable mines
      Of never-failing skill
   He treasures up his bright designs,
      And works his sovereign will.

3. Ye fearful saints, fresh courage take,
      The clouds ye so much dread
   Are big with mercy, and shall break
      In blessings on your head.

4. Judge not the Lord by feeble sense,
      But trust him for his grace;
   Behind a frowning providence
      He hides a smiling face.

5. His purposes will ripen fast,
      Unfolding every hour;
   The bud may have a bitter taste,
      But sweet will be the flower.

6. Blind unbelief is sure to err,
      And scan his work in vain;
   God is his own interpreter,
      And he will make it plain.

WILLIAM COWPER 1731–1800

General

220 NATIONAL ANTHEM 664 6664 probably 17th century
popularized 1745 THOMAS ARNE 1710–78

1. God save our gracious Queen,
   Long live our noble Queen,
      God save the Queen.
   Send her victorious,
   Happy and glorious,
   Long to reign over us:
      God save the Queen.

2. Thy choicest gifts in store
   On her be pleased to pour,
      Long may she reign.
   May she defend our laws,
   And ever give us cause
   To sing with heart and voice:
      God save the Queen.

Gentlemen's Magazine London 1745

General

221 CWM RHONDDA   87 87 47   JOHN HUGHES 1873–1932

1. Guide me, O thou great Redeemer,
    Pilgrim through this barren land;
 I am weak, but thou art mighty,
    Hold me with thy powerful hand:
       Bread of heaven,
 Feed me till I want no more.

2. Open now the crystal fountain
    Whence the healing stream doth flow;
 Let the fire and cloudy pillar
    Lead me all my journey through:
       Strong Deliverer,
 Be thou still my strength and shield.

3. When I tread the verge of Jordan,
    Bid my anxious fears subside;
 Death of death, and hell's destruction
    Land me safe on Canaan's side:
       Songs of praises
 I will ever give to thee.

Welsh WILLIAM WILLIAMS 1717–91
tr. PETER WILLIAMS 1727–96 and others

General

222 GROSSER GOTT *Katholisches Gesangbuch* Vienna c. 1774
78 78 77   adapted Heinrich Bone's *Cantate* 1852

1. Holy God, we praise thy name;
   Lord of all, we bow before thee!
   All on earth thy sceptre own,
   All in heav'n above adore thee.
   Infinite thy vast domain,
   Everlasting is thy reign.

2. Hark! the loud celestial hymn
   Angel choirs above are raising;
   Cherubim and seraphim
   In unceasing chorus praising.
   Fill the heavens with sweet accord,
   Holy, holy, holy Lord.

3. Holy Father, holy Son,
   Holy Spirit, Three we name thee,
   While in essence only One
   Undivided God we claim thee;
   And adoring bend the knee,
   While we own the mystery.

4. Spare thy people, Lord, we pray,
   By a thousand snares surrounded;
   Keep us free from sin today,
   Never let us be confounded;
   Lo, I put my trust in thee—
   Never, Lord, abandon me.

based on the *Te Deum*
Grosser Gott wir loben dich IGNAZ FRANZ 1719–90
tr. CLARENCE WALWORTH 1820–1900

General

223 ST PETER   CM   ALEXANDER REINAGLE 1799–1877

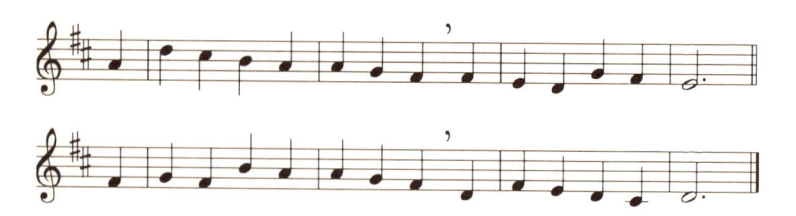

1. How sweet the name of Jesus sounds
 In a believer's ear!
 It soothes his sorrows, heals his wounds,
 And drives away his fear.

2. It makes the wounded spirit whole,
 And calms the troubled breast;
 'Tis manna to the hungry soul,
 And to the weary rest.

3. Dear name! the rock on which I build,
 My shield and hiding-place,
 My never-failing treasury filled
 With boundless stores of grace.

4. Jesus! my Shepherd, Husband, Friend,
 My Prophet, Priest, and King,
 My Lord, my Life, my Way, my End,
 Accept the praise I bring.

5. Weak is the effort of my heart,
 And cold my warmest thought;
 But when I see thee as thou art,
 I'll praise thee as I ought.

6. Till then I would thy love proclaim
 With every fleeting breath;
 And may the music of thy name
 Refresh my soul in death.

JOHN NEWTON 1725–1807

General

224 THAXTED 13 13 13 13 13 13 GUSTAV HOLST 1874–1934
adapted by the composer from *The Planets*

1. I vow to thee, my country—all earthly things above—
   Entire and whole and perfect, the service of my love:
   The love that asks no question, the love that stands the test,
   That lays upon the altar the dearest and the best;
   The love that never falters, the love that pays the price,
   The love that makes undaunted the final sacrifice.

2. And there's another country, I've heard of long ago,
   Most dear to them that love her, most great to them that know;
   We may not count her armies, we may not see her King;
   Her fortress is a faithful heart, her pride is suffering;
   And soul by soul and silently her shining bounds increase,
   And her ways are ways of gentleness and all her paths are peace.

CECIL SPRING-RICE 1859–1918

General

225 ST DENIO 11 11 11 11 Welsh folk tune
adapted JOHN ROBERTS 1822–77

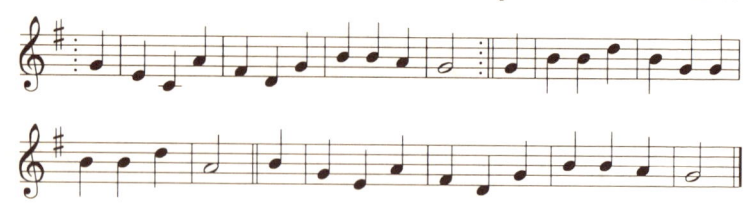

1. Immortal, invisible, God only wise,
In light inaccessible hid from our eyes,
Most blessèd, most glorious, the Ancient of Days,
Almighty, victorious, thy great name we praise.

2. Unresting, unhasting, and silent as light,
Nor wanting, nor wasting, thou rulest in might;
Thy justice like mountains high soaring above
Thy clouds which are fountains of goodness and love.

3. To all life thou givest—to both great and small;
In all life thou livest, the true life of all;
We blossom and flourish as leaves on the tree,
And wither and perish—but nought changeth thee.

4. Great Father of glory, pure Father of light,
Thine angels adore thee, all veiling their sight;
All laud we would render: O help us to see
'Tis only the splendour of light hideth thee.

WALTER CHALMERS SMITH 1824–1908

General

226 EWING 76 76 D ALEXANDER EWING 1830–95
adapted *Hymns Ancient and Modern* 1861

1. Jerusalem the golden,
   With milk and honey blessed,
   Beneath thy contemplation
   Sink heart and voice oppressed.
   I know not, O I know not
   What joys await us there,
   What radiancy of glory,
   What light beyond compare.

2. They stand, those halls of Sion,
   Conjubilant with song,
   And bright with many an angel,
   And all the martyr throng;
   The Prince is ever in them,
   The daylight is serene:
   The pastures of the blessèd
   Are decked in glorious sheen.

3. There is the throne of David,
   And there, from care released,
   The shout of them that triumph,
   The song of them that feast;
   And they who, with their Leader,
   Have conquered in the fight,
   For ever and for ever
   Are clad in robes of white.

4. O sweet and blessèd country,
   Shall I ever see thy face?
   O sweet and blessèd country,
   Shall I ever win thy grace?
   Exult, O dust and ashes,
   The Lord shall be thy part:
   His only, his for ever
   Thou shalt be, and thou art.

Urbs Sion aurea
ST BERNARD OF CLUNY 12th century
tr. JOHN MASON NEALE 1818–66

General

227 ABERYSTWYTH 77 77 D Joseph Parry 1841–1903

1. Jesu, Lover of my soul,
   Let me to thy bosom fly,
   While the nearer waters roll,
   While the tempest still is high:
   Hide me, O my Saviour, hide
   Till the storm of life is past;
   Safe into the haven guide,
   O receive my soul at last.

2. Other refuge have I none,
   Hangs my helpless soul on thee;
   Leave, ah, leave me not alone,
   Still support and comfort me.
   All my trust on thee is stayed,
   All my help from thee I bring;
   Cover my defenceless head
   With the shadow of thy wing.

General

3 Thou, O Christ, art all I want,
    More than all in thee I find:
Raise the fallen, cheer the faint,
    Heal the sick, and lead the blind.
Just and holy is thy name,
    I am all unrighteousness;
False and full of sin I am,
    Thou art full of truth and grace.

4 Plenteous grace with thee is found,
    Grace to cover all my sin;
Let the healing streams abound,
    Make and keep me pure within.
Thou of life the fountain art,
    Freely let me take of thee,
Spring thou up within my heart,
    Rise to all eternity.

CHARLES WESLEY 1707–88

General

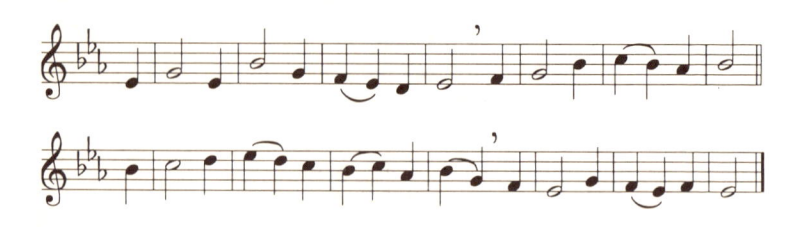

228 ST BOTOLPH CM GORDON SLATER 1896–1979

1. Jesu, the very thought of thee
   With sweetness fills my breast;
   But sweeter far thy face to see,
   And in thy presence rest.

2. Nor voice can sing, nor heart can frame,
   Nor can the memory find,
   A sweeter sound than thy blest name,
   O Saviour of mankind!

3. O hope of every contrite heart,
   O joy of all the meek,
   To those who fall, how kind thou art!
   How good to those who seek!

4. But what to those who find? Ah, this
   Nor tongue nor pen can show;
   The love of Jesus, what it is,
   None but his loved ones know.

5. Jesu, our only joy be thou,
   As thou our prize wilt be;
   Jesu, be thou our glory now,
   And through eternity.

Jesu dulcis memoria c. 12th century
tr. EDWARD CASWALL Cong. Orat. 1814–78

General

229 QUEM PASTORES   88 87   14th century German

This hymn is most suitable for Christmas.

1. Jesus, good above all other,
Gentle Child of gentle Mother,
In a stable born our Brother,
   Give us grace to persevere.

2. Jesus, cradled in a manger,
For us facing every danger,
Living as a homeless stranger,
   Make we thee our King most dear.

3. Jesus, for thy people dying,
Risen Master, death defying,
Lord in heav'n, thy grace supplying,
   Keep us to thine altar near.

4. Jesus, who our sorrows bearest,
All our thoughts and hopes thou sharest,
Thou to man the truth declarest;
   Help us all thy truth to hear.

5. Lord, in all our doings guide us;
Pride and hate shall ne'er divide us;
We'll go on with thee beside us,
   And with joy we'll persevere!

PERCY DEARMER 1867–1936

General

230 ELLACOMBE   DCM   Würtemburg *Gesangbuch* 1784
                                    adapted Mainz *Gesangbuch* 1833

1. Jesus is God! the solid earth,
    The ocean broad and bright,
   The countless stars, like golden dust,
    That strew the skies at night,
   The wheeling storm, the dreadful fire,
    The pleasant wholesome air,
   The summer's sun, the winter's frost,
    His own creations were.

2. Jesus is God! the glorious bands
    Of golden angels sing
   Songs of adoring praise to him,
    Their Maker and their King.
   He was true God in Bethl'em's crib,
    On Calvary's Cross true God,
   He who in heaven eternal reigned
    In time on earth abode.

General

3 Jesus is God! let sorrow come,
    And pain, and every ill;
  All are worthwhile, for all are means
    His glory to fulfil;
  Worthwhile a thousand years of life
    To speak one little word,
  If by our Credo we might own
    The Godhead of our Lord!

4 Jesus is God! O, could I now
    But compass land and sea,
  To teach and tell this single truth,
    How happy should I be!
  O, had I but an angel's voice,
    I would proclaim so loud—
  Jesus, the good, the beautiful,
    Is everlasting God!

FREDERICK WILLIAM FABER Cong. Orat. 1814–63

General

231

FIRST TUNE

WARRINGTON   LM   RALPH HARRISON 1748–1810

SECOND TUNE

TRURO   LM   Thomas Williams' *Psalmodia Evangelica* Part II 1789

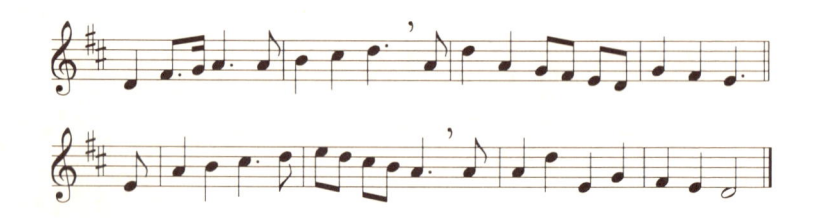

General

1. Jesus shall reign where'er the sun
   Does his successive journeys run;
   His kingdom stretch from shore to shore,
   Till moons shall wax and wane no more.

2. To him shall endless prayer be made,
   And praises throng to crown his head;
   His name like sweet perfume shall rise
   With every morning sacrifice.

3. People and realms of every tongue
   Dwell on his love with sweetest song;
   And infant-voices shall proclaim
   Their early blessings on his name.

4. Blessings abound where'er he reigns,
   The prisoner leaps to lose his chains,
   The weary find eternal rest,
   And all the sons of want are blest.

5. Let every creature rise and bring
   Peculiar honours to our King;
   Angels descend with songs again,
   And earth repeat the long Amen.

based on *Psalm 72*
ISAAC WATTS 1674–1748 *

General

232

FIRST TUNE

NUN DANKET ALL   CM   JOHANN CRÜGER 1598–1662

SECOND TUNE

RICHMOND   CM   THOMAS HAWEIS 1734–1820
adapted SAMUEL WEBBE the younger c. 1770–1843

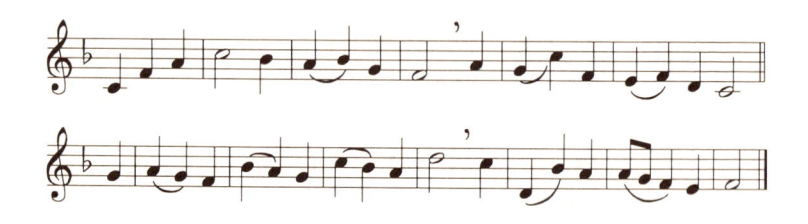

General

1. Jesus, these eyes have never seen
   That radiant form of thine;
   The veil of sense hangs dark between
   Thy blessèd face and mine.

2. I see thee not, I hear thee not,
   Yet art thou oft with me;
   And earth hath ne'er so dear a spot
   As where I met with thee.

3. Yet, though I have not seen, and still
   Must rest in faith alone,
   I love thee, dearest Lord, and will,
   Unseen, but not unknown.

4. When death these mortal eyes shall seal,
   And still this throbbing heart,
   The rending veil shall thee reveal
   All glorious as thou art.

RAY PALMER 1808–87

General

233 GWALCHMAI 74 74 D JOHN DAVID JONES 1827–70

1. King of glory, King of peace,
   I will love thee;
   And that love may never cease,
   I will move thee.
   Thou hast granted my request,
   Thou hast heard me;
   Thou didst note my working breast,
   Thou hast spared me.

2. Wherefore with my utmost art
   I will sing thee,
   And the cream of all my heart
   I will bring thee.
   Though my sins against me cried,
   Thou didst clear me;
   And alone, when they replied,
   Thou didst hear me.

General

3 Seven whole days, not one in seven,
    I will praise thee;
In my heart, though not in heaven,
    I can raise thee.
Small it is, in this poor sort
    To enrol thee:
E'en eternity's too short
    To extol thee.

GEORGE HERBERT 1593–1632

General

234

FIRST TUNE

ALBERTA   10 4 10 4 10 10   WILLIAM HENRY HARRIS 1883–1973

SECOND TUNE

SANDON   10 4 10 4 10 10   CHARLES HENRY PURDAY 1799–1885

General

1 Lead, kindly Light, amid the encircling gloom,
    Lead thou me on;
  The night is dark, and I am far from home,
    Lead thou me on.
  Keep thou my feet; I do not ask to see
  The distant scene; one step enough for me.

2 I was not ever thus, nor prayed that thou
    Shouldst lead me on;
  I loved to choose and see my path; but now
    Lead thou me on.
  I loved the garish day, and, spite of fears,
  Pride ruled my will: remember not past years.

3 So long thy power hath blest me, sure it still
    Will lead me on
  O'er moor and fen, o'er crag and torrent, till
    The night is gone,
  And with the morn those angel faces smile,
  Which I have loved long since, and lost awhile.

    The Venerable JOHN HENRY NEWMAN Cong. Orat. 1801–90

General

235 MANNHEIM 87 87 87 Friedrich Filitz's *Choralbuch* 1847
adapted Thomas Binney's *Congregational Church Music* 1853

1. Lead us, heavenly Father, lead us
    O'er the world's tempestuous sea;
   Guard us, guide us, keep us, feed us,
    For we have no help but thee;
   Yet possessing every blessing,
    If our God our Father be.

2. Saviour, breathe forgiveness o'er us;
    All our weakness thou dost know;
   Thou didst tread this earth before us,
    Thou didst feel its keenest woe;
   Lone and dreary, faint and weary,
    Through the desert thou didst go.

3. Spirit of our God, descending,
    Fill our hearts with heavenly joy,
   Love with every passion blending,
    Pleasure that can never cloy;
   Thus provided, pardoned, guided,
    Nothing can our peace destroy.

JAMES EDMESTON 1791–1867

General

236 LUCKINGTON   10 4 66 66 10 4   BASIL HARWOOD 1859–1949

1. Let all the world in every corner sing,
      My God and King!
   The heavens are not too high,
   His praise may thither fly;
   The earth is not too low,
   His praises there may grow.
   Let all the world in every corner sing,
      My God and King!

2. Let all the world in every corner sing,
      My God and King!
   The Church with psalms must shout,
   No door can keep them out;
   But above all, the heart
   Must bear the longest part.
   Let all the world in every corner sing,
      My God and King!

GEORGE HERBERT 1593–1632

General

237 MONKLAND   77 77   JOHN ANTES 1740–1811
arranged JOHN BERNARD WILKES 1785–1869

1. Let us, with a gladsome mind,
   Praise the Lord, for he is kind:
   For his mercies ay endure,
   Ever faithful, ever sure.

2. Let us blaze his name abroad,
   For of gods he is the God:

3. He with all-commanding might
   Filled the new-made world with light:

4. He the golden-tressèd sun
   Caused all day his course to run:

5. And the hornèd moon by night,
   'Mid her spangled sisters bright:

6. All things living he doth feed,
   His full hand supplies their need:

7. Let us, with a gladsome mind,
   Praise the Lord, for he is kind:
   For his mercies ay endure,
   Ever faithful, ever sure.

based on *Psalm 136*
JOHN MILTON 1608–74 *

General

238 PROVIDENCE   84 84   RICHARD RUNCIMAN TERRY 1865–1938

1. Lord, for tomorrow and its needs
   I do not pray;
   Keep me, my God, from stain of sin,
   Just for today.

2. Let me both diligently work
   And duly pray;
   Let me be kind in word and deed,
   Just for today.

3. Let me be slow to do my will,
   Prompt to obey;
   Help me to mortify my flesh,
   Just for today.

4. Let me no wrong or idle word
   Unthinking say;
   Set thou a seal upon my lips,
   Just for today.

5. And if today my tide of life
   Should ebb away,
   Give me thy sacraments divine,
   Sweet Lord, today.

6. So, for tomorrow and its needs
   I do not pray;
   But keep me, guide me, love me, Lord,
   Just for today.

SISTER MARY XAVIER

General

239 SLANE 10 11 11 12 traditional Irish

1. Lord of all hopefulness, Lord of all joy,
   Whose trust, ever child-like, no cares could destroy,
   Be there at our waking, and give us, we pray,
   Your bliss in our hearts, Lord, at the break of the day.

2. Lord of all eagerness, Lord of all faith,
   Whose strong hands were skilled at the plane and the lathe,
   Be there at our labours, and give us, we pray,
   Your strength in our hearts, Lord, at the noon of the day.

3. Lord of all kindliness, Lord of all grace,
   Your hands swift to welcome, your arms to embrace,
   Be there at our homing, and give us, we pray,
   Your love in our hearts, Lord, at the eve of the day.

4. Lord of all gentleness, Lord of all calm,
   Whose voice is contentment, whose presence is balm,
   Be there at our sleeping, and give us, we pray,
   Your peace in our hearts, Lord, at the end of the day.

JAN STRUTHER 1901–53

General

240 ISTE CONFESSOR   11 11 11 5   Poitiers *Vesperale* 1746

1. Lord of our life, and God of our salvation,
   Star of our night, and hope of every nation,
   Hear and receive thy Church's supplication,
   Lord God Almighty.

2. Lord, thou canst help when earthly armour faileth,
   Lord, thou canst save when deadly sin assaileth;
   Christ, o'er thy rock nor death nor hell prevaileth;
   Grant us thy peace, Lord.

3. Peace in our hearts, our evil thoughts assuaging;
   Peace in thy Church, where brothers are engaging;
   Peace, when the world its busy war is waging:
   Calm thy foes' raging.

4. Grant us thy help till backward they are driven,
   Grant them thy truth, that they may be forgiven;
   Grant peace on earth, and, after we have striven,
   Peace in thy heaven.

Christe du Beistand
MATTHAÜS VON LÖWENSTERN 1594–1648
freely adapted PHILIP PUSEY 1799–1855

General

241 RAVENSHAW (Ave Hierarchia) 66 66 medieval German
adapted WILLIAM HENRY MONK 1823–89

1 Lord, thy word abideth,
And our footsteps guideth;
Who its truth believeth,
Light and joy receiveth.

2 When our foes are near us,
Then thy word doth cheer us,
Word of consolation,
Message of salvation.

3 When the storms are o'er us,
And dark clouds before us,
Then its light directeth,
And our way protecteth.

4 Who can tell the pleasure,
Who recount the treasure
By thy word imparted
To the simple-hearted?

5 Word of mercy, giving
Succour to the living;
Word of life, supplying
Comfort to the dying.

6 O that we discerning
Its most holy learning,
Lord, may love and fear thee,
Evermore be near thee!

HENRY WILLIAMS BAKER 1821–77

General

242 LOVE DIVINE 87 87 JOHN STAINER 1840–1901

An alternative tune will be found at Hymn 150.

1 Love divine, all loves excelling,
    Joy of heaven, to earth come down,
  Fix in us thy humble dwelling,
    All thy faithful mercies crown.

2 Jesu, thou art all compassion,
    Pure unbounded love thou art;
  Visit us with thy salvation,
    Enter every trembling heart.

3 Come, Almighty to deliver,
    Let us all thy life receive;
  Suddenly return, and never,
    Never more thy temples leave.

4 Thee we would be always blessing,
    Serve thee as thy hosts above,
  Pray, and praise thee, without ceasing,
    Glory in thy perfect love.

5 Finish then thy new creation,
    Pure and spotless let us be;
  Let us see thy great salvation,
    Perfectly restored in thee.

6 Changed from glory into glory,
    Till in heaven we take our place,
  Till we cast our crowns before thee,
    Lost in wonder, love and praise!

CHARLES WESLEY 1707–88

General

243 BUNESSAN　　55 54　　　　　　　　　　　　　Gaelic folk tune

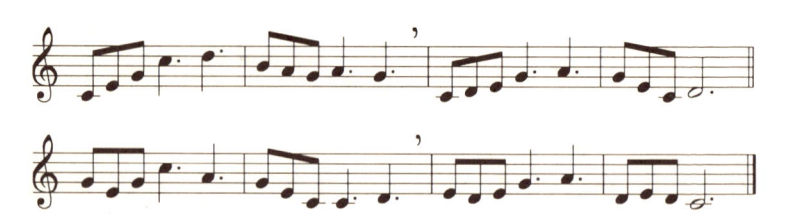

1. Morning has broken
   Like the first morning,
   Blackbird has spoken
   Like the first bird.
   Praise for the singing,
   Praise for the morning,
   Praise for them springing
   Fresh from the Word.

2. Sweet the rain's new fall
   Sunlit from heaven,
   Like the first dewfall
   On the first grass.
   Praise for the sweetness
   Of the wet garden,
   Sprung in completeness
   Where his feet pass.

3. Mine is the sunlight,
   Mine is the morning
   Born of the one light
   Eden saw play.
   Praise with elation,
   Praise every morning,
   God's re-creation
   Of the new day.

ELEANOR FARJEON 1881–1965

General

244 BELMONT CM William Gardiner's *Sacred melodies* 1812
adapted *Islington Psalmody* 1854

1. My God, accept my heart this day,
   And make it wholly thine,
   That I from thee no more may stray,
   No more from thee decline.

2. Before the Cross of him who died,
   Behold, I prostrate fall;
   Let every sin be crucified,
   And Christ be all in all.

3. Anoint me with thy heavenly grace,
   And seal me for thine own;
   That I may see thy glorious face,
   And worship at thy throne.

4. Let every thought and work and word
   To thee be ever given;
   Then life shall be thy service, Lord,
   And death the gate of heaven.

5. All glory to the Father be,
   All glory to the Son,
   All glory, Holy Ghost, to thee,
   While endless ages run.

MATTHEW BRIDGES 1800–94

General

245 WESTMINSTER CM JAMES TURLE 1802–82

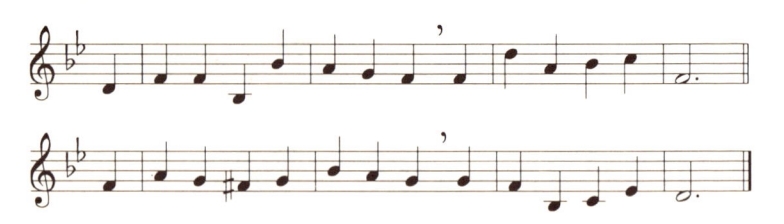

1. My God! how wonderful thou art,
   Thy majesty how bright,
   How beautiful thy mercy-seat
   In depths of burning light!

2. How dread are thine eternal years,
   O everlasting Lord!
   By prostrate spirits day and night
   Incessantly adored!

3. O how I fear thee, living God!
   With deepest, tenderest fears,
   And worship thee with trembling hope
   And penitential tears.

4. Yet I may love thee, living God!
   Almighty as thou art,
   For thou hast stooped to ask of me
   The love of my poor heart.

5. No earthly father loves like thee,
   No mother half so mild
   Bears and forbears, as thou hast done,
   With me, thy sinful child.

6. Father of Jesus, love's reward,
   What rapture will it be,
   Prostrate before thy throne to lie,
   And gaze, and gaze on thee!

FREDERICK WILLIAM FABER Cong. Orat. 1814–63

General

246 NUN DANKET
67 67 66 66

Johann Crüger's *Praxis Pietatis Melica* 1647
arranged FELIX MENDELSSOHN 1809–47
and WILLIAM HENRY MONK 1823–89

1. Now thank we all our God,
With hearts and hands and voices,
Who wondrous things hath done,
In whom his world rejoices;
Who from our mother's arms
Hath blessed us on our way
With countless gifts of love,
And still is ours today.

2. O may this bounteous God
Through all our life be near us,
With ever joyful hearts
And blessèd peace to cheer us;
And keep us in his grace,
And guide us when perplexed,
And free us from all ills
In this world and the next.

3. All praise and thanks to God
The Father now be given,
The Son, and him who reigns
With them in highest heaven,
The one eternal God,
Whom earth and heaven adore;
For thus it was, is now,
And shall be evermore.

based on *Ecclesiasticus 50: 22–3*
Nun danket alle Gott MARTIN RINKART 1586–1649
tr. CATHERINE WINKWORTH 1827–78

General

247

FIRST TUNE

CAITHNESS CM   Scottish *Psalter* 1635

SECOND TUNE

SAN ROCCO CM   Derek Williams born 1945

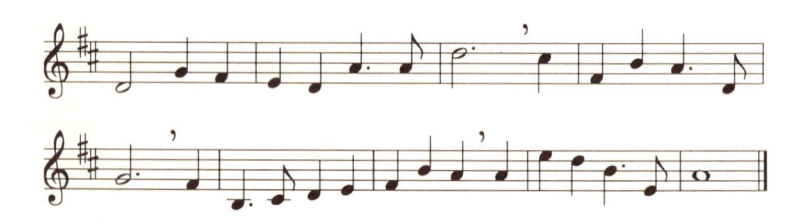

General

1. O for a closer walk with God,
   A calm and heavenly frame,
   A light to shine upon the road
   That leads me to the Lamb!

2. Where is the blessedness I knew
   When first I saw the Lord?
   Where is the soul-refreshing view
   Of Jesus and his word?

3. Return, O holy Dove, return,
   Sweet messenger of rest;
   I hate the sins that made thee mourn
   And drove thee from my breast.

4. The dearest idol I have known,
   Whate'er that idol be,
   Help me to tear it from thy throne,
   And worship only thee.

5. So shall my walk be close with God,
   Calm and serene my frame:
   So purer light shall mark the road
   That leads me to the Lamb.

WILLIAM COWPER 1731–1800

General

248 KING'S LYNN 76 76 D English folk tune
adapted RALPH VAUGHAN WILLIAMS 1892–1958

This hymn was originally written for the tune at Hymn 187.

1. O God of earth and altar,
   Bow down and hear our cry,
   Our earthly rulers falter,
   Our people drift and die;
   The walls of gold entomb us,
   The swords of scorn divide,
   Take not thy thunder from us,
   But take away our pride.

2. From all that terror teaches,
   From lies of tongue and pen,
   From all the easy speeches
   That comfort cruel men,
   From sale and profanation
   Of honour and the sword,
   From sleep and from damnation,
   Deliver us, good Lord!

3. Tie in a living tether
   The prince and priest and thrall,
   Bind all our lives together,
   Smite us and save us all;
   In ire and exultation
   Aflame with faith, and free,
   Lift up a living nation,
   A single sword to thee.

GILBERT KEITH CHESTERTON 1874–1936

General

249 ST ANNE   CM   *A Supplement to the New Version* 1708
attributed WILLIAM CROFT 1678–1727

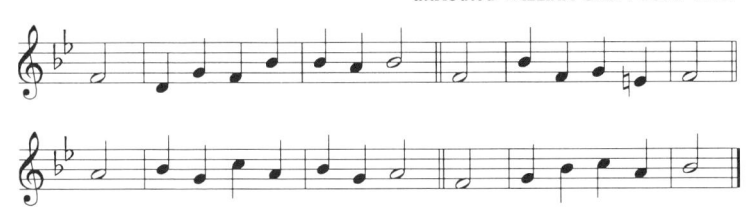

1. O God, our help in ages past,
    Our hope for years to come,
   Our shelter from the stormy blast,
    And our eternal home;

2. Under the shadow of thy throne
    Thy saints have dwelt secure;
   Sufficient is thine arm alone,
    And our defence is sure.

3. Before the hills in order stood,
    Or earth received her frame,
   From everlasting thou art God,
    To endless years the same.

4. A thousand ages in thy sight
    Are like an evening gone,
   Short as the watch that ends the night
    Before the rising sun.

5. Time, like an ever-rolling stream,
    Bears all its sons away;
   They fly forgotten, as a dream
    Dies at the opening day.

6. O God, our help in ages past,
    Our hope for years to come,
   Be thou our guard while troubles last,
    And our eternal home.

based on *Psalm 90*
ISAAC WATTS 1674–1748

General

250 WOLVERCOTE 76 76 D William Harold Ferguson 1874–1950

1. O Jesus, I have promised
   To serve thee to the end;
   Be thou for ever near me,
   My Master and my Friend;
   I shall not fear the battle
   If thou art by my side,
   Nor wander from the pathway
   If thou wilt be my guide.

2. O let me hear thee speaking
   In accents clear and still,
   Above the storms of passion,
   The murmurs of self-will;
   O speak to reassure me,
   To hasten or control;
   O speak, and make me listen,
   Thou guardian of my soul.

3. O Jesus, thou hast promised
   To all who follow thee,
   That where thou art in glory
   There shall thy servant be;
   And, Jesus, I have promised
   To serve thee to the end;
   O give me grace to follow,
   My Master and my Friend.

4. O let me see thy footmarks,
   And in them plant mine own;
   My hope to follow duly
   Is in thy strength alone;
   O guide me, call me, draw me,
   Uphold me to the end;
   And then in heaven receive me,
   My Saviour and my Friend.

John Bode 1816–74

General

251 ELTHAM LM Nathaniel Gawthorne's *Harmonia Perfecta* 1730

An alternative tune will be found at Hymn 161.

1. O love, how deep, how broad, how high!
   How passing thought and fantasy
   That God, the Son of God, should take
   Our mortal form for mortals' sake.

2. He sent no angel to our race
   Of higher or of lower place,
   But wore the robe of human frame,
   And he himself to this world came.

3. For us baptised, for us he bore
   His holy fast, and hungered sore;
   For us temptations sharp he knew;
   For us the tempter overthrew.

4. For us to wicked men betrayed,
   Scourged, mocked, in crown of thorns arrayed;
   For us he bore the Cross's death;
   For us at length gave up his breath.

5. For us he rose from death again,
   For us he went on high to reign,
   For us he sent his Spirit here
   To guide, to strengthen, and to cheer.

O Amor quam ecstaticus
attributed St Thomas à Kempis 1379–1471
tr. Benjamin Webb 1819–85

General

252

FIRST TUNE

HIGHWOOD   11 10 11 10   RICHARD RUNCIMAN TERRY 1865–1938

SECOND TUNE

STRENGTH AND STAY   11 10 11 10   JOHN BACCHUS DYKES 1823–76

General

1 O perfect Love, all human thought transcending,
   Lowly we kneel in prayer before thy throne,
  That theirs may be the love which knows no ending
   Whom thou for evermore dost join in one.

2 O perfect Life, be thou their full assurance
   Of tender charity and steadfast faith,
  Of patient hope, and quiet, brave endurance,
   With childlike trust that fears nor pain nor death.

3 Grant them the joy which brightens earthly sorrow,
   Grant them the peace which calms all earthly strife;
  And to life's day the glorious unknown morrow
   That dawns upon eternal love and life.

DOROTHY FRANCES GURNEY 1858–1932

General

253 LAUDATE DOMINUM   CHARLES HUBERT HASTINGS PARRY 1848–1918
10 10 11 11   from 'Hear my words, ye people'

1. O praise ye the Lord! praise him in the height;
   Rejoice in his word, ye angels of light;
   Ye heavens, adore him by whom ye were made,
   And worship before him, in brightness arrayed.

2. O praise ye the Lord! praise him upon earth,
   In tuneful accord, ye sons of new birth;
   Praise him who hath brought you his grace from above,
   Praise him who hath taught you to sing of his love.

3. O praise ye the Lord, all things that give sound!
   Each jubilant chord re-echo around;
   Loud organs, his glory forth tell in deep tone,
   And sweet harp, the story of what he hath done.

4. O praise ye the Lord! thanksgiving and song
   To him be outpoured all ages along:
   For love in creation, for heaven restored,
   For grace of salvation, O praise ye the Lord!

based on *Psalms 148* and *150*
HENRY WILLIAMS BAKER 1821–77

General

254 HEREFORD LM SAMUEL SEBASTIAN WESLEY 1810–76

1. O thou who camest from above,
   The pure celestial fire to impart,
   Kindle a flame of sacred love
   On the mean altar of my heart.

2. There let it for thy glory burn
   With inextinguishable blaze,
   And trembling to its source return
   In humble prayer, and fervent praise.

3. Jesus, confirm my heart's desire
   To work, and speak, and think for thee;
   Still let me guard the holy fire,
   And still stir up thy gift in me.

4. Ready for all thy perfect will,
   My acts of faith and love repeat,
   Till death thy endless mercies seal,
   And make my sacrifice complete.

CHARLES WESLEY 1707–88

General

255 HANOVER   10 10 11 11   *Supplement to the New Version* 1708
attributed William Croft 1678–1727

1. O worship the King, all-glorious above;
   O gratefully sing his power and his love:
   Our Shield and Defender, the Ancient of Days,
   Pavilioned in splendour, and girded with praise.

2. O tell of his might, O sing of his grace,
   Whose robe is the light, whose canopy space;
   His chariots of wrath the deep thunder-clouds form,
   And dark is his path on the wings of the storm.

3. This earth, with its store of wonders untold,
   Almighty, thy power hath founded of old;
   Hath stablished it fast by a changeless decree,
   And round it hath cast, like a mantle, the sea.

General

4 Thy bountiful care what tongue can recite?
   It breathes in the air, it shines in the light;
   It streams from the hills, it descends to the plain,
   And sweetly distils in the dew and the rain.

5 Frail children of dust, and feeble as frail,
   In thee do we trust, nor find thee to fail;
   Thy mercies how tender, how firm to the end,
   Our Maker, Defender, Redeemer, and Friend.

6 O measureless Might, ineffable Love,
   While angels delight to hymn thee above,
   Thy humbler creation, though feeble their lays,
   With true adoration shall sing to thy praise.

based on *Psalm 104*
ROBERT GRANT 1779–1838

General

256 ST GERTRUDE   65 65 + refrain   ARTHUR SULLIVAN 1842–1900

1   Onward, Christian soldiers,
      Marching as to war,
  With the Cross of Jesus
      Going on before.
  Christ the royal Master
      Leads against the foe;
  Forward into battle,
      See, his banners go!
      Onward, Christian soldiers,
          Marching as to war,
      With the Cross of Jesus
          Going on before.

General

2 At the sign of triumph
    Satan's legions flee;
On then, Christian soldiers,
    On to victory.
Hell's foundations quiver
    At the shout of praise;
Brothers, lift your voices,
    Loud your anthems raise.

3 Like a mighty army
    Moves the Church of God;
Brothers, we are treading
    Where the saints have trod;
We are not divided,
    All one body we,
One in hope and doctrine,
    One in charity.

4 Crowns and thrones may perish,
    Kingdoms rise and wane,
But the Church of Jesus
    Constant will remain;
Gates of hell can never
    'Gainst that Church prevail;
We have Christ's own promise,
    And that cannot fail.

5 Onward, then, ye people,
    Join our happy throng,
Blend with ours your voices
    In the triumph song;
Glory, laud, and honour
    Unto Christ the King;
This through countless ages
    Men and angels sing.

SABINE BARING-GOULD 1834–1924

General

257 SONG 46 (abridged)   10 10   ORLANDO GIBBONS 1583–1625

1 Peace, perfect peace, in this dark world of sin?
  The Blood of Jesus whispers peace within.

2 Peace, perfect peace, by thronging duties pressed?
  To do the will of Jesus, this is rest.

3 Peace, perfect peace, with sorrows surging round?
  In Jesus' arms will nought but calm be found.

4 Peace, perfect peace, with loved ones far away?
  In Jesus' keeping we are safe, and they.

5 Peace, perfect peace, our future all unknown?
  Jesus we know, and he is on the throne.

6 Peace, perfect peace, death shadowing us and ours?
  Jesus has vanquished death and all its powers.

7 It is enough: earth's struggles soon shall cease,
  And Jesus call us to heaven's perfect peace.

EDWARD HENRY BICKERSTETH 1825–1906 *

General

258 PRAISE, MY SOUL   87 87 87   JOHN GOSS 1800-80

1. Praise, my soul, the King of heaven;
   To his feet thy tribute bring.
   Ransomed, healed, restored, forgiven,
   Who like me his praise should sing?
   Praise him! Praise him!
   Praise him! Praise him!
   Praise the everlasting King!

2. Praise him for his grace and favour
   To our fathers in distress;
   Praise him still the same for ever,
   Slow to chide, and swift to bless.
   Praise him! Praise him!
   Praise him! Praise him!
   Glorious in his faithfulness.

3. Father-like he tends and spares us;
   Well our feeble frame he knows;
   In his hands he gently bears us,
   Rescues us from all our foes.
   Praise him! Praise him!
   Praise him! Praise him!
   Widely as his mercy flows.

4. Angels, help us to adore him;
   Ye behold him face to face;
   Sun and moon bow down before him,
   Dwellers all in time and space.
   Praise him! Praise him!
   Praise him! Praise him!
   Praise with us the God of grace!

based on *Psalm 103*
HENRY FRANCIS LYTE 1793–1847

General

259 AUSTRIA   87 87 D   Franz Joseph Haydn 1732–1809

1. Praise the Lord! ye heavens, adore him;
   Praise him, angels, in the height;
   Sun and moon, rejoice before him,
   Praise him, all ye stars and light:
   Praise the Lord! for he has spoken,
   Worlds his mighty voice obeyed;
   Laws, which never shall be broken,
   For their guidance he has made.

2. Praise the Lord! for he is glorious;
   Never shall his promise fail;
   God has made his saints victorious.
   Sin and death shall not prevail.
   Praise the God of our salvation;
   Hosts on high, his power proclaim;
   Heaven and earth, and all creation,
   Laud and magnify his name!

General

3 Worship, honour, glory, blessing,
   Lord, we offer to thy name;
Young and old, thy praise expressing,
   Join their Saviour to proclaim.
As the saints in heaven adore thee,
   We would bow before thy throne;
As thine angels serve before thee,
   So on earth thy will be done.

> based on *Psalm 148*
> Verses 1, 2 *Foundling Hospital Collection* 1796
> Verse 3 EDWARD OSLER 1798–1863

General

260

FIRST TUNE

BILLING   CM   Richard Runciman Terry 1865–1938

1. Praise to the Holiest in the height,
   And in the depth be praise;
   In all his words most wonderful,
   Most sure in all his ways.

2. O loving wisdom of our God!
   When all was sin and shame,
   A second Adam to the fight
   And to the rescue came.

3. O wisest love! that flesh and blood,
   Which did in Adam fail,
   Should strive afresh against the foe,
   Should strive and should prevail.

4. And that a higher gift than grace
   Should flesh and blood refine,
   God's presence and his very self,
   And essence all-divine.

General

SECOND TUNE

CHORUS ANGELORUM   CM   ARTHUR SOMERVELL 1863–1937

A further alternative tune will be found at Hymn 232 (second tune).

5 O generous love! that he, who smote
     In man for man the foe,
   The double agony in man
     For man should undergo;

6 And in the garden secretly,
     And on the Cross on high,
   Should teach his brethren, and inspire
     To suffer and to die.

7 Praise to the Holiest in the height,
     And in the depth be praise;
   In all his words most wonderful,
     Most sure in all his ways.

from *The Dream of Gerontius*
The Venerable JOHN HENRY NEWMAN Cong. Orat. 1801–90

General

261 GOPSAL 66 66 88   GEORGE FREDERICK HANDEL 1685–1759

1. Rejoice, the Lord is King!
    Your Lord and King adore;
   Mortals, give thanks and sing,
    And triumph evermore:
     Lift up your heart, lift up your voice;
     Rejoice, again I say, rejoice.

2. Jesus, the Saviour, reigns,
    The God of truth and love;
   When he had purged our stains,
    He took his seat above:

3. His kingdom cannot fail,
    He rules o'er earth and heaven;
   The keys of death and hell
    Are to our Jesus given:

4. He sits at God's right hand
    Till all his foes submit,
   And bow to his command,
    And fall beneath his feet:

5. Rejoice in glorious hope;
    Jesus the Judge shall come,
   And take his servants up
    To their eternal home:
     We then shall hear th' archangel's voice,
     The trump of God shall sound, Rejoice!

CHARLES WESLEY 1707–88

General

262 EIN' FESTE BURG 87 87 66 677 MARTIN LUTHER 1483–1546
arranged JOHANN SEBASTIAN BACH 1685–1750

1. Rejoice today with one accord,
   Sing out with exultation;
   Rejoice and praise our mighty Lord,
   Whose arm hath brought salvation.
   His works of love proclaim
   The greatness of his name;
   For he is God alone,
   Who hath his mercy shown:
   Let all his saints adore him!

2. When in distress to him we cried,
   He heard our sad complaining;
   O trust in him, whate'er betide,
   His love is all-sustaining.
   Triumphant songs of praise
   To him our hearts shall raise;
   Now every voice shall say,
   O praise our God alway:
   Let all his saints adore him!

HENRY WILLIAMS BAKER 1821–77

General

263 SAVANNAH (Herrnhut) 77 77 Herrnhut *Choralbuch* c. 1740
in John Wesley's *Foundery Collection* 1742

1. Take my life, and let it be
   Consecrated, Lord, to thee;
   Take my moments and my days,
   Let them flow in ceaseless praise.

2. Take my hands, and let them move
   At the impulse of thy love.
   Take my feet, and let them be
   Swift and purposeful for thee.

3. Take my voice, and let me sing
   Always, only, for my King.
   Take my intellect, and use
   Every power as thou shalt choose.

4. Take my will, and make it thine:
   It shall be no longer mine.
   Take my heart; it is thine own:
   It shall be thy royal throne.

5. Take my love; my Lord, I pour
   At thy feet its treasure-store.
   Take myself, and I will be
   Ever, only, all for thee.

FRANCES RIDLEY HAVERGAL 1836–79

General

264 WOODLANDS 10 10 10 10 WALTER GREATOREX 1877–1949

1. Tell out, my soul, the greatness of the Lord:
   Unnumbered blessings, give my spirit voice;
   Tender to me the promise of his word;
   In God my Saviour shall my heart rejoice.

2. Tell out, my soul, the greatness of his name:
   Make known his might, the deeds his arm has done;
   His mercy sure, from age to age the same;
   His holy name, the Lord, the Mighty One.

3. Tell out, my soul, the greatness of his might:
   Powers and dominions lay their glory by;
   Proud hearts and stubborn wills are put to flight,
   The hungry fed, the humble lifted high.

4. Tell out, my soul, the glories of his word:
   Firm is his promise, and his mercy sure.
   Tell out, my soul, the greatness of the Lord
   To children's children and for evermore.

based on the *Magnificat*
TIMOTHY DUDLEY-SMITH born 1926

General

265

FIRST TUNE

ST COLUMBA   87 87   traditional Irish

SECOND TUNE

DOMINUS REGIT ME   87 87   JOHN BACCHUS DYKES 1823–76

General

1. The King of love my shepherd is,
   Whose goodness faileth never;
   I nothing lack if I am his
   And he is mine for ever.

2. Where streams of living water flow
   My ransomed soul he leadeth,
   And where the verdant pastures grow
   With food celestial feedeth.

3. Perverse and foolish oft I strayed,
   But yet in love he sought me,
   And on his shoulder gently laid,
   And home, rejoicing, brought me.

4. In death's dark vale I fear no ill
   With thee, dear Lord, beside me;
   Thy rod and staff my comfort still,
   Thy Cross before to guide me.

5. Thou spread'st a table in my sight;
   Thy unction, grace bestoweth:
   And O what transport of delight
   From thy pure chalice floweth!

6. And so through all the length of days
   Thy goodness faileth never;
   Good Shepherd, may I sing thy praise
   Within thy house for ever.

based on *Psalm 23*
HENRY WILLIAMS BAKER 1821–77

General

266

FIRST TUNE

CRIMOND   CM   Jessie Irvine 1836–87

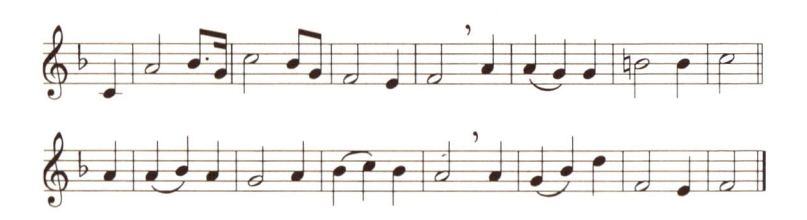

SECOND TUNE

WILTSHIRE   CM   George Smart 1776–1867

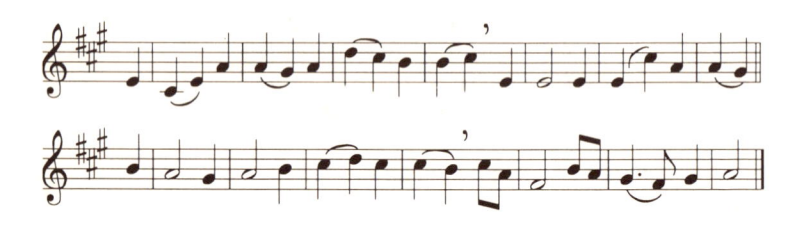

General

1. The Lord's my shepherd, I'll not want.
   He makes me down to lie
   In pastures green; he leadeth me
   The quiet waters by.

2. My soul he doth restore again,
   And me to walk doth make
   Within the paths of righteousness,
   E'en for his own name's sake.

3. Yea, though I walk in death's dark vale,
   Yet will I fear none ill;
   For thou art with me, and thy rod
   And staff me comfort still.

4. My table thou hast furnishèd
   In presence of my foes;
   My head thou dost with oil anoint,
   And my cup overflows.

5. Goodness and mercy all my life
   Shall surely follow me;
   And in God's house for evermore
   My dwelling-place shall be.

based on *Psalm 23*
Scottish *Psalter* 1650

General

267 ADDISON'S (London)   DLM   JOHN SHEELES 1688–1761

1   The spacious firmament on high,
       With all the blue, ethereal sky,
       And spangled heav'ns, a shining frame,
       Their great Original proclaim.
       Th'unwearied sun, from day to day,
       Does his Creator's power display,
       And publishes to every land
       The work of an almighty hand.

General

2 Soon as the evening shades prevail,
　The moon takes up the wondrous tale,
　And nightly to the listening earth
　Repeats the story of her birth;
　Whilst all the stars that round her burn,
　And all the planets in their turn,
　Confirm the tidings as they roll,
　And spread the truth from pole to pole.

3 What though, in solemn silence, all
　Move round the dark terrestrial ball?
　What though nor real voice nor sound
　Amid their radiant orbs be found?
　In reason's ear they all rejoice,
　And utter forth a glorious voice,
　For ever singing, as they shine,
　'The hand that made us is divine'.

based on *Psalm 19*
JOSEPH ADDISON 1672–1719

General

268 ALL FOR JESUS   87 87   JOHN STAINER 1840–1901

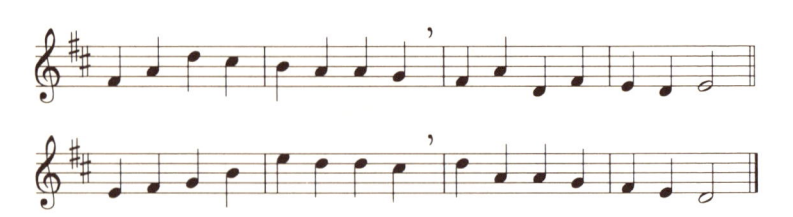

An alternative tune will be found at Hymn 1.

1. There's a wideness in God's mercy
   Like the wideness of the sea;
   There's a kindness in his justice
   Which is more than liberty.

2. There is no place where earth's sorrows
   Are more felt than up in heaven;
   There is no place where earth's failings
   Have such kindly judgement given.

3. For the love of God is broader
   Than the measure of man's mind;
   And the heart of the Eternal
   Is most wonderfully kind.

General

4 There is welcome for the sinner,
   And more graces for the good;
  There is mercy with the Saviour;
   There is healing in his Blood.

5 There is plentiful redemption
   In the Blood that has been shed;
  There is joy for all the members
   In the sorrows of the Head.

6 If our love were but more simple,
   We should take him at his word;
  And our lives would be all gladness
   In the joy of Christ our Lord.

            FREDERICK WILLIAM FABER Cong. Orat. 1814–63

General

269 MOSCOW   664 66 64   FELICE GIARDINI 1717–96
                                                                                later form of last three bars

1 Thou, whose eternal word
   Chaos and darkness heard,
      And took their flight,
   Hear us, we humbly pray,
   And, where the gospel-day
   Sheds not its glorious ray,
      Let there be light!

2 Thou, who didst come to bring
   On thy redeeming wing
      Healing and sight,
   Health to the sick in mind,
   Sight to the inly blind,
   O now, to all mankind,
      Let there be light!

General

3 Spirit of truth and love,
　Life-giving, holy Dove,
　　　Speed forth thy flight;
　Move o'er the waters' face,
　Bearing the lamp of grace,
　And, in earth's darkest place,
　　　Let there be light!

4 Blessèd and holy Three,
　Glorious Trinity,
　　　Wisdom, Love, Might;
　Boundless as ocean's tide
　Rolling in fullest pride,
　Through the world, far and wide,
　　　Let there be light!

　　　　　　　　　　JOHN MARRIOTT 1780–1825

General

270 ORIEL 87 87 87 Caspar Ett's *Cantica Sacra* 1840

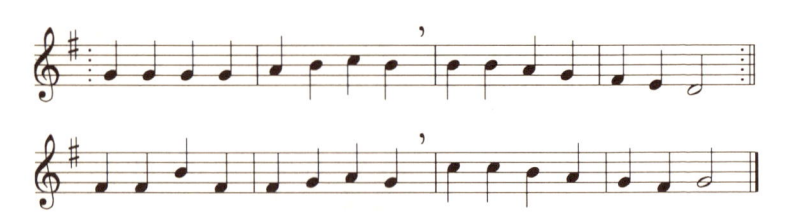

1. To the name that brings salvation
   Honour, worship, laud we pay:
   That for many a generation
   Hid in God's foreknowledge lay;
   But to every tongue and nation
   Holy Church proclaims today.

2. 'Tis the name of adoration,
   'Tis the name of victory;
   'Tis the name for meditation
   In the vale of misery;
   'Tis the name for veneration
   By the citizens on high.

3. 'Tis the name by right exalted
   Over every other name:
   That when we are sore assaulted
   Puts our enemies to shame:
   Strength to them that else had halted,
   Eyes to blind, and feet to lame.

4. Jesu, we thy name adoring,
   Long to see thee as thou art:
   Of thy clemency imploring
   So to write it in our heart,
   That hereafter, upward soaring,
   We with angels may have part.

Gloriosi Salvatoris c. 15th century
tr. JOHN MASON NEALE 1818–66

General

271 BOW BRICKHILL   LM   SYDNEY NICHOLSON 1875–1947

An alternative tune will be found at Hymn 102.

1 We sing the praise of him who died,
   Of him who died upon the Cross;
The sinner's hope let men deride,
   For this we count the world but loss.

2 Inscribed upon the Cross we see
   In shining letters, 'God is love.'
He bears our sins upon the Tree,
   He brings us mercy from above.

3 The Cross! it takes our guilt away,
   It holds the fainting spirit up;
It cheers with hope the gloomy day,
   And sweetens every bitter cup.

4 It makes the coward spirit brave,
   And nerves the feeble arm for fight;
It takes the terror from the grave,
   And gilds the bed of death with light.

5 The balm of life, the cure of woe,
   The measure and the pledge of love;
The sinner's refuge here below,
   The angels' theme in heaven above.

THOMAS KELLY 1769–1855

General

272 LAUDES DOMINI   666 D   Joseph Barnby 1838–96

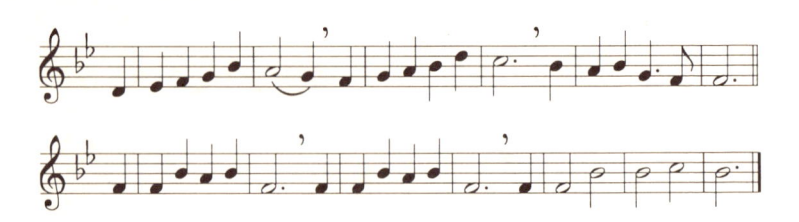

1. When morning gilds the skies,
   My heart awaking cries,
       May Jesus Christ be praised:
   Alike at work and prayer
   To Jesus I repair;
       May Jesus Christ be praised.

2. The night becomes as day,
   When from the heart we say,
       May Jesus Christ be praised:
   The powers of darkness fear,
   When this sweet chant they hear,
       May Jesus Christ be praised.

3. In heaven's eternal bliss
   The loveliest strain is this,
       May Jesus Christ be praised:
   Let air, and sea, and sky
   From depth to height reply,
       May Jesus Christ be praised.

4. Be this, while life is mine,
   My canticle divine,
       May Jesus Christ be praised:
   Be this the eternal song
   Through all the ages on,
       May Jesus Christ be praised.

Beim frühen Morgenlicht
Anonymous Würzburg 1828
tr. Edward Caswall Cong. Orat. 1814–78

General

273 MONKS GATE   65 65 66 66   English folk tune 'Our Captain Calls'
adapted RALPH VAUGHAN WILLIAMS 1872–1958

1. Who would true valour see,
   Let him come hither;
   One here will constant be,
   Come wind, come weather;
   There's no discouragement
   Shall make him once relent
   His first avowed intent
      To be a pilgrim.

2. Who so beset him round
   With dismal stories
   Do but themselves confound;
   His strength the more is.
   No lion can him fright;
   He'll with a giant fight;
   But he will have a right
      To be a pilgrim.

3. Hobgoblin nor foul fiend
   Can daunt his spirit;
   He knows he at the end
   Shall life inherit.
   Then fancies fly away,
   He'll fear not what men say;
   He'll labour night and day
      To be a pilgrim.

from *Pilgrim's Progress*
JOHN BUNYAN 1628–88

General

274   DARWALL'S 148th   66 66 44 44   JOHN DARWALL 1731–89

1. Ye holy angels bright,
   Who wait at God's right hand,
   Or through the realms of light
   Fly at your Lord's command,
   Assist our song,
   For else the theme
   Too high doth seem
   For mortal tongue.

2. Ye blessèd souls at rest,
   Who ran this earthly race,
   And now, from sin released,
   Behold the Saviour's face,
   God's praises sound,
   As in his sight
   With sweet delight
   Ye do abound.

General

3 Ye saints, who toil below,
   Adore your heavenly King,
And onward as ye go
   Some joyful anthem sing;
     Take what he gives
       And praise him still,
       Through good or ill,
     Who ever lives!

4 My soul, bear thou thy part,
   Triumph in God above:
And with a well-tuned heart
   Sing thou the songs of love!
     Let all thy days
       Till life shall end,
       Whate'er he send,
     Be filled with praise.

                     JOHN HAMPDEN GURNEY 1802–62
                        after RICHARD BAXTER 1615–91

General

275 LASST UNS ERFREUEN   *Geistliche Kirchengesäng* Cologne 1623
88 44 88 + alleluias   arranged RALPH VAUGHAN WILLIAMS 1872–1958

1. Ye watchers and ye holy ones,
   Bright seraphs, cherubim and thrones,
     Raise the glad strain, Alleluia!
   Cry out dominions, princedoms, powers,
   Virtues, archangels, angels' choirs,
     Alleluia, Alleluia, Alleluia, Alleluia,
       Alleluia!

2. O higher than the cherubim,
   More glorious than the seraphim,
     Lead their praises, Alleluia!
   Thou Bearer of the eternal Word,
   Most gracious, magnify the Lord,
     Alleluia, Alleluia, Alleluia, Alleluia,
       Alleluia!

General

3 Respond, ye souls in endless rest,
  Ye patriarchs and prophets blest,
    Alleluia, Alleluia!
  Ye holy twelve, ye martyrs strong,
  All saints triumphant, raise the song,
    Alleluia, Alleluia, Alleluia, Alleluia,
      Alleluia!

4 O friends, in gladness let us sing,
  Supernal anthems echoing,
    Alleluia, Alleluia!
  To God the Father, God the Son,
  And God the Spirit, Three in One,
    Alleluia, Alleluia, Alleluia, Alleluia,
      Alleluia!

ATHELSTAN RILEY 1858–1945

Benediction

276 MELCOMBE   LM   SAMUEL WEBBE the elder 1740–1816

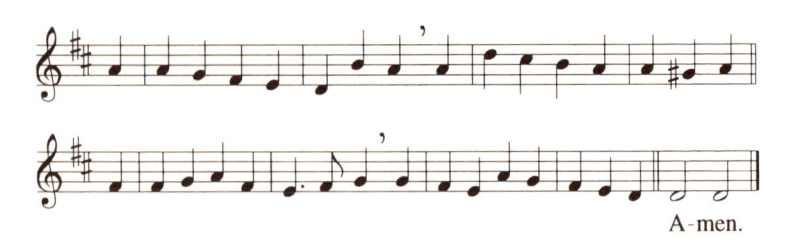

A-men.

1 O salutáris Hóstia,
    Quae caeli pandis óstium,
    Bella premunt hostília,
    Da robur, fer auxílium.

2 Uni trinóque Dómino
    Sit sempitérna glória,
    Qui vitam sine término
    Nobis donet in pátria.   Amen.

ST THOMAS AQUINAS 1227–74

Benediction

277

Translation suitable for singing

1 O saving Victim, opening wide
   The gate of heav'n to man below;
  Our foes press hard on every side;
   Thine aid supply, thy strength bestow.

2 All praise and thanks to thee ascend
   For evermore, blest One in Three;
  O grant us life that shall not end,
   In our true native land with thee. Amen.

Verbum supernum prodiens
ST THOMAS AQUINAS 1227–74
tr. JOHN MASON NEALE 1818–66 and others

Benediction

278 ST THOMAS   87 87 87   John Francis Wade's MS book c. 1740

A - men.

1. Tantum ergo Sacraméntum
   Venerémur cérnui:
   Et antíquum documéntum
   Novo cedat rítui;
   Praestet fides suppleméntum
   Sénsuum deféctui.

2. Genitóri, Genitóque
   Laus et jubilátio,
   Salus, honor, virtus quoque
   Sit et benedíctio;
   Procedénti ab utróque
   Compar sit laudátio.   Amen.

St Thomas Aquinas 1227–74

V. Panem de caelo praestitísti eis. [Allelúia.]
R. Omne delectaméntum in se habéntem. [Allelúia.]

Benediction

279

Translation suitable for singing

1. Therefore we, before him bending,
   This great Sacrament revere;
   Types and shadows have their ending,
   For the newer rite is here;
   Faith, our outward sense befriending,
   Makes the inward vision clear.

2. Glory let us give, and blessing
   To the Father and the Son;
   Honour, might, and praise addressing,
   While eternal ages run;
   Ever too his love confessing,
   Who from both, with both is one. Amen.

V. Thou didst give them bread from heaven. [Alleluia.]
R. Containing in itself all sweetness. [Alleluia.]

Pange lingua gloriosi corporis mysterium
ST THOMAS AQUINAS 1227–74
tr. JOHN MASON NEALE 1818–66 and others

Benediction

280 ADOREMUS Tone VI

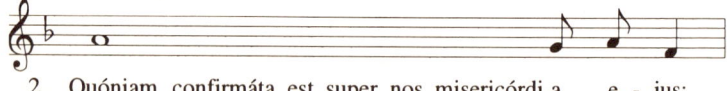

Antiphon

A - do - ré - mus in ae - tér - num San - ctís - si - mum Sa - cra - mén - tum.

Psalm 117

1. Laudáte Dóminum omnes gentes: laudáte eum omnes pópuli.

2. Quóniam confirmáta est super nos misericórdi-a e - jus: et véritas Dómini manet in ae - tér - num.

3. Glória Patri et Fí - li - o; et Spirí - tu - i Sancto.

Benediction

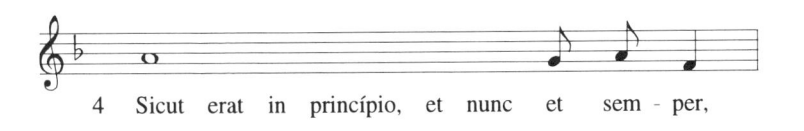

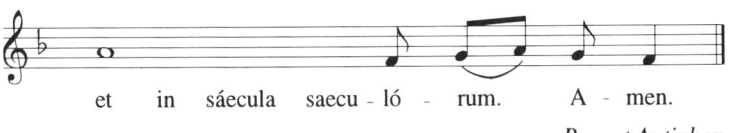

4 Sicut erat in princípio, et nunc et sem-per,
et in sáecula saecu-ló-rum. A-men.

Repeat Antiphon

from Easter to Pentecost this Antiphon is used:

Al-le-lú-ia, al-le-lú-ia, al-le-lú-ia.

Translation

Let us adore for evermore the most Holy Sacrament.

Praise the Lord, all ye nations: praise him, all ye people.
Because his mercy is confirmed upon us; and the truth of the
 Lord remaineth for ever.
Glory be to the Father, and to the Son, and to the Holy Ghost.
As it was in the beginning, is now, and ever shall be,
 world without end. Amen.

Let us adore for ever the most Holy Sacrament.

Antiphons of the Blessed Virgin Mary

281 ALMA REDEMPTORIS MATER — Mode V

From Advent to the Presentation (2nd February)

Alma* Redemptóris Mater,

quae pérvia caeli porta manes, Et stella maris,

succúrre cadénti súrgere qui curat pópulo:

Tu quae genuísti, natúra miránte,

tuum sanctum Genitórem: Virgo prius

ac postérius, Gabriélis ab ore

Antiphons of the Blessed Virgin Mary

su-mens il-lud A - ve, pec-ca-tó-rum mi-se-ré - re.

HERMANN THE LAME died 1054

In Advent

    V. Angelus Dómini nuntiávit Maríae.
    R. Et concépit de Spíritu Sancto.

From Christmas Day to the Presentation (2nd February)

    V. Post partum Virgo invioláta permansísti.
    R. Dei Génitrix intercéde pro nobis.

Translation

> Mother of Christ! hear thou thy people's cry,
> Star of the deep, and portal of the sky!
> Mother of him who thee from nothing made,
> Sinking we strive, and call to thee for aid:
> Oh, by that joy which Gabriel brought to thee,
> Thou Virgin first and last, let us thy mercy see.

In Advent

    V. The angel of the Lord declared unto Mary.
    R. And she conceived of the Holy Ghost.

From Christmas Day to the Presentation (2nd February)

    V. Thou, who after thy child-bearing didst remain a pure virgin.
    R. Mother of God, make intercession for us.

Antiphons of the Blessed Virgin Mary

282 AVE REGINA Mode VI

From the Presentation to Maundy Thursday

A - ve Re - gí - na cae - ló - rum, * A - ve
Dó - mi - na An - ge - ló - rum: Sal - ve ra - dix,
sal - ve por - ta, Ex qua mun - do lux est or - ta:
Gau - de Virgo glo - ri - ó - sa, Su - per om - nes
spe - ci - ó - sa: Va - le, o val - de de - có - ra,
Et pro no - bis Chri - stum ex - ó - ra.

12th century

Antiphons of the Blessed Virgin Mary

V. Dignáre me laudáre te Virgo sacráta.
R. Da mihi virtútem contra hostes tuos.

Translation

    Hail, O Queen of heav'n enthron'd!
    Hail, by angels mistress own'd,
    Root of Jesse! Gate of morn!
    Whence the world's true light was born:
    Glorious Virgin, joy to thee,
    Loveliest whom in heaven they see.
    Fairest thou where all are fair!
    Plead with Christ our sins to spare.

V. Reject not my praise, Virgin all holy.
R. Strengthen me to resist all thy enemies.

Antiphons of the Blessed Virgin Mary

283 REGINA CAELI   Mode VI

From Easter to Pentecost Sunday

Re - gí - na cae - li * lae - tá - re, al - le - lú - ia:

Qui - a quem me - ru - í - sti por - tá - re,

al - le - lú - ia: Re - sur - ré - xit, si - cut di - xit,

al - le - lú - ia: O - ra pro no - bis De - um,

al - le - lú - ia.

12th century

V. Gaude et laetáre Virgo María, allelúia.
R. Quia surréxit Dóminus vere, allelúia.

Antiphons of the Blessed Virgin Mary

Translation

    Queen of heaven, rejoice, alleluia:
    For he whom thou wast worthy to bear, alleluia:
    Is risen as he promised, alleluia:
    Pray for us to God, alleluia.

V.   Rejoice and be glad, O Virgin Mary; alleluia.
R.   For the Lord is risen indeed; alleluia.

Antiphons of the Blessed Virgin Mary

284 SALVE REGINA   Mode V

After Pentecost until Advent

Sal - ve, Re - gí - na, * ma - ter mi - se - ri - cór - di - ae:

Vi - ta, dul - cé - do, et spes nos - tra, sal - ve.

Ad te cla - má - mus, éx - su - les, fí - li - i He - vae.

Ad te sus - pi - rá - mus, ge - mén - tes et flen - tes

in hac la - cri - má - rum val - le. E - ia er - go,

Ad - vo - cá - ta nos - tra, il - los tu - os

Antiphons of the Blessed Virgin Mary

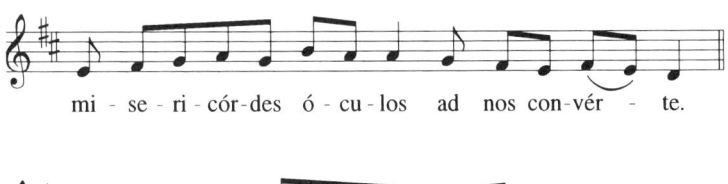

misericórdes óculos ad nos convérte.

Et Jesum, benedíctum fructum ventris tui,

nobis post hoc exsílium osténde.

O clemens, O pia, O

dulcis Virgo María.

HERMANN THE LAME died 1054

V. Ora pro nobis sancta Dei Génitrix.
R. Ut digni efficiámur promissiónibus Christi.

Antiphons of the Blessed Virgin Mary

Translation

Hail, holy Queen, Mother of mercy; hail, our life, our sweetness and our hope. To thee do we cry, poor banished children of Eve; to thee we send up our sighs, mourning and weeping in this vale of tears.

Turn, then, most gracious advocate, thine eyes of mercy towards us; and after this our exile, show unto us the blessed fruit of thy womb, Jesus. O clement, O loving, O sweet Virgin Mary.

V. Pray for us, O holy Mother of God.
R. That we may be made worthy of the promises of Christ.

Mass VIII (de Angelis)

285

KYRIE ELEISON   15th–16th century Mode V

twice

Ký-ri - e   *   e - lé-i-son.

twice

Chri-ste   e - lé-i-son.

Ký-ri-e   e - lé-i-son.

Ký-ri-e   *   **

e - lé-i-son.

Mass VIII (de Angelis)

GLORIA 16th century Mode V

Celebrant
Gló - ri - a in ex - cél - sis Dé - o.

All
Et in ter - ra pax ho - mí - ni - bus bo - nae vo - lun - tá - tis. Lau - dá - mus te. Be - ne - dí - ci - mus te. A - do - rá - mus te. Glo - ri - fi - cá - mus te. Grá - ti - as á - gi - mus ti - bi prop - ter ma - gnam gló - ri - am tu - am. Dó - mi - ne De - us, Rex cae - lé - stis.

Mass VIII (de Angelis)

De - us Pa - ter om - ní - po - tens. Dó-mi-ne Fi - li u - ni - gé - ni - te, Je - su Chri - ste. Dó - mi - ne De - us, A-gnus De - i, Fí - li - us Pa - tris. Qui tol - lis pec-cá-ta mun - di, mi-se-ré - re no - bis. Qui tol - lis pec - cá - ta mun - di, sú - sci - pe de - pre - ca - ti - ó - nem

Mass VIII (de Angelis)

no - stram. Qui se-des ad déx-te-ram Pa - tris,

mi - se - ré - re no - bis. Quó - ni - am tu

so - lus sanc - tus. Tu so-lus Dó - mi - nus.

Tu so-lus Al - tís - si - mus, Je - su Chri - ste.

Cum San - cto Spí - ri - tu, in gló - ri - a

De - i Pa - tris. A - men.

Mass VIII (de Angelis)

SANCTUS　　　　　　　　　　　　　　　　　　　　　　　12th century Mode VI

San - ctus,* San - ctus, San - ctus Dó - mi - nus Deus Sá - ba - oth. Ple - ni sunt cae - li et ter - ra gló - ri - a tu - a. Ho-sán - na in ex - cél - sis. Be - ne - dí - ctus qui ve - nit in nó - mi - ne Dó - mi - ni.

Mass VIII (de Angelis)

Ho-sán - na in ex - cél - sis.

AGNUS DEI 15th century Mode VI

A - gnus De - i, * qui tol - lis pec-cá-ta mun - di: mi-se-ré-re no - bis. A-gnus De - i, * qui tol - lis pec-cá-ta mun - di: mi-se-ré-re no - bis. A - gnus De - i, * qui tol - lis pec-cá-ta mun - di: do-na no - bis pa - cem.

Mass XI (Orbis Factor)

286

KYRIE ELEISON   10th century adapted 14th–16th century Mode I

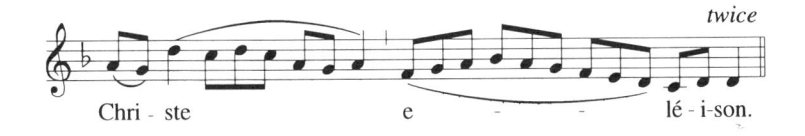

twice

Ký - ri - e * e - - - lé - i - son.

twice

Chri - ste e - - lé - i - son.

Ký - ri - e e - - lé - i - son.

Ký - ri - e e - - lé - i - son.

GLORIA   10th century Mode II

Celebrant   *All*

Gló - ri - a in ex - cél - sis De - o. Et in ter - ra

Mass XI (Orbis Factor)

pax ho-mí-ni-bus bo-nae vo-lun-tá-tis.

Lau-dá-mus te. Be-ne-dí-ci-mus te.

A-do-rá-mus te. Glo-ri-fi-cá-mus te.

Grá-ti-as á-gi-mus ti-bi prop-ter

ma-gnam gló-ri-am tu-am. Dó-mi-ne

De-us, Rex cae-lé-stis, De-us Pa-ter

Mass XI (Orbis Factor)

om - ní - po - tens. Dó - mi - ne Fi - li -

u - ni - gé - ni - te Je - su Chri - ste.

Dó - mi - ne De - us, A - gnus De - i,

Fí - li - us Pa - tris. Qui tol - lis pec - cá - ta

mun - di, mi - se - ré - re no - bis.

Qui tol - lis pec - cá - ta mun - di, sú - sci - pe

Mass XI *(Orbis Factor)*

deprecatiónem nostram. Qui sedes ad déxteram Patris, miserére nobis. Quóniam tu solus sanctus. Tu solus Dóminus. Tu solus Altíssimus, Jesu Christe. Cum Sancto Spíritu, in glória Dei Patris. Amen.

Mass XI (Orbis Factor)

SANCTUS 11th century Mode II

San - ctus,* San - ctus, San - ctus Dó - mi - nus.

De - us Sá - ba - oth. Ple - ni sunt cae - li et

ter - ra gló - ri - a tu - a. Ho - sán - na in

ex - cél - sis. Be - ne - dí - ctus qui ve - nit

in nó - mi - ne Dó - mi - ni.

Ho - sán - na in ex - cél - sis.

Mass XI (Orbis Factor)

AGNUS DEI   14th century Mode I

Agnus Dei,* qui tollis peccata mundi: miserére nobis. Agnus Dei,* qui tollis peccata mundi: miserére nobis. Agnus Dei,* qui tollis peccata mundi: dona nobis pacem.

Mass XVIII (Latin)

287

KYRIE (*Deus genitor alme*)   11th century Mode IV

twice

Ký - ri - e * e - lé - i - son. Chri - ste

twice

e - lé - i - son. Ký - ri - e e - lé - i - son.

Ký - ri - e e - lé - i - son.

KYRIE (*At Masses of the Dead*)   Mode VI

twice

Ký - ri - e * e - lé - i - son. Chri - ste

twice

e - lé - i - son. Ký - ri - e e - lé - i - son.

Ký - ri - e e - lé - i - son.

Mass XVIII (Latin)

GLORIA XV 　　　　　　　　　　　　　　　　　　　10th century Mode IV

Celebrant 　　　　　　　　　　　　　　*All*

Gló - ri - a in ex - cél - sis De - o.　Et in ter - ra

pax ho - mí - ni - bus　bo - nae vo - lun - tá - tis.

Lau - dá - mus te.　Be - ne - dí - ci - mus te.

A - do - rá - mus te.　Glo - ri - fi - cá - mus te.

Grá - ti - as á - gi - mus ti - bi　prop - ter ma - gnam

gló - ri - am tu - am.　Dó - mi - ne De - us,

Mass XVIII (Latin)

Rex cae - lé - stis,   De - us Pa - ter om - ní - po - tens.

Dó - mi - ne   Fi - li   u - ni - gé - ni - te

Je - su Chri - ste.   Dó - mi - ne De - us,   A - gnus De - i,

Fí - li - us Pa - tris.   Qui tol - lis pec - cá - ta mun - di,

mi - se - ré - re no - bis.   Qui tol - lis pec - cá - ta

mun - di   sú - sci - pe de - pre - ca - ti - ó - nem no - stram.

Mass XVIII (Latin)

Qui se-des ad déx-te-ram Pa-tris, mi-se-ré-re no-bis. Quó-ni-am tu so-lus san-ctus. Tu so-lus Dó-mi-nus. Tu so-lus Al-tís-si-mus, Je-su Chri-ste. Cum San-cto Spí-ri-tu, in gló-ri-a De-i Pa-tris. A-men.

Mass XVIII (Latin)

SANCTUS 13th century

Sanctus, * Sanctus, Sanctus Dóminus Deus Sábaoth. Pleni sunt caeli et terra glória tua. Hosánna in excélsis. Benedíctus qui venit in nómine Dómini. Hosánna in excélsis.

Mass XVIII (Latin)

AGNUS DEI   12th century

A - gnus De - i, * qui tol - lis pe - cá - ta mun - di:

twice

mi - se - ré - re no - bis.   A - gnus De - i, * qui tol - lis

pec - cá - ta mun - di: do - na no - bis pa - cem.

Mass XVIII (English)

288

KYRIE   adapted P.R.

twice   *twice*

Lord * have mer-cy. Christ have mer-cy.

Lord have mer-cy. Lord have mer-cy.

GLORIA XV   adapted *The English Kyriale* 1991

Celebrant   *All*

Glo-ry to God in the high-est, and peace to his

peo-ple on earth. Lord God, hea-ven-ly King,

al-migh-ty God and Fath-er, we wor-ship you,

Mass XVIII (English)

we give you thanks, we praise you for your glo - ry.

Lord Je - sus Christ, on - ly Son of the Fa - ther.

Lord God, Lamb of God, you take a - way the

sin of the world: have mer - cy on us; you are

sea - ted at the right hand of the Fa - ther:

re - ceive our prayer. For you a - lone are the Ho - ly One,

Mass XVIII (English)

you a-lone are the Lord, you a-lone are the Most High,

Je-sus Christ, with the Ho-ly Spi-rit, in the

glo-ry of God the Fa - ther. A - men.

SANCTUS   adapted *The Roman Missal* 1974

Ho-ly, * ho-ly, ho-ly Lord, God of power and might,

hea-ven and earth are full of your glo - ry, Ho-san-na

Mass XVIII (English)

in the high - est. Bles-sed is he who comes in the name of the Lord. Ho - san - na in the high - est.

AGNUS DEI   adapted P.R.

Lamb of God, * you take a - way the sins of the world: have mer - cy on us. Lamb of God, you

twice

take a - way the sins of the world: grant us peace.

Mass Ordinary

289 CREDO III 17th century Mode V

Celebrant Credo in unum Deum, *All* Patrem omnipoténtem, factórem caeli et terrae, visibílium ómnium, et invisibílium. Et in unum Dóminum Jesum Christum, Fílium Dei unigénitum. Et ex Patre natum ante

Mass Ordinary

ómni-a sáe - cu - la. De-um de De - o,

lu-men de lú-mi-ne, De-um ve-rum de

De-o ve-ro. Gé-ni-tum, non fac - tum,

con-sub-stan-ti-á-lem Pa-tri, per quem

óm-ni-a fac-ta sunt. Qui prop-ter nos hó-mi-nes,

et prop-ter no-stram sa-lú-tem, de-scén-dit de

Mass Ordinary

caelis. Et incarnátus est de Spíritu Sancto, ex María Vírgine: Et homo factus est. Crucifíxus étiam pro nobis: sub Póntio Piláto, passus et sepúltus est. Et resurréxit tértia die, secúndum Scriptúras.

Mass Ordinary

Et a-scén-dit in cae - lum: se-det ad

déx-te-ram Pa - tris. Et í-te-rum ven-tú-rus

est cum gló-ri-a, ju-di-cá-re vi-vos et

mór-tu-os; cu-jus re-gni non e-rit fi-nis.

Et in Spí-ri-tum San-ctum, Dó-mi-num,

et vi-vi-fi-cán-tem, qui ex Pa-tre

Mass Ordinary

Fi - li - ó - que pro - cé - dit. Qui cum Pa - tre et
Fí - li - o, si - mul ad - o - rá - tur, et
con - glo - ri - fi - cá - tur: qui lo - cú - tus est per
Pro - phé - tas. Et u - nam san - ctam ca - thó - li - cam
et a - pos - tó - li - cam Ec - clé - si - am.
Con - fí - te - or u - num bap - tís - ma

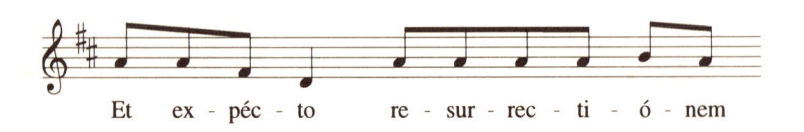

Mass Ordinary

in re-mis-si-ó-nem pec-ca-tó-rum.

Et ex-péc-to re-sur-rec-ti-ó-nem

mor-tu-ó-rum. Et vi-tam ven-tú-ri sáe-cu-li.

A - - - - - - - men.

Mass Ordinary

290 RESPONSES AT THE EUCHARISTIC PRAYER and PATER NOSTER

RESPONSES AT THE EUCHARISTIC PRAYER

Cel: Dó-mi-nus vo-bís-cum. *R:* Et cum spí-ri-tu tu-o. *C:* Sur-sum cor-da. *R:* Ha-bé-mus ad Dó-mi-num. *C:* Grá-ti-as a-gá-mus Dó-mi-no De-o no-stro. *R:* Di-gnum et ju-stum est.

leading to Sanctus

after Consecration

C: My-sté-ri-um fí-de-i. *R:* Mor-tem tu-am

Mass Ordinary

annuntiámus Dómine, et tuam resurrectiónem confitémur, donec vénias.

at conclusion of Eucharistic Prayer

C:... per ómnia sáecula saeculorum. R: Amen.

Mass Ordinary

Pater Noster (The Lord's Prayer)

Cel. ... au - dé - mus dí - ce - re: *All:* Pa - ter no - ster,

qui es in cae - lis: san - cti - fi - cé - tur no - men

tu - um; ad - vé - ni - at regnum tu - um; fi - at

vo - lún - tas tu - a, si - cut in cae - lo et in

ter - ra. Pa - nem no - strum co - ti - di - á - num da

no - bis hó - di - e; et di - mít - te no - bis

Mass Ordinary

débita nostra, sicut et nos dimíttimus debitóribus nostris; et ne nos indúcas in tentatiónem; sed líbera nos a malo.

C: ... et advéntum Salvatóris nostri Jesu Christi.

R: Quia tuum est regnum, et potéstas, et glória in sáecula.

Latin Hymns

291 ADORO TE

Paris *Processionale* 1697

* ♪ in vv. 2 and 6

1. Adoro te devóte, latens Déitas,
   Quae sub his figúris vere látitas:
   Tibi se cor meum totum súbjicit,
   Quia te contémplans totum déficit.

2. Visus, tactus, gustus in te fállitur,
   Sed audítu solo tuto créditur:
   Credo quidquid dixit Dei Fílius,
   Nil hoc verbo veritátis vérius.

3. In cruce latébat sola Déitas,
   At hic latet simul et humánitas;
   Ambo tamen credens, atque cónfitens,
   Peto quod petívit latro póenitens.

4. Plagas sicut Thomas non intúeor,
   Deum tamen meum te confíteor;
   Fac me tibi semper magis crédere,
   In te spem habére, te dilígere.

5. O memoriále mortis Dómini,
   Panis vivus vitam praestans hómini:
   Praesta meae menti de te vívere,
   Et te illi semper dulce sápere.

6. Pie pellicáne, Jesu Dómine,
   Me immúndum munda tuo sánguine:
   Cujus una stilla salvum fácere
   Totum mundum quit ab omni scélere.

7. Jesu, quem velátum nunc aspício,
   Oro fiat illud, quod tam sítio,
   Ut te reveláta cernens fácie,
   Visu sim beátus tuae glóriae.
   Amen.

attributed St Thomas Aquinas 1227–74

For translations see Hymns 117 and 124.

Latin Hymns

292 ATTENDE DOMINE (The Lent Prose)   Mode V

Atténde Dómine, et miserére,
Quia peccávimus tibi.

1. Ad te Rex summe, ómnium redémptor,
   Oculos nostros sublevámus flentes:
   Exáudi, Christe, supplicántum preces.

2. Déxtera Patris, lapis anguláris,
   Via salútis, janua caeléstis,
   Ablue nostri máculas delícti.

3. Rogámus Deus tuam majestátem:
   Auribus sacris gémitus exáudi:
   Crímina nostra plácidus indúlge.

4. Tibi fatémur crímina admíssa:
   Contríto corde pándimus occúlta:
   Tua, Redémptor, píetas ignóscat.

5. Innocens captus, nec repúgnans ductus,
   Téstibus falsis pro ímpiis damnátus:
   Quos redemísti, tu consérva, Christe.

The Lent Prose
traditional, The Roman Rite

Latin Hymns

293

Translation suitable for singing

> *Hear us, O loving Lord, hear and have mercy,*
> *For we have sinnèd against thee.*

1 To thee, highest King, all the world's Redeemer,
  Raise we our weeping eyes in holy pleading;
  Hearken, O Christ, and grant our supplication.

2 Thou chief corner-stone, right hand of the Father,
  Way of salvation, gateway of the heavens,
  Wash thou away the stains of our offences.

3 God of majesty, humbly we implore thee,
  Bow down and hearken to our lamentation:
  For all our sins, O grant us thy forgiveness.

4 To thee we confess all our sins committed:
  With contrite heart disclose we our offences:
  In loving kindness pardon, O Redeemer.

5 Innocent, captive, taken unresisting,
  Unjustly sentenced for the sake of sinners,
  Save us, O Christ, save those thou hast redeemèd.

tr. cento
The London Oratory

Latin Hymns

294 AVE MARIA Mode I

A - ve Ma - rí - a, * grá - ti - a ple - na,

Dó - mi - nus te - cum, be - ne - díc - ta

tu in mu - li - é - ri - bus, et

be - ne - díc - tus fruc - tus ven - tris tu - i

Je - sus. Sanc-ta Ma - rí - a, Ma-ter De - i,

o - ra pro no - bis pec - ca - tó - ri - bus,

Latin Hymns

nunc et in ho - ra mor-tis no - strae. A - men.

Translation

> Hail Mary, full of grace, the Lord is with thee; blessed art thou among women and blessed is the fruit of thy womb, Jesus. Holy Mary, Mother of God, pray for us sinners now and at the hour of our death. Amen.

295 AVE MARIS STELLA — Mode I

1. Ave maris stella,
   Dei Mater alma,
   Atque semper Virgo,
   Felix caeli porta.

2. Sumens illud Ave
   Gabriélis ore,
   Funda nos in pace,
   Mutans Hevae nomen.

3. Solve vincla reis,
   Profer lumen caecis,
   Mala nostra pelle,
   Bona cuncta posce.

4. Monstra t*e* esse matrem,
   Sumat per te preces,
   Qui pro nobis natus
   Tulit esse tuus.

Latin Hymns

5 Virgo singuláris,
   Inter omnes mitis,
   Nos culpis solútos
   Mites fac et castos.

6 Vitam praesta puram,
   Iter para tutum,
   Ut vidéntes Jesum,
   Semper collaetémur.

7 Sit laus Deo Patri,
   Summo Christo decus,
   Spirítui Sancto,
   Tribus honor unus. Amen.

9th century
Office hymn for feasts of
the Blessed Virgin Mary

For translation see Hymn 160.

Latin Hymns

296 AVE VERUM   Mode VI

A - ve verum Corpus natum de Ma - rí - a
Ve - re pas-sum, im-mo-lá-tum in Cru - ce pro

Vír - gi - ne: Cu-ius la-tus per-fo-rá - tum
hó - mi - ne: Es-to no-bis prae-gu-stá - tum

flu - xit a - qua et sán - gui - ne:
mor - tis in ex - á - mi - ne:

O Je - su dul - cis! O Je - su pi - e!

O Je - su, fi - li Ma - rí - ae.

attributed POPE INNOCENT VI died 1362

297

Translation suitable for singing

> Hail true Body, born of Mary
> Spotless Virgin's virgin birth;
> Thou who truly hangest weary
> On the Cross for sons of earth;
> Thou whose sacred side was riven,
> Whence flowed the water and the blood,
> O may'st thou, dear Lord, be given
> At death's hour to be my food;
> O Jesu most kind, O Jesu glorious One!
> O Jesu, holy Mary's Son!

tr. HENRY NUTCOMBE OXENHAM 1829–88 *

Latin Hymns

298 CHRISTUS VINCIT
(Acclamations)

13th century Worcester Cathedral *Antiphonal*
arranged Laurence Bévenot O.S.B. 1901–1991

Cantor: Chri - stus vin - cit: Chri - stus re - gnat: Chri - stus im - pe - rat.

All: CHRI-STUS VIN - CIT: CHRI-STUS RE - GNAT: CHRI - STUS IM - PE - RAT.

Cantor: Ex - au - di Chri - ste. *All:* EX - AU - DI CHRI - STE.

Cantor: Sum - mo Pon - ti - fi - ci et u - ni - ver - sa - li Pa - pae: *All:* VI - TA. *Cantor:* Sal - va - tor mun - di:

Latin Hymns

All / *Cantor*
TU IL-LUM AD - JU - VA. San-cta Ma-ri - a:

All / *Cantor*
TU IL-LUM AD - JU - VA. San-cte Pe - tre:

All / *Cantor*
TU IL-LUM AD - JU - VA. San-cte Pau - le:

All / *Cantor*
TU IL-LUM AD - JU - VA. San-cte Phi-lip - pe:*

All
TU IL-LUM AD - JU - VA. CHRI-STUS VIN - CIT:

CHRI-STUS RE - GNAT: CHRI-STUS IM - PE - RAT.

* or other saint

Latin Hymns

Rex re - gum! CHRI- STUS VIN - CIT. Rex no - ster! CHRI- STUS RE - GNAT. Glo - ri - a no - stra! CHRI- STUS IM - PE - RAT. Ip - si so - li im - pe - ri - um glo - ri - a et po - te - stas, per im - mor - ta - li - a sae - cu - la sae - cu - lo - rum. A - men. CHRI- STUS VIN - CIT:

Latin Hymns

CHRI-STUS RE - GNAT: CHRI-STUS IM - PE - RAT.

Translation

        Christ is victorious: Christ is king: Christ is Lord.
        Christ is victorious: Christ is king: Christ is Lord.

        Graciously hear us, O Christ.
        Graciously hear us, O Christ.

        To the supreme Pontiff and Pope of the world, grant life.
        Saviour of the world: do thou assist him.
        Holy Mary: do thou assist him.
        Saint Peter: do thou assist him.
        Saint Paul: do thou assist him.
        Saint Philip*: do thou assist him.
        Christ is victorious: Christ is king: Christ is Lord.

        King of kings: Christ is victorious.
        Our king: Christ is king.
        Our glory: Christ is Lord.

        To him alone be dominion, glory and power,
           through unending ages for ever. Amen

        Christ is victorious: Christ is king: Christ is Lord.

* or other saint

                                      tr. The London Oratory

299 JESU DULCIS MEMORIA — Mode I

A - men.

1. Jesu dulcis memória,
   Dans vera cordis gáudia:
   Sed super mel, et ómnia,
   Ejus dulcis praeséntia.

2. Nil cánitur suávius,
   Nil audítur jucúndius,
   Nil cogitátur dúlcius,
   Quam Jesus Dei Fílius.

3. Jesu spes poeniténtibus,
   Quam pius es peténtibus!
   Quam bonus te quaeréntibus!
   Sed quid inveniéntibus?

4. Nec lingua valet dícere,
   Nec líttera exprímere:
   Expértus potest crédere,
   Quid sit Jesum dilígere.

5. Sis, Jesu, nostrum gáudium,
   Qui es futúrus praémium:
   Sit nostra in te glória,
   Per cuncta semper saécula. Amen.

c. 12th century

Latin Hymns

300

Translation suitable for singing

1 Jesus to cast one thought upon
Makes gladness after he is gone.
But more than honey and honeycomb
Is to come near and take him home.

2 Song never was so sweet in ear,
Word never was such news to hear,
Thought half so sweet there is not one
As Jesus, God the Father's Son.

3 Jesu, their hope who go astray,
So kind to those who ask the way,
So good to those who ask for thee,
To those who find what must thou be?

4 To speak of that no tongue will do,
Nor letters suit to spell it true:
But they can guess who've tasted of
What Jesus is and what is love.

5 Be our delight, O Jesu, now,
As by and by our prize art thou,
And grant our glorying may be
World without end alone in thee. Amen.

tr. GERARD MANLEY HOPKINS S.J. 1844–89

301 LUCIS CREATOR

Mode VIII

A - men.

1. Lucis Créator óptime
   Lucem diérum próferens,
   Primórdiis lucis novae
   Mundi parans oríginem.

2. Qui mane junctum vésperi
   Diem vocári praécipis,
   Illábitur tetrum chaos;
   Audi preces cum flétibus.

3. Ne mens graváta crímine
   Vitae sit exsul múnere,
   Dum nil perénne cógitat,
   Seséque culpis ílligat.

4. Caeléste pulset óstium:
   Vitále tollat praémium:
   Vitémus omne nóxium:
   Purgémus omne péssimum.

5. Praesta, Pater piíssime,
   Patríque compar Unice,
   Cum Spíritu Paráclito
   Regnans per omne saéculum. Amen.

Office hymn for Sunday Vespers of the year
6th century

Latin Hymns

302

Translation suitable for singing

1 O blest Creator of the light!
    Who dost the dawn from darkness bring
And framing nature's depth and height,
    Didst with the light thy work begin;

2 Who gently blending eve with morn,
    And morn with eve, didst call them day—
Thick flows the flood of darkness down;
    Oh, hear us as we weep and pray!

3 Keep thou our souls from schemes of crime,
    Nor guilt remorseful let them know;
Nor, thinking but on things of time,
    Into eternal darkness go.

4 Teach us to knock at heav'n's high door;
    Teach us the prize of life to win;
Teach us all evil to abhor,
    And purify ourselves within.

5 Father of mercies! hear our cry;
    Hear us, O sole-begotten Son!
Who, with the Holy Ghost most high,
    Reignest while endless ages run. Amen.

tr. EDWARD CASWALL Cong. Orat. 1814–78

303 PANGE LINGUA — Mode III

A - men.

1. Pange lingua gloriósi
    Córporis mystérium,
   Sanguinísque pretiósi,
    Quem in mundi prétium
   Fructus ventris generósi
    Rex effúdit géntium.

2. Nobis datus, nobis natus
    Ex intácta Vírgine,
   Et in mundo conversátus,
    Sparso verbi sémine,
   Sui moras incolátus
    Miro clausit órdine.

3. In suprémae nocte coenae
    Recúmbens cum frátribus,
   Observáta lege plene
    Cibis in legálibus,
   Cibum turbae duodénae
    Se dat suis mánibus.

Latin Hymns

4 Verbum caro, panem verum
   Verbo carnem éfficit,
 Fitque sanguis Christi merum,
   Et si sensus déficit,
 Ad firmándum cor sincérum
   Sola fides súfficit.

5 Tantum ergo Sacraméntum
   Venerémur cérnui,
 Et antíquum documéntum
   Novo cedat rítui:
 Praestet fides suppleméntum
   Sénsuum deféctui.

6 Genitóri, Genitóque
   Laus et jubilátio,
 Salus, honor, virtus quoque
   Sit et benedíctio:
 Procedénti ab utróque
   Compar sit laudátio. Amen.

Office hymn for Corpus Christi
ST THOMAS AQUINAS 1227–74

For translation suitable for singing see Hymn 127.

Latin Hymns

304 PANIS ANGELICUS (Sarum) — Mode VII

1. Panis angélicus fit panis hóminum;
   Dat panis caélicus figúris términum;
   O res mirábilis! mandúcat Dóminum
   Pauper, servus, et húmilis!

2. Te trina Déitas únaque póscimus,
   Sic nos tu vísita, sicut te cólimus:
   Per tuas sémitas duc nos quo téndimus,
   Ad lucem quam inhábitas. Amen.

St Thomas Aquinas 1227–74

Translation

1. Man makes repast in this banquet supernal;
   Shadows fade fast in this sunlight eternal;
   Wondrous our heritage, Lord, in receiving thee.
      Earth's poor slaves—yet believing thee.

2. O gracious Trinity, fill, we implore thee,
   With thy Divinity hearts that adore thee;
   Dwelling in light, to that light bring us home again.
      From thy paths ne'er to roam again.

tr. Ronald Arbuthnott Knox 1888–1957

Latin Hymns

305 RORATE CAELI (The Advent Prose) — Mode I

Refrain

Ro - rá - te cae - li dé - su - per et nu - bes

Repeat first time

plu - ant ju - stum.

Verse 1

Ne i - ra - scá - ris Dó - mi - ne, ne ul - tra
me - mí - ne - ris in - i - qui - tá - tis: ec - ce
cí - vi - tas San - cti fa - cta est de - sér - ta:
Si - on de - sér - ta fa - cta est:

Latin Hymns

Jerúsalem desoláta est:
domus sanctificatiónis tuae
et glóriae tuae, ubi
laudavérunt te patres nostri.

repeat Refrain

Verse 2
Peccávimus, et facti sumus tamquam
immúndus nos, et cecídimus quasi

Latin Hymns

fó - li - um u - ni - vér - si: et in - i - qui - tá - tes

nos - trae qua - si ven - tus ab - stu - lé - runt nos:

ab - scon - dí - sti fá - ci - em tu - am

a no - bis, et al - li - sí - sti nos in

repeat Refrain

ma - nu in - i - qui - tá - tis nos - trae.

Verse 3

Vi - de Dó - mi - ne af - fli - cti - ó - nem

Latin Hymns

pó - pu - li tu - i, et mit - te
quem mi - sú - rus es: e - mít - te A - gnum
do - mi - na - tó - rem ter - rae, de pe - tra de - sér - ti
ad mon-tem fí - li - ae Si - on: ut au - fe - rat

repeat Refrain

ip - se ju - gum cap - ti - vi - tá - tis nos - trae.

Verse 4

Con - so - lá - mi - ni, con - so - lá - mi - ni,

Latin Hymns

pópule meus: cito véniet salus tua: quare moeróre consúmeris, quia innovávit te dolor? Salvábo te, noli timére, ego enim sum Dóminus Deus tuus, Sanctus Israel, redémptor tuus.

repeat Refrain

The Advent Prose
traditional, The Roman Rite

Translation overleaf

Latin Hymns

Translation

Refrain Drop down dew, ye heavens, from above, and let the clouds rain down the Just One.

1   Be not angry, O Lord, and remember no longer our iniquity: behold, the city of thy Holy One is become a desert: Sion is become a desert: Jerusalem is desolate: the house of thy sanctification and of thy glory, where our fathers praised thee. *Refrain*

2   We have sinned and are become as one that is unclean: and we have all fallen as a leaf, and our iniquities like the wind have carried us away: thou hast hidden thy face from us, and hast crushed us in the hold of our iniquity. *Refrain.*

3   Behold, O Lord, the affliction of thy people, and send forth him who is to come: send forth the Lamb, the ruler of the earth, from the rock of the desert, to the mount of the daughter of Sion: that he may take away the yoke of our captivity. *Refrain*

4   Be comforted, be comforted, my people: thy salvation cometh quickly: why art thou consumed with grief? for sorrow hath estranged thee: I will save thee; fear not, for I am the Lord thy God, the Holy One of Israel, thy redeemer. *Refrain*

Latin Hymns

306 TE DEUM LAUDAMUS (Tonus Simplex)   Mode III

Te Deum laudámus: * te Dóminum confitémur. Te aetérnum Patrem omnis terra venerátur. Tibi omnes ángeli, tibi caeli et univérsae potestátes: Tibi chérubim et séraphim incessábili voce proclámant:

Latin Hymns

Sanctus: Sanctus: Sanctus
Dóminus Deus Sábaoth. Pleni sunt
caeli et terra majestátis glóriae
tuae. Te glorió - sus Apostolórum
chorus: Te prophetárum laudábilis
númerus: Te mártyrum candidátus

Latin Hymns

lau-dat ex - ér - ci - tus. Te per or-bem ter - rá - rum

san - cta con - fi - té - tur Ec - clé - si - a:

Pa - trem im - mén-sae ma-jes - tá - tis:

Ve - ne - rán-dum tu - um ve - rum et ú - ni - cum

Fí - li - um: San-ctum quo - que Pa - rá - cli - tum

Spí - ri - tum, Tu Rex gló - ri - ae, Chri - ste.

Latin Hymns

Tu Patris sempitérnus es Fílius.

Tu ad liberándum susceptúrus hóminem, non horruísti Vírginis úterum.

Tu devícto mortis acúleo, aperuísti credéntibus regna caelórum.

Tu ad déxteram Dei

Latin Hymns

se - des, in gló - ri - a Pa - tris. Ju - dex cré - de - ris

es - se ven - tú - rus. Te er - go quaé - su - mus, tu - is

fá - mu - lis súb - ve - ni, quos pre - ti - ó - so

sán - gui - ne re - de - mí - sti. Ae - tér - na fac

cum san - ctis tu - is in gló - ri - a nu - me - rá - ri.

Sal - vum fac pó - pu - lum tu - um Dó - mi - ne,

Latin Hymns

et bé - ne - dic hae - re - di - tá - ti tu ae.

Et re - ge e - os, et ex - tól - le il - los

us - que in ae - tér - num. Per sín - gu - los di - es,

be - ne - dí - ci - mus te. Et lau - dá - mus no - men

tu - um in saé - cu - lum, et in saé - cu - lum

saé - cu - li. Di - gná - re Dó - mi - ne di - e

Latin Hymns

isto sine peccáto nos custodíre.
Miserére nostri Dómine, miserére nostri. Fiat misericórdia tua Dómine super nos, quemádmodum sperávimus in te. In te Dómine sperávi: non confúndar in aetérnum.

ascribed St Nicetas 335–415

Versicles and Responses overleaf

Latin Hymns

V. Benedicámus Patrem et Fílium cum Sancto Spíritu.
R. Laudémus et superexaltémus eum in sáecula.

V. Benedíctus es Dómine in firmaménto caeli.
R. Et laudábilis, et gloriósus, et superexaltátus in sáecula.

V. Dómine, exáudi orationem meam.
R. Et clamor meus ad te véniat.

V. Dóminus vobíscum.
R. Et cum spíritu tuo.

Latin Hymns

307 TE LUCIS ANTE TERMINUM (Ferial) — Mode VIII

1. Te lucis ante términum,
   Rerum Creátor póscimus,
   Ut pro tua cleméntia,
   Sis praesul et custódia.

2. Procul recédant sómnia,
   Et nóctium phantásmata;
   Hostémque nostrum cómprime,
   Ne polluántur córpora.

3. Praesta, Pater piíssime,
   Patríque compar Unice,
   Cum Spíritu Paráclito,
   Regnans per omne saéculum.
   Amen.

Office hymn for Compline
7th century

308 *Translation suitable for singing*

1. Now with the fast-departing light,
   Maker of all! we ask of thee,
   Of thy great mercy, through the night
   Our guardian and defence to be.

2. Far off let idle visions fly;
   No phantom of the night molest:
   Curb thou our raging enemy,
   That we in chaste repose may rest.

3. Father of mercies! hear our cry;
   Hear us, O sole-begotten Son!
   Who, with the Holy Ghost most high,
   Reignest while endless ages run. Amen.

tr. EDWARD CASWALL Cong. Orat. 1814–78

Latin Hymns

309 UBI CARITAS　　　　　　　　　　　　　　　　　　　　Mode VI

Ubi cáritas et amor, Deus ibi est. Congregávit nos in unum Christi amor. Exultémus et in ipso jucundémur. Timeámus et amémus Deum vivum. Et ex corde diligámus nos sincéro. Amen.

Latin Hymns

2 Ubi cáritas et amor, Deus ibi est.
 Simul ergo cum in unum congregámur,
 Ne nos mente dividámur caveámus.
 Cessant júrgia malígna, cessent lites,
 Et in médio nostri sit Christus Deus.

3 Ubi cáritas et amor, Deus ibi est.
 Simul quoque cum beátis videámus
 Gloriánter vultum tuum, Christe Deus;
 Gáudium quod est imménsum, atque probum;
 Saécula per infiníta saeculórum. Amen.

Mass of Maundy Thursday
9th–10th century

Translation

1 Where is love and loving-kindness, God is fain to dwell.
 Flock of Christ, who loved us, in one fold contained,
 Joy and mirth be ours, for mirth and joy he giveth;
 Fear we still and love the God who ever liveth,
 Each to other joined by charity unfeignèd.

2 Where is love and loving-kindness, God is fain to dwell.
 Therefore, when we meet, the flock of Christ, so loving,
 Take heed lest bitterness be there engendered;
 All our spiteful thoughts and quarrels be surrendered,
 Seeing Christ is there, divine among us moving.

3 Where is love and loving-kindness, God is fain to dwell.
 So may we be gathered once again, beholding
 Glorified the glory, Christ, of thy unveiling,
 There, where never ending joys, and never failing
 Age succeeds to age eternally unfolding. Amen.

tr. RONALD ARBUTHNOTT KNOX 1888–1957

Latin Hymns

310 VENI CREATOR — Mode VIII

A - men.

1. Veni, Creátor Spíritus,
   Mentes tuórum vísita,
   Imple supérna grátia
   Quae tu creásti péctora.

2. Qui díceris Paráclitus,
   Altíssimi donum Dei,
   Fons vivus, ignis, cáritas,
   Et spiritális únctio.

3. Tu septifórmis múnere,
   Dígitus patérnae déxterae,
   Tu rite promíssum Patris
   Sermóne ditans gúttura.

4. Accénde lumen sénsibus,
   Infúnde amórem córdibus,
   Infírma nostri córporis
   Virtúte firmans pérpeti.

5. Hostem repéllas lóngius,
   Pacémque dones prótinus;
   Ductóre sic te praévio,
   Vitémus omne nóxium.

6. Per te sciámus da Patrem,
   Noscámus atque Fílium,
   Teque utriúsque Spíritum
   Credámus omni témpore.

7. Deo Patri sit glória,
   Et Fílio qui a mórtuis
   Surréxit, ac Paráclito,
   In saeculórum saécula. Amen.

Office hymn for Pentecost
attributed RABANUS MAURUS 776–856

Latin Hymns

311

Translation suitable for singing

1. Come, O Creator Spirit, come
   And make within our hearts thy home;
   To us thy grace celestial give,
   Who of thy breathing move and live.

2. O Comforter, that name is thine,
   Of God most high the gift divine;
   The well of life, the fire of love,
   Our souls' anointing from above.

3. Thou dost appear in sevenfold dower
   The sign of God's almighty power;
   The Father's promise, making rich
   With saving truth our earthly speech.

4. Our senses with thy light inflame,
   Our hearts to heavenly love reclaim;
   Our bodies' poor infirmity
   With strength perpetual fortify.

5. Our mortal foe afar repel,
   Grant us henceforth in peace to dwell;
   And so to us, with thee for guide,
   No ill shall come, no harm betide.

6. May we by thee the Father learn,
   And know the Son, and thee discern,
   Who art of both; and thus adore
   In perfect faith for evermore.

7. All glory to the Father be,
   All glory risen Son to thee,
   Who with the Paraclete art one,
   Reigning while endless ages run.   Amen.

tr. ROBERT BRIDGES 1844–1930
v. 7 ANONYMOUS

Latin Hymns

312 VENI SANCTE SPIRITUS (Gregorian)   Mode I

1. Veni Sancte Spíritus, Et emítte cáelitus Lucis tuae rádium.
2. Veni pater páuperum, Veni dator múnerum, Veni lumen córdium.
3. Consolátor óptime, Dulcis hospes ánimae, Dulce refrigérium.
4. In labóre réquies, In aestu tempéries, In fletu solátium.
5. O lux beatíssima, Reple cordis íntima Tuórum fidélium.
6. Sine tuo númine, Nihil est in hómine, Nihil est innóxium.

Latin Hymns

7 Lava quod est sórdidum, Riga quod est áridum, Sana quod est sáucium.
8 Flecte quod est rígidum, Fove quod est frígidum, Rege quod est dévium.

9 Da tuis fidélibus, In te confidéntibus, Sacrum septenárium.
10 Da virtútis méritum, Da salútis éxitum, Da perénne gáudium.

optional: Amen. Allelúia.

Sequence for Pentecost
attributed STEPHEN LANGTON died 1228

Translation suitable for singing overleaf

Latin Hymns

313

Translation suitable for singing

   1 Holy Spirit, Lord of light,
      From the clear celestial height,
         Thy pure beaming radiance give.

   2 Come, thou Father of the poor,
      Come with treasures which endure:
         Come, thou Light of all that live!

3 Thou, of all consolers best,
    Thou, the soul's delightsome guest,
      Dost refreshing peace bestow:

4 Thou in toil art comfort sweet;
    Pleasant coolness in the heat;
      Solace in the midst of woe.

5 Light immortal, Light divine,
    Visit thou these hearts of thine,
      And our inmost being fill:

6 If thou take thy grace away,
    Nothing pure in man will stay;
      All his good is turned to ill.

   7 Heal our wounds, our strength renew;
      On our dryness pour thy dew;
         Wash the stains of guilt away:

   8 Bend the stubborn heart and will;
      Melt the frozen, warm the chill;
         Guide the steps that go astray.

   9 Thou, on those who evermore
      Thee confess and thee adore,
         In thy sevenfold gifts descend:

  10 Give them comfort when they die;
      Give them life with thee on high;
         Give them joys that never end.
         Amen. Alleluia.

tr. EDWARD CASWALL Cong. Orat. 1814–78

314 VEXILLA REGIS

Mode I

A- men.

1 Vexílla Regis pródeunt
 Fulget Crucis mystérium,
 Qua vita mortem pértulit,
 Et morte vitam prótulit.

2 Quae vulneráta lánceae
 Mucróne diro, críminum
 Ut nos laváret sórdibus,
 Manávit unda et sánguine.

3 Impléta sunt, quae cóncinit
 David fidéli cármine,
 Dicéndo natiónibus:
 Regnávit a ligno Deus.

4 Arbor decóra et fúlgida,
 Ornáta Regis púrpura,
 Elécta digno stípite
 Tam sancta membra tángere.

5 Beáta, cujus bráchiis
 Prétium pepéndit saéculi,
 Statéra facta córporis,
 Tulítque praedam tártari.

6 O Crux, ave, spes única
 Hoc Passiónis témpore †
 Piis adáuge grátiam
 Reísque dele crímina.

7 Te, fons salútis Trínitas,
 Collaúdet omnis spíritus:
 Quibus Crucis victóriam
 Largíris, adde praémium.
            Amen.

Office hymn for Passiontide
VENANTIUS FORTUNATUS 530–609

For translation suitable for singing see Hymn 70.

† (Sept. 14 Exaltation of the Holy Cross) In hac triúmphi glória

Latin Hymns

315 VICTIMAE PASCHALI LAUDES Mode I

Víc - ti - mae Pas - chá - li lau - des * ím - mo - lent

Chri - sti - á - ni. A - gnus re - dé - mit o - ves: Chri - stus

ín - no - cens Pa - tri re - con - ci - li - á - vit pec - ca - tó - res

Mors et vi - ta du - él - lo con - fli - xé - re mi - rán - do:

dux vi - tae mór - tu - us, re - gnat vi - vus.

Dic no - bis Ma - rí - a, quid vi - dí - sti in vi - a?

Latin Hymns

Se-púl-chrum Christi vi-vén-tis, et gló-ri-am vidi re-sur-gén-tis: An-gé-li-cos testes, su-dá-ri-um, et ve-stes. Sur-ré-xit Chrístus spes me-a: prae-cé-det su-os in Ga-li-lé-am. Sci-mus Christum sur-re-xís-se a mór-tu-is ve-re: tu no-bis,

optional:

vic-tor Rex, mi-se-ré-re. A-men. Al-le-lú-ia.

Sequence for Easter
WIPO OF BURGUNDY 11th century

Translation suitable for singing overleaf

Latin Hymns

316

Translation suitable for singing

> Christians, to the Paschal Victim
> Offer your thankful praises!
>
> A Lamb the sheep redeemeth:
> Christ, who only is sinless,
> Reconcileth sinners to the Father.
>
> Death and life have contended
> In that combat stupendous:
> The Prince of Life, who died, reigns immortal.
>
> Speak Mary, declaring
> What thou sawest wayfaring:
>
> 'The tomb of Christ, who is living,
> The glory of Jesu's resurrection:
>
> Bright angels attesting,
> The shroud and napkin resting.
>
> Yea, Christ my hope is arisen:
> To Galilee straight he goes before you.'
>
> Christ indeed from death is risen,
> Our new life obtaining.
> Have mercy, victor King, ever reigning!
>
> Amen. Alleluia.

tr. cento
The London Oratory

Index of First Lines and Tunes

A great and mighty wonder	11	Es ist ein'Ros' entsprungen	
Abide with me: fast falls the eventide	192	Eventide	
Accept, Almighty Father	101	Pearsall	
Accept, O Father, in thy love	102	Breslau	
Adeste fideles	12	Adeste fideles	
Adoremus in aeternum	280	Adoremus	
Adoro te devote latens Deitas	291	Adoro te	
Ah, holy Jesu, how hast thou offended	59	Herzliebster Jesu	
All creatures of our God and King	198	Lasst uns erfreuen	
All glory, laud and honour	60	Valet will ich dir geben	
All hail the power of Jesu's name!	199	Miles Lane	
All my heart this night rejoices	14	Warum sollt'ich	
All my hope on God is founded	200	Michael	
All people that on earth do dwell	201	Old Hundredth	
All things bright and beautiful	202	All things bright and beautiful	
All ye who seek a comfort sure	133	St Bernard	
Alleluia, sing to Jesus	112	Hyfrydol	
Alma Redemptoris Mater	281	Alma Redemptoris Mater	
Amazing grace! how sweet the sound	203	Amazing Grace	
And did those feet in ancient time	204	Jerusalem	
And now, O Father, mindful of the love	113	Unde et memores	
Angel-voices ever singing	205	Angel voices	
Angels we have heard on high	15	Les anges dans nos campagnes	
As pants the hart for cooling streams	206	1. Martyrdom 2. Abridge	
As with gladness men of old	41	Dix (Treuer Heiland)	
At the Cross her station keeping	61	Stabat Mater	
At the Lamb's high feast we sing	73	Salzburg	
At the name of Jesus	207	Evelyns	
Attende Domine, et miserere	292	Attende Domine (The Lent Prose)	
Ave Maria, gratia plena	294	Ave Maria	

Index of First Lines and Tunes

Ave maris stella	295	Ave maris stella
Ave Regina caelorum	282	Ave Regina
Ave verum, Corpus natum	296	Ave verum
Awake, my soul, and with the sun	189	Morning Hymn
Away in a manger, no crib for a bed	16	1. Cradle Song
		2. Normandy Carol
Battle is o'er, hell's armies flee	74	Surrexit
Bethlehem, of noblest cities	42	Stuttgart
Blest are the pure in heart	208	Franconia
Breathe on me, Breath of God	91	Mount Ephraim
Brightest and best of the sons of the morning	43	Epiphany
Bring flowers of the rarest	144	Queen of the Angels
By the blood that flowed from thee	138	Westminster Old
Christ is made the sure Foundation	209	Westminster Abbey
Christ, the fair glory of the holy angels	178	Coelites plaudant
Christ the Lord is risen again	75	Orientibus partibus
Christ the Lord is ris'n today	76	St George's Windsor
Christians awake! salute the happy morn	17	Stockport
Christians, to the Paschal Victim	316	Victimae Paschali laudes
Christus vincit: Christus regnat	298	Christus vincit
Come down, O Love divine	92	Down Ampney
Come, Holy Ghost, Creator, come	93	Tallis's Ordinal
Come, let us join our cheerful songs	210	Nativity
Come, O Creator Spirit, come	311	Veni Creator
Come, thou holy Paraclete	94	Veni Sancte Spiritus
Come, thou long-expected Jesus	1	Cross of Jesus
Come, thou Redeemer of the earth	18	Puer nobis nascitur
Come, ye faithful, raise the strain	77	Ave virgo virginum
Come, ye thankful people, come	211	St George's Windsor
Credo in unum Deum	289	Credo III
Cross of Jesus, Cross of sorrow	62	Cross of Jesus
Crown him with many crowns,	141	Diademata
Daily, daily, sing to Mary	145	Daily daily
Dear Lord and Father of mankind	212	Repton
Dear Maker of the starry skies	2	Creator alme
Dearest Jesu, we are here	103	Liebster Jesu
Deck thyself, my soul, with gladness	114	Schmücke dich
Ding dong! merrily on high	19	Branle de l'official

Index of First Lines and Tunes

Draw nigh, and take the Body of the Lord	115	1. Ellers
		2. Song 24
Eternal Father, strong to save	213	Melita
Faith of our fathers, living still	183	Sawston
Father, hear the prayer we offer	214	Sussex
Father of heaven, whose love profound	215	Dunedin
Father of mercy, God of consolation	216	Christe sanctorum
Father, we praise thee, now the night is over	190	Diva servatrix
Father, we thank thee who hast planted	116	Rendez à Dieu
Firmly I believe and truly	217	1. Shipston
		2. Halton Holgate
For all the saints	166	Sine Nomine
Forth in thy name, O Lord, I go	191	Song 34 (Angels' Song)
Forty days and forty nights	50	Aus der tiefe
Full in the panting heart of Rome	184	Wiseman
Give me the wings of faith to rise	167	Song 67
Glorious things of thee are spoken	218	Abbot's Leigh
Glory be to Jesus	139	Wem in Leidenstagen (Caswall)
Glory to thee, my God, this night	193	Tallis's Canon (The Eighth Tune)
God moves in a mysterious way	219	London New
God of mercy and compassion	51	Au sang qu'un Dieu
God rest you merry, gentlemen	20	God rest you merry
God save our gracious Queen	220	National Anthem
Godhead here in hiding, whom I do adore	117	Adoro te
Good Christian men, rejoice and sing	78	Vulpius (Gelobt sei Gott)
Great Saint Andrew, friend of Jesus	175	Omni die
Guide me, O thou great Redeemer	221	Cwm Rhondda
Hail, glorious Saint Patrick, dear saint of our isle	177	St Patrick
Hail, holy Joseph, hail!	171	Maria jung und zart
Hail, holy Queen enthroned above	146	Salve Regina coelitum
Hail, Jesus, hail! who for my sake	140	Cornwall
Hail, Queen of heav'n, the ocean star	147	Stella
Hail Redeemer, King divine	142	King Divine
Hail the day that sees him rise	87	Llanfair

Index of First Lines and Tunes

Hail to the Lord who comes	44	St Cecilia
Hail to the Lord's Anointed,	3	Crüger
Hail true Body, born of Mary	297	Ave verum
Hark! a herald voice is sounding	4	Merton
Hark! hark, my soul! Angelic songs are swelling	179	Pilgrims
Hark the glad sound! the Saviour comes	5	Bristol
Hark! the herald angels sing	21	Mendelssohn
Hear, O thou bounteous Maker, hear	52	Commandments
Hear thy children, gentlest Mother	148	Drakes Boughton
Hear us, O loving Lord	293	Attende Domine
Help, Lord, the souls that thou hast made	181	Burford
Her Virgin eyes saw God incarnate born	149	Farley Castle (Lawes' Psalm 72)
Holy God, we praise thy name	222	Grosser Gott
Holy, Holy, Holy! Lord God Almighty	96	Nicaea
Holy light on earth's horizon	150	Blaenwern
Holy Mary, we implore thee	151	Abbot's Leigh
Holy Spirit, come, confirm us	95	Marching
Holy Spirit, Lord of light	313	Veni Sancte Spiritus (Gregorian)
Holy Virgin, by God's decree	152	Vierge Sainte
How brightly beams the morning star	45	Wie schön leuchtet
How sweet the name of Jesus sounds	223	St Peter
I bind unto myself today	97	St Patrick's Breastplate, Gartan
I vow to thee, my country	224	Thaxted
I'll sing a hymn to Mary	153	Turris Davidica
Immaculate Mary! our hearts are on fire	154	Lourdes Hymn
Immortal, invisible, God only wise	225	St Denio
In dulci jubilo	22	In dulci jubilo
In the bleak mid-winter	23	Cranham
Infant holy, Infant lowly	24	W żłobie leży
It came upon the midnight clear	25	Noel
Jerusalem the golden	226	Ewing
Jesu dulcis memoria	299	Jesu dulcis memoria
Jesu, grant me this, I pray	134	Song 13
Jesu, Lover of my soul	227	Aberystwyth
Jesu, meek and lowly	63	St Martin

Index of First Lines and Tunes

Jesu, the very thought of thee	228	St Botolph
Jesus Christ is risen today	79	Easter Hymn
Jesus, good above all other	229	Quem pastores
Jesus is God! the solid earth	230	Ellacombe
Jesus, my Lord, my God, my all	118	Corpus Christi
Jesus shall reign where'er the sun	231	1. Warrington
		2. Truro
Jesus, these eyes have never seen	232	1. Nun danket all
		2. Richmond
Jesus to cast one thought upon	300	Jesu dulcis memoria
Just as I am, without one plea	119	Saffron Walden
King of glory, King of peace	233	Gwalchmai
Lead, kindly Light, amid the encircling gloom	234	1. Alberta
		2. Sandon
Lead us, heavenly Father, lead us	235	Mannheim
Leader now on earth no longer	174	Swavesey
Let all mortal flesh keep silence	120	Picardy
Let all on earth their voices raise	168	Brockham
Let all the world in every corner sing	236	Luckington
Let us with a gladsome mind	237	Monkland
'Lift up your hearts!' We lift them, Lord, to thee	104	Woodlands
Like the dawning of the morning	6	Our Lady's Expectation
Lo! he comes with clouds descending	7	Helmsley
Long live the Pope! His praises sound	185	Wolvercote
Lord, accept the gifts we offer	105	Gott des Himmels
Lord, enthroned in heav'nly splendour	121	St Helen
Lord, for tomorrow and its needs	238	Providence
Lord Jesus, think on me	53	Southwell
Lord of all hopefulness, Lord of all joy	239	Slane
Lord of our life, and God of our salvation	240	Iste confessor
Lord, thy word abideth	241	Ravenshaw (Ave Hierarchia)
Lord, we gather at your altar	106	Freu' dich sehr
Lord, who throughout these forty days	54	St Flavian
Love divine, all loves excelling	242	Love Divine
Love of the Father, love of God the Son	98	Song 22
Love's redeeming work is done	80	Savannah (Herrnhut)
Loving Father, from thy bounty	107	Rhuddlan

Index of First Lines and Tunes

Lucis Creator optime	301	Lucis Creator
Maiden, yet a Mother	155	Une vaine crainte
Man of sorrows, wrapt in grief	64	Arfon (O vous dont les tendres ans)
Mary Immaculate, star of the morning	156	Liebster Immanuel
Mass VIII (de Angelis)	285	
Mass XI (Orbis Factor)	286	
Mass XVIII with Gloria XV	287	
Mass XVIII with Gloria XV (English version)	288	
Merciful Saviour, hear our humble prayer	182	Old 124th
Morning has broken	243	Bunessan
Most ancient of all mysteries	99	Bangor
My God, accept my heart this day	244	Belmont
My God! how wonderful thou art	245	Westminster
My God I love thee, not because	55	Everlasting Love
My song is love unknown	65	Love Unknown
Now is the healing time decreed	56	Jena (Das neugeborne Kindelein)
Now thank we all our God	246	Nun danket
Now the green blade riseth	81	Nouvel nouvelet
Now with the fast-departing light	308	Te lucis ante terminum (Ferial)
O blest Creator of the light	302	Lucis Creator
O Bread of heaven, beneath this veil	122	Tynemouth
O Christ, our true and only light	57	Whitehall (Lawes' Psalm 8)
O Christ our joy, to whom is given	88	Gonfalon Royal
O come, all ye faithful	13	Adeste fideles
O come and mourn with me awhile	66	1. Old Hall Green 2. St Cross
O come, O come, Emmanuel	8	Veni Emmanuel
O English hearts, what heart can know	186	O Mensch bewein'
O Food of men wayfaring	123	In allen meinen Thaten
O for a closer walk with God	247	1. Caithness 2. San Rocco
O God of earth and altar	248	King's Lynn
O God, our help in ages past	249	St Anne

Index of First Lines and Tunes

O God, we give ourselves today	108	Irish
O Godhead hid, devoutly I adore thee	124	Aquinas
O great Saint David, still we hear thee call us	176	St David
O Jesus Christ, remember	125	Munich
O Jesus, I have promised	250	Wolvercote
O King of might and splendour	109	Von Gott ich nicht lassen
O Little One sweet, O Little One mild	26	O Jesulein süss
O little town of Bethlehem	27	Forest Green
O Love, how deep, how broad, how high!	251	Eltham
O Mother blest, whom God bestows	157	St Ursula
O Mother! I could weep for mirth	158	Immaculate, Immaculate
O perfect Love, all human thought transcending	252	1. Highwood 2. Strength and Stay
O praise ye the Lord!	253	Laudate Dominum
O purest of creatures! sweet Mother, sweet Maid	159	Maria zu lieben
O sacred head sore wounded	67	Passion Chorale
O Sacred Heart, our home lies deep in thee	135	Laurence
O salutaris Hostia	276	Melcombe
O saving Victim, opening wide	277	Melcombe
O thou, who at thy Eucharist didst pray	126	Song 1
O thou who camest from above	254	Hereford
O thou who dost accord us	58	Innsbruck
O what their joy and their glory must be	169	Regnator orbis
O worship the Lord in the beauty of holiness	46	Was lebet
O worship the King, all glorious above	255	Hanover
Of the Father's heart begotten	28	Divinum Mysterium
Of the glorious Body telling	127	Neander (Unser Herrscher)
On Christmas night all Christians sing	29	Sussex Carol
On Jordan's bank the Baptist's cry	9	Winchester New
Once in royal David's city	30	Irby
Once, only once, and once for all	128	Albano
Onward, Christian soldiers	256	St Gertrude
Pange lingua gloriosi	303	Pange lingua
Panis angelicus fit panis hominum	304	Panis angelicus (Sarum)
Peace, perfect peace, in this dark world of sin	257	Song 46
Personent hodie	31	Personent hodie
Praise, my soul, the King of heaven	258	Praise, my soul
Praise the Lord! ye heavens, adore him	259	Austria

Index of First Lines and Tunes

Praise to the Holiest in the height	260	1. Billing
		2. Chorus Angelorum
Praise to the Lord, the Almighty, the King of creation!	110	Lobe den Herrn
Quem pastores laudavere	32	Quem pastores
Regina coeli laetare, alleluia	283	Regina coeli
Rejoice, the Lord is King!	261	Gopsal
Rejoice today with one accord	262	Ein' feste Burg
Responses at the Eucharistic Prayer and Pater Noster	290	
Ride on, ride on in majesty!	68	Winchester New
Rorate caeli desuper	305	Rorate caeli (The Advent Prose)
Round me falls the night	194	Seelenbraütigam
Salve Regina, mater misericordiae	284	Salve Regina
See, amid the winter's snow	34	Oxford
See the Conqueror mounts in triumph	89	Lux Eoi
See us, Lord, about thine altar	111	Redhead No. 46
Silent night, holy night	35	Stille Nacht
Sing, my tongue, the glorious battle	69	Brompton Road
Songs of thankfulness and praise	47	Salzburg
Soul of my Saviour, sanctify my breast	129	Anima Christi
Star of sea and ocean	160	St Martin
Sun of my soul, thou Saviour dear	195	1. Abends
		2. Fulda
Sweet Sacrament divine	130	Divine Mysteries
Sweet Saviour, bless us ere we go	196	Sunset (St Philip)
Take my life, and let it be	263	Savannah (Herrnhut)
Tantum ergo Sacramentum	278	St Thomas
Te Deum laudamus	306	Te Deum laudamus (Tonus Simplex)
Te lucis ante terminum	307	Te lucis ante terminum (Ferial)
Tell out, my soul, the greatness of the Lord	264	Woodlands
The angel Gabriel from heaven came	36	Gabriel's message
The beauteous light of God's eternal majesty	172	Annue Christi
The Church's one foundation	187	Aurelia

Index of First Lines and Tunes

The Day of Resurrection	82	Ellacombe
The day thou gavest, Lord, is ended	197	St Clement
The first Nowell the angel did say	37	The first Nowell
The God whom earth, and sea, and sky	161	Eisenach
The great God of heaven is come down to earth	38	A virgin unspotted
The head that once was crowned with thorns	90	St Magnus
The heavenly Word proceeding forth	131	Wareham
The King of love my Shepherd is	265	1. St Columba 2. Dominus regit me
The Lord's my shepherd, I'll not want	266	1. Crimond 2. Wiltshire
The race that long in darkness pined	48	Dundee
The royal banners forward go	70	Vexilla Regis
The spacious firmament on high	267	Addison's (London)
The strife is o'er, the battle done	83	Victory
The thirteenth of May	162	A treize de Maio (Fatima Ave)
There is a green hill far away	71	Horsley
There's a wideness in God's mercy	268	All for Jesus
Therefore we, before him bending	279	St Thomas
They come, God's messengers of love	180	Angelus
This joyful Eastertide	84	This joyful Eastertide
Thou whom shepherds worshipped	33	Quem pastores
Thou, whose eternal word	269	Moscow
Thy hand, O God, has guided	188	Thornbury
'Tis good, Lord, to be here	100	Carlisle
To Christ, the Prince of Peace	136	Narenza (Ave Maria klare)
To Christ the Lord of worlds we sing	143	Deus tuorum militum
To Jesus' Heart, all burning	137	Cor Jesu
To the name that brings salvation	270	Oriel
Ubi caritas et amor, Deus ibi est	309	Ubi caritas
Unto us is born a Son	39	Puer nobis
Veni, Creator Spiritus	310	Veni Creator
Veni Sancte Spiritus	312	Veni Sancte Spiritus (Gregorian)
Vexilla Regis proderunt	314	Vexilla Regis
Victimae Paschali	315	Victimae Paschali laudes

Index of First Lines and Tunes

Virgin-born, we bow before thee	163	Mon Dieu, prête moi l'oreille
Virgin, wholly marvellous	164	Nun komm der Heiden Heiland
Wake, O wake! with tidings thrilling	10	Wachet auf
We sing the praise of him who died	271	Bow Brickhill
What star is this with beams so bright	49	St Venantius
When I survey the wondrous Cross	72	Rockingham
When morning gilds the skies	272	Laudes Domini
While shepherds watched their flocks by night	40	Winchester Old
Who are these, like stars appearing	170	All Saints
Who would true valour see	273	Monks Gate
With all the powers my poor soul hath	132	Uffingham
Wouldst thou a patron see	173	Monks Gate
Ye choirs of New Jerusalem	85	St Fulbert
Ye holy angels bright	274	Darwall's 148th
Ye sons and daughters of the Lord	86	O filii et filiae
Ye watchers and ye holy ones	275	Lasst uns erfreuen
Ye who own the faith of Jesus	165	1. Regent Square 2. Daily daily

The Catholic Hymn Book

Oratorian Supplement

Oratorian Supplement

317 ST PHILIP'S DEATH   886 886   GEORGE HERBERT 1817–1906

1. Day set on Rome! its golden morn
   Had seen the world's Creator borne
   Around St Peter's square;
   Trembling and weeping all the way,
   God's Vicar with his God that day
   Made pageant brave and rare!

2. Oh, come to Father Philip's cell,
   Rome's rank and youth, they know it well,
   Come ere the moment flies!
   The feast hath been too much for him;
   His heart is full, his eye is dim,
   And Rome's Apostle dies!

3. Come, O Creator Spirit! come,
   Take thine elect unto his home,
   Thy chosen one, sweet Dove!
   'Come to thy rest,' he hears thee say;
   He waits not—he hath passed away
   In mortal trance of love.

4. When Rome in deepest slumber slept,
   Our father's children knelt and wept
   Around his little bed;
   He raised his eyes, then let them fall
   With marked expression upon all;
   He blessed them, and was dead.

5. One half from earth, one half from heaven,
   Was that mysterious blessing given;
   Just as his life had been
   One half in heaven, one half on earth,
   Of earthly toil and heavenly mirth
   A wondrous woven scene!

6. O Jesus, Mary, Joseph, bide,
   With kind Saint Raphael, by my side
   When death shall come for me;
   And, Philip! leave me not that day;
   But let my spirit pass away,
   Leaning, dear Sire, on thee!

FREDERICK WILLIAM FABER Cong. Orat. 1814–63

Oratorian Supplement

318 NOEL   DCM   ARTHUR SULLIVAN 1842–1900
                                     after a traditional English melody

1. Look down from heaven, Father dear,
   From that bright mount above,
   On us who in this vale of tears
   So sorely need thy love:
   Look from thy peaceful haven, from
   Thy place of well-earned rest,
   On us who in this storm-tossed sea
   With perils are oppressed.

2. No longer can earth's shadows or
   Its darkness dim thy sight,
   But clearly into all things dost
   Thou see in God's own light:
   Remember then thy vineyard here,
   The work thy hand hath wrought,
   Which thou didst plant with so much toil,
   And so much anxious thought.

3. Into thy hands we place ourselves,
   From thee we seek for aid,
   Thine army rule, for see the hosts
   Of hell 'gainst us arrayed:
   Beneath thy kind protecting care
   If thou wilt let us live,
   To thee the rudder of our lives
   With all our hearts we give.

4. So steer this little ship of thine,
   And from thy place on high,
   Lead us in safety 'mid the rocks
   Which all around us lie:
   And if our pilot thou wilt be,
   If thou wilt be our guide,
   We'll safely come to port and be
   For ever by thy side.

RALPH FRANCIS KERR Cong. Orat. 1874–1932

Oratorian Supplement

319 NORTHERN COASTS CM ANONYMOUS

1. On northern coasts our lot is cast,
   Where faithful hearts are few;
   Still are we Philip's children dear,
   And Peter's soldiers true.

2. Founder and Sire! to mighty Rome,
   Beneath St Peter's shade,
   Thy early vow of loyal love
   And ministry was paid.

3. The ample porch and portal high
   Of Peter was thy home;
   The world's apostle he, and thou
   Apostle of his Rome.

4. And first in the old catacombs,
   In galleries long and deep,
   Where martyr popes had ruled their flock,
   And slept their glorious sleep.

5. There in the night the youthful saint
   To heaven his prayers addressed,
   Till a new Pentecost came down,
   And burned within his breast.

6. And in that heart-consuming love
   He walked the city wide;
   He lured the noble and the young,
   From Babel's pomp and pride;

7. And gathering them within his cell,
   Unveiled the lustre bright
   And beauty of his inner soul,
   And won them by the sight.

8. And when he died, he did but go
   In other lands to dwell,
   A traveller now, who in his life
   Ne'er left that one dear cell.

9. He travelled, and he travelled on,
   He crossed the swelling sea,
   He sought our island's very heart,
   And here at length is he.

10. Glory to God, who framed a Saint
    So beautiful and sweet:
    Who brought him from St Peter's side,
    And placed us at his feet.

The Venerable JOHN HENRY NEWMAN Cong. Orat. 1801–90

Oratorian Supplement

320 ST PHILIP NERI   11 11 11 5   *Oratory Vesper Tunes* date unknown

1. This is the Saint of gentleness and kindness,
   Cheerful in penance, and in precept winning;
   Patiently healing of their pride and blindness,
   Souls that are sinning.

2. This is the Saint, who, when the world allures us,
   Cries her false wares, and opes her magic coffers,
   Points to a better city, and secures us
   With richer offers.

3. Love is his bond, he knows no other fetter,
   Asks not our all, but takes whate'er we spare him,
   Willing to draw us on from good to better,
   As we can bear him.

4. When he comes near to teach us and to bless us,
   Prayer is so sweet, that hours are but a minute;
   Mirth is so pure, though freely it possess us,
   Sin is not in it.

5. Thus he conducts, by holy paths and pleasant,
   Innocent souls, and sinful souls forgiven,
   Towards the bright palace, where our God is present,
   Throned in high heaven.

The Venerable JOHN HENRY NEWMAN Cong. Orat. 1801–90

Oratorian Supplement

321 WUNDERSCHÖN PRÄCHTIGE
779 D + refrain

Swiss published Einsiedeln 1773
arranged RALPH DOWNES 1904–93

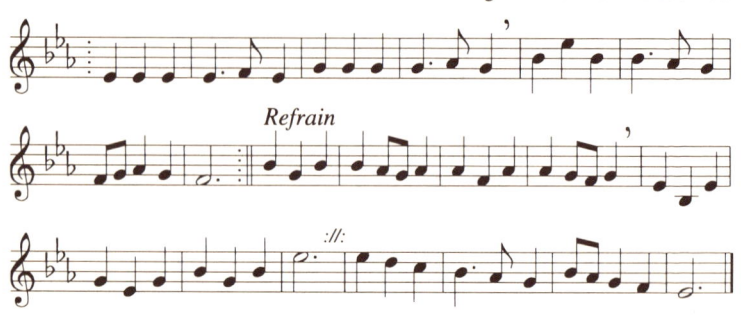

1. True sons of Philip, raise
Heav'nward your strain of praise,
Ever rejoicing in God as he taught;
Learn from Saint Philip still
In body, mind and will
Truly our Lord to serve, counting self as naught.

2. Trust in Saint Philip's prayers
Let him relieve our cares,
Ease for us gain in temptations and stress.
Once we his aid invoke
Riven is Satan's yoke
And we are stronger our Saviour to bless.

Songs therefore let us bring,
Praises to Jesus sing,
Now and forever our Lord and our God.

3. Turn, as Saint Philip bade,
Often to Mary's aid,
Refuge and help she refuses to none;
Years have not dimmed her power
In this and ev'ry hour
New grace she wins us by prayer with her Son.

4. Love was Saint Philip's school,
Ours let us make his rule,
Now Holy Ghost, fill our hearts with thy love;
Daily thy grace bestow
On our fight here below,
Nor let us fail till we join the saints above.

PATRICK BUSHELL Cong. Orat. 1912–93

Oratorian Supplement

322 NARENZA SM
(Ave Maria klare)

Johann Leisentritt's
Catholicum Hymnologium Germanicum 1584
adapted WILLIAM HENRY HAVERGAL 1793–1870

1. When many sought a guide
 In times of stress and storm,
 The fortunate in Philip found
 A wisdom firm but warm.

2. He influenced the great,
 Yet was a humble priest;
 Pure servant of a loving Lord,
 Devoted to the least.

3. When weary pilgrim bands
 Their way to Rome did wend,
 They found in him a sanctuary,
 A father and a friend.

4. The truth he could discern,
 From sin he could set free;
 He followed in his Master's steps
 In true humility.

5. The noble youth of Rome
 Encouraged he, and taught
 The essence of a virtuous life;
 To hold the world as naught.

6. To English Mission priests
 He gave a fond farewell:
 'Salvete, flores martyrum!'
 Their end he could foretell.

7. We sing of Philip's heart,
 So full of burning love;
 His message to an erring world
 To honour God above.

8. As Philip, let us pray
 That God may bless us all;
 The Father, Son and Holy Ghost,
 And raise us when we fall.

DOMINIC JACOB Cong. Orat. born 1960
and AMANDA HILL born 1943